Apollo's Chariot

Apollo's Chariot

The Meaning of the Astrological Sun

Liz Greene

The Wessex Astrologer

Published in 2023 by
The Wessex Astrologer Ltd
PO Box 9307
Swanage
BH19 9BF
England

For a full list of our titles go to www.wessexastrologer.com

First published 2001 by the CPA Press, BCM Box 1815
London WC1N 3XX, England
www.cpalondon.com
2nd printing 2004
1900869179

Copyright © 2001 by Liz Greene
Liz Greene asserts the moral right to be identified as the author of this work.

ISBN 9781916625082

A catalogue record for this book is available at The British Library

No part of this book may be reproduced or used in any form or by any means without the written permission of the publisher.
A reviewer may quote brief passages.

To Charles

on whom the Sun will always shine,

in loving memory

Table of Contents

Part One: The Meaning of the Natal Sun

Introduction..	1
The political incorrectness of the Sun....................	1
The plan for the day..	3
Non-Greek solar deities..	5
Marduk...	6
The Buddha...	7
Mithras...	8
Apollo...	9
The carrier of divine fire...	11
The one who makes things ripen...........................	13
A story needs a plot...	18
The god of healing..	20
The god of music..	21
Solar play...	23
Solar joy...	26
Apollo and the Python...	29
Apollo the curse-breaker...	30
Creative speech...	32
The lonely god..	36
Apollo and the Muses..	38
An example chart..	43
Creative mediumship: the Sun in the 12th house..	43
Sun and Moon in square...	49
The actor's gift..	52
Problems with boundaries.......................................	56
More example charts...	58
The eternal quest: the Sun in Sagittarius...............	58
Creative idealism: the Sun in the 11th house........	61
Collective rejection of the Sun................................	65
Creative serpent-slaying: the Sun in the 8th house	69
The 8th house and fate...	72
When the Sun doesn't shine...	75
Father and Sun..	75
An unaspected Sun..	76
The Sun aspecting the outer planets.....................	78
The narcissistic wound..	80
The formation of the ego...	84
Narcissistic wounding down the generations......	87

The father and the solar spirit	91
The Sun aspecting Saturn or Chiron	93
Sun-Pluto aspects	97
More solar themes	98
The Sun in a grand cross	98
The problem of perfectionism	101
The acceptance of limits	103
Envy	106
Inner choices	112
Bibliography	114

Part Two: The Sun, Creativity, and Vocation

The Sun and the creative process	116
The nature of creativity	116
The divine child	119
Playing and reality	119
The mythic creator-gods	123
Solar selfishness	125
The "transitional object"	127
Creativity and embodiment	132
The artist and the magician	134
The sustenance of the Sun	136
The Sun at work	142
Creativity and the 5th house	142
The creativity of Sun-Uranus	145
The Sun in the 6th: inspiration from everyday life	148
Charts from the group	151
The Sun in the 4th: inherited creativity	153
The creativity of Sun-Chiron	156
The Sun in the 11th in Aries: crusading for others	160
Solar light on Pluto's inheritance	164
The creativity of Sun-Moon	166
The challenge of Chiron in Capricorn	169
Family curses and family gifts	170
Sun-sign astrology	172
The developing Sun	175
Solar progressions	175
The progressed solar cycle	175
The progressed Sun changing signs	179
The progressed Sun aspecting natal planets	182
Shedding light on dark places	183

Applying and separating solar progressions	184
Progressed Sun separating from natal Pluto	185
Progressed Sun applying to natal Jupiter	187
Progressed Sun applying to natal Moon	188
Progressed Sun trine natal Uranus	192
Transits to the natal Sun	195
The creativity of Sun-Mars and Sun-Pluto	197
Transiting Uranus opposing natal Sun	203
The Pluto in Leo generation group	204
The Sun and vocation	207
Sun-Pluto in the political arena	207
The Sun in Capricorn in the 2nd house	209
The creativity of Sun-Uranus-Pluto	211
The 1960s generation	212
Vocation and the call of the Sun	214
Walking the dangerous edge	216
Bibliography	221

Part One: The Meaning of the Natal Sun

This seminar was given on 1 November 1998 at Regents College, London as part of the Autumn Term of the seminar programme of the Centre for Psychological Astrology.

Introduction

The political incorrectness of the Sun

Good morning, and welcome to the seminar. The Sun is so bright today that we have had to draw the blinds against the glare. That seems to me rather ironic, given the theme we are dealing with. But perhaps we can best understand the astrological Sun when we don't try to stare straight at it. I assume all of you know that today is the first part of a two-part exploration. Inevitably, some of you are going to want to ask things which I will have to answer by saying, "Wait until next week." I hope that won't prove too frustrating.

Although the first thing the astrological student learns about is the Sun, and the first contact the lay person has with astrology is the description of his or her Sun-sign in the newspapers, I believe we lack understanding of this fundamental astrological building-block. We use terms like "self-expression" and "individuality" in relation to the Sun but, as with so many keywords, we may not be very clear about what we mean by them. Although every astrological textbook starts with the Sun, it is an extremely elusive and complex symbol. I often feel that we never get to the bottom of the Sun (or perhaps the top might be a better metaphor), whatever we are given to read and whatever we are taught about it. There seem to be so many levels and layers to the Sun, and we will see the vast scope of these layers when we examine the mythology of the Sun-gods a bit later this morning.

At the present time there are powerful currents at work on a collective level, concurrent with Uranus and Neptune transiting through Aquarius, which emphasise the opposite of solar values. I might even go as far as suggesting that placing too much importance on the astrological Sun is not, at this time, politically correct. And if we accept the concept of astrological "ages" reflected by the precession of the spring equinoctial point through the constellations, then we must also recognise that we are on the threshold of the Aquarian Age[1] – once again, the opposite of solar concerns. There is a great deal in the collective psyche mitigating against the solar realm at the moment. I am not suggesting that this is "wrong" or "bad". It simply *is*, and we can only hope that it reflects a necessary and ultimately positive stage in the cycle of human evolution. But whenever something is strongly emphasised on a collective level, the individual needs to be able to respond as an individual – even if, in the end, it is the welfare of the group that takes priority. Therefore it is important for us to understand the Sun as deeply as we possibly can, and get a clearer sense of how to work with it, live it, and express it in an individual way. Then we are in a position to respond creatively and intelligently to the *zeitgeist*, rather than being swallowed up by it.

Jung, whose birth chart contains the polarity of Sun in Leo and Aquarius on the Ascendant, was convinced that the only antidote to a general slide into mass unconsciousness, with all its potential blind destructiveness, is a sense of individual identity and individual values. At the moment, individuality is not very fashionable. The word "global" is forever on our lips. Nationalism is nasty, elitism is offensive, political correctness appears to be reaching obscene extremes, and the current "dumbing down" process afflicting the British media has reduced intellectual standards to the lowest common denominator in the name of not offending those who cannot be bothered to aspire. We are not supposed to think in selfish, "What about me?" terms. We are encouraged to think in collective terms, with the accent on "sharing" and "participating", and this is reflected in the kinds of governments that we have voted into power right across Europe since Uranus and Neptune entered the sign of the Water-bearer. That is undoubtedly right and appropriate at the moment – the world is merely enacting, or reflecting, what the transits portray on an archetypal level.

Nevertheless, I believe it is imperative that we are conscious of what we are doing, and are able to choose and discriminate. We need to understand the Sun better because, as astrologers, we work with individuals. We do not work with collectives, except in the context of

---

[1] For a provocative discussion on the non-existence of the Aquarian Age, see Nicholas Campion, *Astrology, History and Apocalypse*, CPA Press, London, 2000.

seminars and supervision groups; and these are usually small groups designed to help the individual student develop his or her interpretive skills. We offer consultations to individual people who come to us to have their horoscopes interpreted because they are concerned about what is happening in their individual lives. Whatever the current *zeitgeist,* it is not our role to tell these people they should be thinking globally and not personally – even if their vocation points to a contribution to the collective. And in order to understand what they are and need as individuals, we must first understand the Sun in the birth chart.

The plan for the day

I would like to start with the mythology of the Sun. Myth speaks to us on emotional and imaginative levels and extends our minds beyond current thought structures. Myth portrays universal truths and fundamental human patterns which do not alter, and which stand outside the trends of any particular time. The human themes which myth describes are not confined to a particular way of looking at things at a particular juncture of history or in a particular kind of society. Myths are archetypal, timeless, and universal. They are free of political polemics. They arise from deep levels of the psyche that the ego cannot control, and no government legislation can eradicate their power, importance, and truth.

Although myths about the Sun exist in every culture in every epoch of history, I want to focus specifically on the mythology of Apollo. He is not the only solar deity worthy of mention, and we will be looking briefly at several others. But he is the most refined and fully developed of all the ancient Sun-gods. As I discuss the myths of Apollo, I want to link them with some possible psychological interpretations. Mythic attributes and stories tell us something about who and what we are. At the same time, I would also like to try to connect some of these mythic and psychological principles with actual Sun placements in individual birth charts. In other words, I will be asking, "What does this myth have to do with the Sun in the 2nd house? What can this mythic figure tell us about the Sun in Pisces? How does this story relate to the Sun opposite Saturn? What can this motif tell us about the Sun conjunct Jupiter?"

Then I want to start looking at the issue of father, and all that this implies. The Sun is, of course, one of our most important symbols of father-ness, both on an inner level and in terms of what the Sun in the birth chart tells us about our paternal inheritance. Along with this material, I would like to look at what kinds of problems and conflicts, internal and external, might stop the Sun from shining in an individual's life. There is always a problem with the Sun. It is the nature of the Sun to have to struggle in order to give light. There is no person in existence who is not, in some way, still in the process of developing the Sun. There doesn't seem to be such a thing as a complete, finished Sun, or a person in whom the Sun is fully realised. Its very nature implies that the psychological principle portrayed by the Sun involves a constant cyclical process of struggle and re-emergence. That is its essence. All of us, in one way or another, are still grappling with the work of the Sun in our charts. Whatever our age, and however much we are managing to express solar light, our solar work is never finished.

However, we need to look at what kinds of things hurt the Sun, and why an individual might have greater difficulty in expressing it. Some people seem entirely blocked, and the Sun is all but invisible. Many of us have had the experience of making an appointment with a client, doing the preliminary work on the chart, and forming a preconception, based on the Sun, that this is going to be a certain kind of person. We might see the Sun in fire, strongly aspected to Jupiter and Mars, and we think, "This is going to be a really powerful client, full of confidence and energy." Then a grey, diffident creature comes in and hovers timidly in the corner of the room, and we wonder what on earth has happened. Where is the Sun? Why is it not shining? Many kinds of emotional and psychic difficulties and creative blocks, often given interesting but ultimately unhelpful psychological labels, are linked with the Sun being blocked, undermined, bottled up, unexpressed, or unformed. Why does this happen? What can the individual do about it? That is going to be an important part of what we will be looking at today.

I have some example charts that might be fun to play around with. Many of you will have brought your own charts as well. Today we won't be talking about transits to the Sun. That is on the agenda for next week. Vocation is another theme we will explore next week, although vocation is strongly linked to the natal Sun. It is birth chart Sun placements we are going to be dealing with today – house, sign, aspects, paternal inheritance, and the difficulties for the Sun that may arise with certain kinds of natal configurations as well as certain kinds of early experiences.

Non-Greek solar deities

However far back we go in exploring myth, we always find the Sun. The earliest human formulations of religious worship are linked to the Sun, in every culture and in every quarter of the globe. Neolithic monuments such as Stonehenge are understood by many archaeologists to be solar temples[2]; and even when creation myths such as those of Babylon, Egypt, and Sumeria present us with images of a primordial sea as the source of life, a solar deity invariably emerges coincident with and responsible for the creation of the world and of humanity.[3] The physical Sun is, after all, hard to miss, and is the greatest thing in the heavens; and it was apparent to early humans that they were dependent on this Great Light for their survival.

Very early religious worship is difficult for us to comprehend, for we have no written records which might allow us to enter imaginatively into the world-view of the worshippers. We don't know whether the solar cycle which was clearly so important to the builders of Stonehenge was understood as God literally or symbolically. In late antiquity, the physical Sun in the heavens was understood not as a god in itself, but as the symbol of something transcendent and ineffable. But despite the claims of some modern theologians and historians that monotheism originated with the Judeo-Christian religious perspective, monotheism has in fact always existed in solar worship, and the Sun has always been perceived as cosmic centre and cosmocrator, even when other gods were accorded honour and value.

---

[2] See Robin Heath, *Sun, Moon and Stonehenge,* Bluestone Press, Cardigan, Wales, 1998.
[3] See Liz Greene, *The Astrological Neptune and the Quest for Redemption,* Part One, Samuel Weiser Inc, York Beach, ME, 1996.

Marduk

The Babylonian Sun-god Marduk can help to give us valuable insights into the meaning of the astrological Sun. Although he isn't as well-defined a personality as the later Greek Apollo, his battle with and victory over the mother-goddess Tiamat is a powerful image of the solar struggle against the darkness of the collective and the instinctual compulsions of the body.[4] We have a wonderful poetic description of Marduk from the Babylonian epic, the *Enuma Elish*, which I would like to read to you.

> Perfect were his manners beyond comprehension,
> Unsuited for understanding, difficult to perceive.
> Four were his eyes, four were his ears;
> When he moved his lips, fire blazed forth.
> Large were all four hearing organs,
> And the eyes, like in number, scanned all things.
> He was the loftiest of the gods, surpassing was his stature;
> His members were enormous, he was exceedingly tall.
> "My son, my little son!
> My son, the Sun! Sun of the heavens!"
> Clothed with the halo of ten gods, he was strong to the utmost,
> As their awesome flashes were heaped upon him.[5]

The image of the Sun's eyes "scanning all things" appears also in the Egyptian Sun-god, Re, and his daughter Sekhmet, the "Eye of Re" who enacts her father's will on earth and avenges wrongs done against him. We will also meet it later in the figure of Apollo "Longsight". The implication is that solar consciousness is connected with the ability to be aware, to see, to pay attention, both inwardly and in the outer world. But most importantly, Marduk must fight and destroy his mother in order to survive. Out of her dismembered body, he creates heaven and earth. We might say that out of the conflict and suffering which arise from the experience of separation, individual creative potential is generated and fuelled. Later I will talk more about this solar necessity to

---

[4] For more interpretations of the myth of Marduk and Tiamat, see Greene, *The Astrological Neptune and the Quest for Redemption*, ibid.

[5] From *The Orphic Poems*, M. L. West, Oxford University Press, 1983, quoted on p. 211, *Enuma Elish*, 93-104, trans. E. A. Speiser in *ANET* 62.

separate from the family matrix in order to become an individual, and the price which must be paid. But the mythic figure of Marduk tells us something very important about a process which is essentially solar, and necessary for the psychological emergence and survival of the individual. There are many failed Marduks wandering about who are unwilling, or perhaps unable, without sufficient help, to do battle with the primordial source and emerge with their light fully shining. We will talk more about that later.

The Buddha

According to Joseph Campbell, the mythology of the Buddha is solar.[6] He is called the Lion of the Shakya Clan, who sits upon the Lion Throne. Lions seem to be linked with the Sun as far back as Egypt, when the Pharoah, deemed to be the son of the Sun-god Re, sat on a lion-legged throne, and the goddess Sekhmet, daughter of Re, was portrayed with a lion's head. The symbol of the Buddha's teaching is the Sun Wheel, and the reference of his doctrine is to a state that is no state, of which the only appropriate image is light. And the father of the Buddha was of the Dynasty of the Sun.

The purity of solar light is emphasised in the myths of Buddhist India, as opposed to the mixture of light and darkness represented by the Moon. T he light of the Sun is also eternal, whereas the light of the Moon, waxing and waning, is at once mortal and immortal. In the Sankhya philosophy, this eternal light which lies at the core of the individual as well as of the universe may be activated by certain yoga practices. When the agitated "matter" or "mind stuff" within the individual mind is stilled, an unbroken image of the true essence is beheld, the false idea of the ego disappears; and one's identity with that undying, Sun-like source of life, that state which is no state but can only be portrayed as light, is at last recognised. When we begin to examine the myths of Apollo later, we will see that he is the carrier of the Sun, not the Sun itself. And we might look at this Buddhist portrayal of solar light and consider that the astrological Sun is the individual carrier, like the Greek Apollo, of something indescribable, ineffable, and eternal.

---

[6] Joseph Campbell, *Oriental Mythology*, Penguin Books, New York, 1982.

Mithras

Mithras is another ancient solar deity, whose origins lie in Persia. Before he became Romanised, he was a god of oaths and a mediator between his father Ahura Mazda, the god of light and goodness, and humanity. He has much in common with Apollo, who also plays this role for Zeus. Like Marduk, Mithras must struggle, but in his case the enemy is not a monstrous mother-dragon; it is a bull. Mithras also possesses a unique attribute which can give us another important insight into the Sun: he is a redeemer-god, not unlike the figure of Christ, and is often portrayed in ancient iconography in similar ways. The solar rays which surround his head serve the same symbolic purpose as the halo portrayed around the head of Christ – they represent immortality. Like Christ, Mithras suffers to redeem humanity, beginning with his birth into mortal flesh from a virgin's body. In Mithraic myth, the god incarnates in earthly form at the time of the winter solstice, around 23rd December, when the light of the Sun in the northern hemisphere is at its weakest but heralds the beginning of the new solar cycle. It is not accidental that the myth of Jesus' birth is also linked with this solstice, and the ancient Roman cult of Sol Invictus, the Unconquered Sun – connected but not identical with the cult of Mithras – also shared with Christianity this symbolic emphasis on the winter solstice. The theme of redemption through the Sun runs through the early mystery religions like a golden thread, suggesting that it is through realisation of our inner divinity that we are redeemed from the suffering of mortal flesh. As the Emperor Julian wrote:

> "...He [the Sun] has generated my soul from eternity, and rendered it an attendant on his divinity."[7]

Solar initiations such as those in the mysteries of Mithras usually involved a series of grades or steps through which the initiate passed, gradually increasing in consciousness and understanding, until he or she had full realisation of the spark of divine life which animates, and has its existence independent of, the physical form. This is not the

---

[7] Thomas Taylor, trans., *Collected Writings on the Gods and the World*, "The Emperor Julian's Oration to the Sovereign Sun", p. 75, Prometheus Trust, Frome, Somerset, 1994.

Part One: The Meaning of the Natal Sun

same as the Neptunian initiation into dissolution. It is an enhancement of life, rather than a repudiation or relinquishing of it. The cult of Mithras placed enormous emphasis on a strict adherence to oaths and promises, suggesting that one of the important psychological dimensions of the Sun in the horoscope is that mysterious quality we call integrity.

Apollo

We could spend all morning perusing the realm of solar myth. I have only mentioned a handful of solar deities, and have neglected the Celtic, Norse, Teutonic, North and South American, Slavic, and Chinese and Japanese mythic portrayals of solar light. I'm limited by time rather than by any lesser importance on the part of these overlooked deities. But you can all do your own homework if these myths interest you. We need to move on to the Greek Sun-god Apollo, who can provide us with an enormous amount of insight into the astrological Sun. Those of you seated at the back probably won't be able to read the material I am now putting up on the overhead projector, but I will go through it with you. On the left, I have listed the chief attributes of Apollo the Sun-god. On the right I have given parallel attributes belonging to the astrological Sun. I would like to work through these and consider what they might mean psychologically. Hopefully, we can also start looking at some specific Sun placements in the context of these attributes.

The nature of the Sun-god	The astrological Sun
1. God of light, without being the Sun itself	Vessel for the spirit
2. Makes the fruits of the earth ripen	Brings innate potentials to flower in worldly life
3. God of sudden death, through shooting his arrows; brings the souls of the dead to heaven in his chariot	Determines the life span; guardian of the immortal spirit

4. God of healing	The will to live and the healing power of consciousness
5. God of divination and prophecy	A sense of destiny or the unfolding of a purposeful pattern
6. God of music	Creative power as an expression of the spirit
7. Colonising god who founds cities	The will to civilise and create below what is above
8. Cosmocrator	Gives order to and governs the inner solar system of the individual
9. Breaker of family curses, enemy of the Erinyes	Consciousness releases the individual from the power of family complexes
10. Failure in love and fathering	Individuality is not conducive to close family ties
11. Lover/companion/father of the Muses	Inspiration through all the arts: Calliope (epic poetry), Urania (astrology), Polyhymnia (mime), Erato (singing), Thalia (comedy), Clio (history), Euterpe (flute-playing), Terpsichore (dance), Melpomene (tragedy)

Part One: The Meaning of the Natal Sun

12. Killing of the Python/creating the Pythoness	Mastering and humanising of the chthonic and prophetic power of the instincts
13. Sharing of Delphi with Dionysus	Relationship of Sun and Neptune, individual and collective

The carrier of divine fire

Apollo is presented in myth, not as the actual physical Sun that shines in the sky, but as the *carrier* of the Sun. That is extremely important. Any anthropomorphised image in myth is concerned with human attributes, and this is true of the gods as well as of the mortals. This god, because he *is* a god, symbolises something within us that is linked to immortality. But he is not the light itself. He is a divine being who carries the Sun in his golden chariot from east to west every day. Apollo is a vessel, a container for something that the Greek mind did not anthropomorphise – the One, the fiery core of godhead. The philosopher Herakleitos believed that fire was the primal element, the basic stuff of creation. We are humans, and although we may carry a divine spark, we are not, in ourselves, the One. But we have within us something described by the image of Apollo, who can give us many hints about what the Sun means as an astrological symbol. The Sun in the horoscope is not divinity itself. None of us is God. We all have the Sun in our birth chart, but so does every cat, dog, chicken, and bumblebee. If Apollo is an image of some archetypal quality within us, and he is equivalent to the astrological Sun, then the Sun in the horoscope symbolises a vessel, a container for something else which lies outside the horoscope and beyond mortal life – but which, as the Emperor Julian said, engenders and infuses our incarnate existence.

The Sun in the chart seems to make this statement: "I am born into a mortal body. My span is finite. But I am the carrier for that which is eternal and cannot be imaged in form, except as divine fire." A being comes into mortal existence on this plane of reality, and they are carrying something. We have huge lists of words to try to define that something, and we get nowhere with it. We can call it spirit, we can call it God, we can call it the One, we can call it the spark of divinity, we can call it the Self. Or we can merely call it the life-force, a term which is non-spiritual but nevertheless just as awesome. We can call it anything we like, using religious, psychological, or biological terminology. All we seem to understand is that it isn't me or you, and yet it is the life-bearing spark that allows each of us to be alive. This life-bearing spark is contained by the Sun in all living organisms. When we die, it isn't there anymore, and there is simply a lump of flesh whose organs have ceased to function. There is an animating life-principle which incarnates into, or is carried by, our mortal selves. This is what Apollo does: he carries this light. When we get glimpses of it, something very important happens to us.

Probably everyone in this room, at one time or another, has had a sense of that spark. Some of you may have experienced it through very specific efforts of a spiritual kind, in guided imagery exercises or meditation or yoga, or in more conventional forms of prayer. Some people experience it spontaneously: One goes out for a walk in the woods in the autumn, and everything is very beautiful and magical, and all the trees are turning colour, and there is a sudden sense of something in life that both *is* life and is *beyond* life. Why is it that we feel ill when we don't get enough sunlight? It is impossible to describe, but I think all of you understand. It is more, far more, than physical light and warmth.

Some people experience it when they are in love. Some people experience it when they are creating something. Very often it can come upon us when we are working with astrology. Plato, we should remember, thought that the studies of astrology, geometry, and music were the great gateways to the "eternal realities" of which the solar circle is a symbol. It is like a door opening through which light flows in, and there is a sense of connection with one's own specialness and purpose which is very hard to describe. This doesn't imply that no one else is special. But there is a sense of being someone unique who is not the same as anyone else, someone whose life has a unique purpose and a unique place in the larger order. It is a profound experience of "myself", of I-ness. It is very different from the Neptunian experience of being taken "out of" oneself, losing oneself in the greater whole. It is a gaining of self, not a losing. The Sun in the birth chart seems to point to where we are closest to that experience – where the door can open most easily. The placement of the Sun hints at the way in which we get nearest to that sense of being a vessel for something. When we look at

Part One: The Meaning of the Natal Sun

the Sun by house and sign, that is where we get closest to the realisation of being someone special, of carrying a destiny, of having a purpose, of having a reason to be here.

The one who makes things ripen

Apollo, who is the carrier of the Sun, is also the god who presides over the process of maturation. He makes the fruits of the earth ripen. He is not the one who plants them; he puts no seed in the ground. But without him, no seed would sprout and achieve its potential. He also presides over the rites and rituals by which young men and women celebrate their entry into adulthood and take their place in society. Apollo is the god of the *ephebe*, the youth who stands poised on the threshold between childhood and maturity. What is this mythic image telling us? Think about it. What does the Sun's ripening power mean for us as humans? I have written it on the diagram. The Sun brings potentials into flower and fruit. It actualises possibilities and makes them real in life. The Sun's light makes our personalities mature. We realise our full selves in sunlight.

When we look at a birth chart, we see all kinds of configurations. We say, "Ah, this trine signifies this talent; that square indicates that problem; this semi-sextile represents this gift; that opposition indicates that conflict." Every chart is a dog's breakfast, in terms of consistency of theme. The contradictions all seem to cancel each other out. When we first begin to study astrology, we don't know where to begin, because there are so many contradictory statements in every birth chart. Which configuration are we? Are we the Moon-Saturn square or the Venus-Jupiter trine? And if we are both, what holds them together? What impels their development? We don't know where we are in this mass of competing planetary aspects and configurations, all of which describe potentials. There is something about the solar principle that brings these possibilities to fruition. It makes them ripen, and also connects them into a unified story. Can you understand what this means psychologically?

Audience: There is no guarantee that anything in a chart will ripen. There can be a potential talent, but it might never be used. There isn't any centre to the personality, without the Sun. Is that what you are saying?

Liz: Yes, that is what I am saying. Something acts as a centre around which everything else orbits. That something is what we call individual identity. It is very mysterious. A chart is a mass of potentials. We can take any birth chart, and we have no idea what the individual has made or will make out of it. We don't have a coherent story. We have only a mass of fragments. It is something within the individual that makes these fragments into a story, like placing isolated beads on a string to make a necklace. Have any of you ever worked with beads? There, on the table, is a pile of ceramic beads of various sizes and shapes and colours. There is no pattern. We work out how many of each we have, and then we say, "I think I will put a blue one first, and then three green ones, followed by a big amber one. Then I'll have another blue one, and then another three green ones." The finished necklace has order, design, harmony, intent. Before our intervention, the pile of beads did not.

The experiences of our lives, reflected by the configurations in our birth charts, also have no order or design until they are bound together by the cord of an individual identity. A birth chart is simply a moment in time. It might be the chart of a human. It could be the birth chart of one's cat. It could be the birth chart of the CPA. It could be any entity that comes into life, born at a certain moment and partaking in the qualities of that moment. We don't know what story can emerge from the possibilities in a birth chart. We have only a map of archetypal potentials. They are like the bones of a skeleton, but we don't know what order they need to be placed in, or what kind of flesh will grow on that bare structure. It is the Sun that brings things to maturity, that ripens potentials. The Sun makes sense of the bones, and impels us to grow a certain kind of flesh that will knit them together.

We may have a tough aspect in our chart, like Mars opposite Saturn or Moon square Pluto; or a comfortable aspect, like Venus conjunct Jupiter or Mercury trine Mars. We have many levels of interpretation for any aspect, depending on our perspective. For example, we can take Mars in Capricorn opposite Saturn in Cancer and read it in many different ways. If we see it in the chart of a young person – say, an eight-year-old, or a thirteen-year-old – we might safely assume that this person is being bounced back and forth by the aspect. We cannot expect a child to have sufficient coherence – or, put another

Part One: The Meaning of the Natal Sun

way, a sufficiently developed ego – to contain, let alone work creatively with, the conflict of energies and needs described by the aspect. He or she will be identified with the Capricorn Mars one moment, strong and tenacious and tough. And then, the next moment, he or she becomes the Cancerian Saturn, loses confidence, becomes apathetic and depressed, and thinks, "I can't do it. I'll fail. No one will love me. I'm not even going to try."

Without the sense of a coherent individual core, we are flung around from planet to planet and aspect to aspect, because there is no centre that can contain these things and bring them to maturity. The Sun seems to represent something inside us which, if it is shining, has the capacity to mature the chart. One is no longer Mars this moment and Saturn the next moment, not knowing which one is, feeling completely overwhelmed and impotent, and repeating the same compulsive patterns over and over again. One *has* a Mars, rather than *being* Mars; one has feelings and passions rather than being compulsively driven by feelings and passions. One has fears, rather than becoming the fear to the point where one is paralysed and incapable of action. In some schools of psychology, this is called dis-identification. It is not about controlling the chart, or transcending it. It is about the different components of the chart making sense in relation to each other and fitting into a whole because there is someone at the centre. Another way of putting it is that consciousness of self allows us to take responsibility for how we deal with what is within us. It does not make the difficulties of a Mars-Saturn opposition go away. But we may experience the difficulties differently, and we may have a greater capability of developing the creative potentials inherent in the aspect.

Whatever this centre is, it has the power to alter the way we experience the ingredients of the chart, which, in mythic symbolism, are really the seeds with which we begin life. For these seeds to mature, we need the Sun. Otherwise, the chart remains a series of fragments, like episodes in a story that don't have any connecting theme. One doesn't realise they are part of a single book. One's life makes no sense. The feeling of continuity, which is so important for self-confidence, is lost or has never been present, because we are flung about from one emotional state to another, from one complex to another. That would be how I understand this image of maturing or ripening the fruits of the earth.

It is very hard to describe what happens when we are expressing an aspect unconsciously, and how it changes when we are conscious of it. By "conscious of it" I don't mean merely intellectually aware of it, but able to experience and observe it deeply on every level. Mars-Saturn, if we are unconscious of it, may be regularly projected. It may constantly appear in the world outside us, and it may seem as though other people are constantly obstructing us. Other people are Mars, pushing aggressively against our boundaries, or other people are Saturn, stopping us from going where we want to go. Life is a hardship; authority is malevolent. One does not feel in charge of one's own journey. One doesn't even know one is on a journey. One is at the mercy of the aspect as it manifests in outer life. And as it manifests inside, one is at the mercy of one's compulsions.

Audience: Yes, but I think that, when you are able to ask the question, "What do I really want?", that makes a difference.

Liz: Oh, yes. It makes a huge difference. But when you ask the question, "What do I really want?", who is the "I" you are referring to? Many people say, "I want this or that," but the "I" is suspect – it may not reflect the centre, the deeper individual. It may merely reflect the collective, or one of many chart configurations temporarily elbowing its way onto the stage. A woman says, "All I want is to get married and have a family," and we cannot be sure who is speaking – the "real" woman or the voice of parents and society, which insists that all women get married and have families. Who is the "real" person? What do marriage and family mean to that particular person at that particular stage in life? If an individual says he or she "really wants" something, and it is flagrantly in contradiction to the Sun in the chart, then perhaps it is not a bad idea to question the authenticity of this voice. That does not imply lying or dishonesty, or that the desire is "wrong". But it may suggest that something fundamental at the core of the personality is still unformed or unexpressed.

One can say about one's Mars-Saturn opposition, "Yes, I know I have a very aggressive, uncompromising element in my personality. I become very resentful when I don't get what I want. But there are some 'up' sides to that. I am tenacious and hard-working and determined. I find it very hard to accept any thwarting of my will. But I can learn to contain my frustration better. I can try to understand where my own anxieties and negative expectations block me. And most importantly, I can try to focus my tenacity on goals which really matter to me." One

Part One: The Meaning of the Natal Sun

can imagine this kind of dialogue around any aspect. The Sun, the "I", says "I have these qualities, I feel and want these things, but I will choose to do this with my life rather than that. I may not always succeed. I may make a mess of it. But I will try because I believe in something strongly enough to make it worth the effort." It is this "I" inside that has values and ideals, and the values make us feel we can choose one thing over another. If we don't have any values, or if we don't have any inner morality – and I don't mean the word "morality" in a conventional sense – how can we know what we "really" want? How can we make a choice? What do we base our choices on? All this is connected with the maturing of the chart through consciousness of self.

Audience: Even more than choosing, it sounds as if the Sun makes the story. So it has to have a sense of self – "I am important enough to have a story." It not necessarily moral, not in the ordinary sense. But it says, "I am important, and this is my story."

Liz: Yes. As I said, I am not using the word "moral" in the colloquial sense. For a great many people, morality is rooted in childhood religious teachings, or parental dictates, or social definitions of right and wrong. It is not heartfelt, and does not come from inside. It is acquired, and may be rooted more in the fear of consequences than in a genuine inner set of values. But inner morality is not really concerned with the rules as they are set by the outer world. Rightness and wrongness arise from a measuring of life against an inner standard. It is a sense of allegiance to something, and the something is not one's ordinary, everyday self.

Audience: It is the Self, with a capital S. It's got to be.

Liz: This term is certainly the one many people would use, especially those involved in Jungian or transpersonal psychology. There are other terms as well. None of them can do any justice to the experience, because language is limited when it attempts to describe such inner states. How many of you aspire to be a good person, whatever your definition of "good" might be? How many of you hope to become a better person, to achieve a standard which you have set from within – not necessarily in terms of behaviour, but perhaps in your astrological or creative work, or in how you relate to other people? Virtually all of you have put your hands up. There is something within us that makes us want to become more than what we are – some image of high value which reflects what we feel to be our true potential. Is there anyone here devoid of this? Well, you probably wouldn't dare raise your hand if you were. This is something of what I mean by inner morality. It is connected to what we perceive as the "highest good", which is very close to, if not identical with, religious aspiration – although conventional religious terminology might never come into it. Perhaps it is the Self with a capital S. I am inclined to just call it the astrological Sun, which also has a capital S.

Audience: Hard to describe, I guess.

Liz: Yes, very hard to describe. That is why we use symbols.

A story needs a plot

Audience: I think that people with the Sun in Leo, or a strong chart emphasis in Leo, are very good at telling stories about themselves. I am thinking of a friend with the Sun in Leo, who makes up stories. They are funny, and they are good stories. The point is that she is always the star, the centre of these really hot stories.

Liz: Yes, it is a Leonine quality, as we might expect, since Leo is ruled by the Sun. A story has a plot that threads people and occurrences together. The idea of a plot is really very profound. It is hard to define, but we know when there is no plot, or when the plot is poorly conceived. If we read a bad novel or see a bad film, we say, "The plot was terrible," or, "There wasn't any plot, just lots of car chases and sex scenes." It is like the string of beads I mentioned earlier. The plot is both the string and the order or pattern in which the beads are placed. The events and people described are the beads themselves. If there is no string and no pattern, there is no necklace, just a pile of beads rattling around.

A story implies a continuity of something that runs all the way through. In a novel, the continuity usually comes either from the narrator or from a protagonist described in the third person. Sometimes it can come from a series of observations by different people about the same character or event. But there is always a linking thread, an idea or a point or a message or an observation. We might equate the Sun's plot with the individual's myth or, as Socrates once put it, the individual *daimon*. Interestingly, the Greek word *mythos* has two meanings: it can be a story, or it can be a plot or structure.

The Sun's plot is the story that makes an individual life coherent. We should not be surprised at the fact that in the Greek world, the bard – the poet-singer who recited the great sagas and tales – was sacred to, and inspired by, Apollo. We may not be poet-singers in a literal sense. But something inside us is singing our story. We can say to ourselves, "I am someone special. I have a story. However unexciting it might seem to others, there is a continuity in my life – someone unique who is always there. Perhaps I change, perhaps I see things differently at different times. Perhaps I have been quite transformed by certain experiences. But there is within me a self that continues."

Audience: Is it a sense of integrity?

Liz: Yes, it is a kind of integrity, in the sense of something whole, something that is complete and "right" and loyal to itself. A lot of our work as astrologers involves trying to help the client get in touch with that solar essence, that central principle. Many people have difficulty experiencing it, and struggle to find some point to their lives. It is also a major reason why many of us take up the study of astrology in the first place. We are looking for something that will give us the sense of a story. We want to understand our birth chart, which we hope will reveal our uniqueness, our purpose, our continuity.

How many times have you heard a client ask, "Is my chart unusual? Is it very different from others you have seen?" As astrologers, we deal with clients who, in one form or another, are asking the same underlying questions we ourselves ask: "Who am I? What is my story? What is the meaning of the things that have happened to me? What is my destiny? What is my purpose? Don't tell me about how important others are. Tell me *I* am important." If we can get just a little glimpse of an answer, then we have a reason to keep going and, more importantly, to aspire to become the best of what we potentially are.

The god of healing

Now I would like to look at Apollo as the god of healing. We use this word "healing" a lot in astrological, psychological, and esoteric circles. We want to go to healers or become healers, or we say, "Astrology is healing. Psychotherapy is healing." What are we talking about? What does it mean to be healed?

Audience: Integrating things.

Liz: Go on.

Audience: To function again, after not being able to function.

Liz: Keep going.

Audience: Healing is wholeness.

Liz: Many of you have had experiences where you feel something wounded or damaged or sick was healed. What happened?

Audience: It felt like a connection with the life-force.

Audience: Consciousness.

Audience: A sense of relief.

Audience: The wound closed up.

Audience: Things made sense and fell into place.

Liz: Once again, we are facing the limits of language. On a physical level, something that is not functioning properly begins to function again. It is restored to health, which is to say, it becomes entirely itself again, according to its essential purpose. Your skin is healed of its rash. Your heart is healed of its irregular heartbeat. Your asthma goes away. Your headaches stop. What does this mean? The organ which is meant to be fulfilling a certain purpose can now fulfil that purpose without being compromised by pain, inflammation, or blockage. It will not infect or destroy other parts of the body, or endanger life. "Healthy" skin does not produce a rash, and a "healthy" heart does not beat irregularly. When it has been "healed", the "sick" organ is restored to what it was meant to be in the first place. It has its integrity back.

The form of healing we favour – whether it is orthodox or alternative medicine, spiritual or psychological healing – may, in the end, be less important than our subjective experience of being healed. Moreover, the line of demarcation between a physical and a psychological wound or illness may be far more blurred than we think. When we seek healing on the inner level, we are looking for something that can help us return to the kind of integral functioning we know we are meant to perform. Then we say, "I feel something has healed. A wound inside is no longer destroying or limiting my life. A condition of disease, or dis-ease, has been removed." We see and feel the wound or disease differently. We are no longer identified with it. We are no longer stuck in poison and misery, anger and pain, loneliness and fear. We may still feel the hurtful feelings, and perhaps even suffer the same physical symptoms. But we are not the wound any more. We are a person who experiences a wound. Because we are restored to what we are meant to be, the wound no longer has the power to prevent us being what we are.

All of this is connected with the kind of healing the Sun offers, and it is the essence of the healing that went on in those centres of the ancient world where Apollo and Aesklepios, his son, were worshipped. We don't know a lot about the techniques used at these healing centres, other than that music and dream work were important. The scientific community is gradually realising that – *mirabile dictu!* - there might be something in it. Recently there was an article in *The Times* about a great new discovery: music actually has an effect on the body! Astounding! The Greeks worked this out 2500 years ago. They were well aware of the connection between harmony in music, harmony in the psyche, and harmony in the body. I don't need to remind you that Apollo was the god of music, and that his characteristic mode of manifestation was thought to be through the revelations of dreams.

The god of music

The idea that there is a cosmic harmony – personified by Apollo as cosmocrator, "he who puts the heavenly bodies in order" – seems to have first been structured into a philosophical system by Pythagoras in the 7th century BCE. At least, this is the earliest reference we have, although the idea probably existed long before. This harmony was understood to be based on number and expressed through music, which echoes the music made by the planets in their orbits. Plato took up this idea and developed it, drawing on the cosmology of the Orphic cults which portrayed Orpheus, also (like Aesklepios) the son of Apollo, as the poet-singer who articulated the cosmic order through his music. Order in this context means a sense of proportion, balance, and interrelationship. Everything has its appropriate place in the whole, functioning according to its purpose. The idea is that, if one plays or listens to music that echoes the cosmic harmonies, this will have a powerful healing effect on the psyche and the body. "Give your grief to Apollo in a song," says Theseus in Mary Renault's wonderful novel, *The King Must Die,* "and he will take the grief away."

Any of you who love music will know what a powerful effect it can have on many levels. This may be one of the reasons why a great deal of "modern" music of the intellectual, theoretical kind leaves us cold and does not touch our hearts in the same way as music which has been composed through genuine inspiration. Eric Clapton's blues may move us far more than Peter Maxwell-Davies' intricate and discordant mathematical constructions, because blues and jazz draw on fundamental, visceral and heartfelt harmonies and rhythms. But Clapton is not currently deemed to be a "proper" composer, while Maxwell-Davies is. We are told by the composers of these kinds of works, and by certain music critics, that we are too ignorant to "understand" this kind of modern music properly, and that is why we do not respond. But perhaps something in us understands all too well, and recognises that the Sun-god is not present.

One of the major functions of Apollo in myth is to serve as the ordering principle in the cosmos, and his power to heal and inspire through music is a reflection of that order. In the same way, one of the major functions of the astrological Sun in the chart is as the ordering principle in the psyche, which acts as a healing agent because it generates and restores inner harmony – the individual harmony appropriate for each birth chart. We need to learn to hear, and play, our own special form of inner music.

Solar play

Let's say that a person has the Sun in the 5th house. Does anyone here have the Sun in the 5th? Two of you? Good. Now, bear in mind everything we have been talking about, and try giving me an interpretation of that placement. Let's say you have a male client coming to see you, who has the Sun in the 5th. What is needed by this individual in order to experience his own integrity, in order to feel he is functioning as he is meant to function, in order to feel connected with his own essential life-giving force?

Audience: He needs to have a sense of being able to create.

Liz: Go on. What does "create" mean?

Audience: Express himself.

Liz: Keep going. We use these words "create" and "express" very liberally. But what do they really mean? Try formulating it another way.

Audience: He needs to feel special.

Liz: When you create, what are you doing?

Audience: Part of myself comes out into life in some form.

Liz: Yes. Something intangible emerges spontaneously from inside – an idea, a feeling, an image, an intuition – and you are making something out of it, something that didn't exist before.

Audience: Is it just for yourself?

Liz: Yes, it's just for yourself – or perhaps just for your Self. Otherwise you can't create. There must be a loyalty to the thing which emerges from within. If you try to create something merely to please those around you, you are betraying the inner vision. Hopefully, pleasing others will be a by-product, but that is not where it begins. There is a certain attentive attitude, a certain listening quality which encourages creative images to arise. Will and intent to control have the opposite effect. Elgar, Mozart, and many other composers claimed they simply listened to music they heard in their minds, and then wrote it down like scribes. The willingness to listen – which is really an act of devotion, an act of love – is directed within, not to the world outside.

Audience: I was thinking of somebody with the Sun in the 5th who loves to play games, like ice hockey.

Liz: Playing is also concerned with making something out of nothing. A creative sportsman or sportswoman is different from a technician. If you watch football matches on television, you will know that there are some teams that play like machines. There is no inspiration in their playing. They simply grind on. They are very boring to watch, even if they win. Then we catch a glimpse of an Italian team, or a French one, and the commentator says, "This is wonderful creative playing!" What does he mean? The individuals are doing their own thing. The idea of being merely one of a team does not motivate the exceptional kick, the amazing, unexpected goal. These players are stars. They are responding in the moment in an entirely individual way.

Audience: I didn't know you liked football.

Liz: I don't. But sometimes discretion is the better part of valour, if one is in Italy at a friend's house when an important match is on.

Audience: There is a certain unconcerned quality about this thing of creative playing. It is not unconcerned in the sense that you don't care about what happens or what comes of it. It is unconcerned in terms of that immediate, spontaneous response to the inner call. It is the loyalty to the ideal.

Liz: Yes, creative play is absolutely self-centred. Perhaps we should remember that, in myth, Apollo was born on an island – the Aegean island of Delos, which was deemed to be at the centre of the world.

Audience: Is it really unconcerned? I think you do want to show others what you have done.

Liz: Of course there is an element of wanting others to see and share in what one has created. We all want to be loved and appreciated. Also, for some people – perhaps especially those with the Sun in the 9th or 3rd, or in Gemini or Sagittarius, where there is a need to communicate ideas and inspire others – creative power is linked with a message which needs to be promulgated. But I am not sure this impulse to share springs from the creative process itself. When solar inspiration is at work in us, through whatever house or sign, the motivating energy is not other people. That comes afterward. Through creative activity we seek, and perhaps achieve, a connection with something that makes us feel we are, indeed, a child of the divine. We become a vessel for something. The next step may be the desire to give it to others, but not because they are essential to the process. And some people don't experience this need to share what they create. The act of doing it is sufficient. It is almost as if the Sun's very nature is to shine – it is a necessity, whether others are there to see it or not.

In fact, the Sun in the birth chart will not shine if there is too much concern for other people's acceptance. This is one of the things that we will look at more carefully later. When an individual is too preoccupied with other people's good opinions, things often go wrong with the solar principle. It may be blocked, or its expression may be badly distorted by the need to be affirmed by others. This is why the Sun is considered "in fall" in Libra. The Sun's light requires an absolute loyalty to something inside. If other people are warmed by it, that is wonderful, and one feels especially good. But even if no one is warmed by it, the Sun still requires that loyalty, although it may be painful to give it.

Audience: You could even take it further, and say, "Unless the Sun is itself, other people will not be warmed by it."

Liz: I believe that is true. We cease to be authentic without that loyalty, and what we create has something false in it and therefore not genuinely warming to others. When we see something which purports to be creative but is really all show, we know it straight away. It doesn't touch our hearts.

Audience: I have a sense, sometimes, when I have managed to create something authentic, that there is a deep stillness inside – a feeling of no longer needing to chase after things.

Liz: That is because you have touched the centre. Everything else is in motion around it, but the centre is still.

Audience: The joy is in the doing, and sometimes you don't even know you have been happy until after you have done it.

Liz: Can I take you up on that word "happy"? First you used the word "joy", and then the word "happy". They are not the same thing. Happiness is something we spend a great deal of time pursuing, because we believe we should have it. But I am not sure whether the Sun has anything at all to do with happiness in the sense we ordinarily use the word. I suspect that happiness, in that sense, is connected with other things in the chart.

Solar joy

Audience: So you would associate the Sun with joy?

Liz: Yes. I would also associate it with a sense of fulfillment. One can be absolutely miserable on the emotional level, or feel very unhappy and frustrated in a relationship, and yet there is a sense of meaningfulness in solar expression which conveys a special kind of joy. I think this is what you meant when you said, "The joy is in the doing, and you don't know you have been happy until afterward." The Sun does not leap about shouting, "Whoopee!" Apollo may be the lord of music, but he always has dignity. When we feel ourselves as the Sun, we feel real. We are at peace with our lives, even if we are unhappy. When we know we are being what we truly are, even if only for a little while, it gives us a reason to keep going, even if we are faced with great inner or outer hardship.

But without that sense of meaning, that experience of "I"-ness, we need other people to keep feeding us. Without them, we cannot find a reason to keep going. Happiness then keeps eluding us, because it depends on others to provide the illusory centre that we lack within ourselves. A separation may have devastating consequences, because it is more than an emotional loss. It is the loss of our centre, which has been projected elsewhere. We can be contented or happy when we experience the Moon or Venus. But the moment one's relationship network is disturbed or there is an emotional disappointment, one loses faith in life and in oneself. Many of the dreadful states people get into because of relationship disappointments are connected with the Sun not shining. The way we experience our emotional disappointments is very powerfully affected by the Sun. This doesn't mean that solar light will protect us from feeling miserable, wretched, hurt, rejected, abandoned, and awful if someone walks out on us or disappoints us or dies. But we have a reason to go on living beyond that relationship. We have our own purpose, our own destiny.

It's interesting to consider Beethoven's "Ode to Joy", which comes at the end of his Ninth (and last) Symphony. Beethoven wasn't exactly a happy chap when he wrote it. Did any of you see the film in which Gary Oldman starred, called *Immortal Beloved*? I would recommend it, as it is relevant to our theme. At the end of the film, Beethoven is old and ill, a miserable, lonely, stone-deaf wreck. His life has fallen apart around him. He is totally alienated from the young man he believes to be his son, the only human being with whom he still has any emotional connection. Yet somehow he manages to write the "Ode to Joy". Where has it come from? It is not joy in the sense of personal happiness. The music speaks of something else – the joy of the whole of creation, the music of the cosmos, which the film manages to convey in the image of the child lying with his face turned toward the infinite heavens. No one could be more unhappy than Beethoven was at the end of his life. Yet this music has the power to inspire joy in the listener.

Audience: Even though you might be going through a miserable situation, something pulls you out – a connection with something.

Liz: Yes, there is something inside that says, "You are worth something. There is a reason why you are alive, and whatever you go through, it serves the deeper purpose of your existence." It is this profound conviction of individual purpose which the Sun conveys. It makes sense of the senselessness of existence, although not through any rational philosophy or neatly packaged set of spiritual beliefs. Life is very unfair, and it deals extremely painful, unmerited blows to people who do not deserve such suffering. If we look at life with a realistic rather than a childish eye, we can see its injustice with horrible clarity. No matter how good and enlightened we are, we still get walloped. Neither innocence nor wisdom can offer any protection. Neptune may offer solace with a vision of the bliss of post-incarnate unity, but it cannot provide a motivation to live and go on creating. Jupiter may offer the intuition of a meaningful cosmos, but the vision is not personal and does not define one's own specialness. Saturn may offer endurance, but if that is all we have, it's incredibly dreary and depressing. Without the solar principle, life is a pretty joyless place.

Audience: Is the Sun the plane of the eternal? Looking at it is like looking at a reflection of what you might be if you were perfect.

Liz: We need to remember that Apollo the Sun-god is the carrier of the light, not the light itself. Our astrological glyph for the Sun is identical with the symbol used for Apollo on ancient coins – a point within a circle. The circle is perfect, without beginning and without end, but it is incarnate only at the central point, which is bound by space and time and anchored in an imperfect world. At Delphi, this point was symbolised by the *omphalos,* the navel-stone – the place of earthly birth. The astrological Sun is equivalent to the mythic Apollo. What Apollo carries is Plato's idea of the One. The god is its vessel. In that sense, we each carry a little spark of the eternal life-force, the One, which is perfect. This is what we are connected to when we are engrossed in creative play, which is why we experience a timeless kind of joy. It does not usually last, and we cannot guarantee its reappearance. But because we carry it in a highly individual form, we sense that there is some special place for us in the universe, even if we don't understand what that place is, and even if we fail to live up to our ideal of it.

Audience: We may just get a glimpse of it, like Beethoven. Even though he was miserable, if he had made the right decisions, he could have lived that "Ode to Joy", not just glimpsed it.

Liz: Why do you say he didn't live it? Perhaps he lived it so deeply and completely that there was no room for personal happiness. We will deal with that issue more thoroughly later. But we can see this conundrum demonstrated in the world of music in dramatic ways. Many composers seem to be deeply connected with the solar principle, yet so many have the most appalling lives. Often the need to create is so consuming that any possibility of personal happiness is willingly and ruthlessly sacrificed. We are not in a position to say that they merely "glimpsed" joy.

Audience: I thought there was a link between music and Neptune.

Liz: I'm sure there is. But for an individual to translate the "music of the spheres" through the highly individual vehicle of personal creativity and personal style, the participation of the Sun is required.

Apollo and the Python

Audience: Is the Sun activated by crisis? The creative spirit comes out when someone faces a stormy sea. They have to survive. They swim three miles to shore. That is a creative act.

Liz: They do say that necessity is the mother of invention. I think I mentioned at the beginning of the seminar that the Sun must struggle. The Sun cannot develop its capacity to give light without a struggle. This is why, in every solar myth, the Sun-god must battle with a dragon, a snake, a monster, or some other horrible creature from the depths in order to fulfil his destiny. Osiris must battle with Set. Mithras must slay the bull. Marduk must conquer Tiamat. Apollo must conquer the Python in order to take his rightful place at Delphi. In some solar myths, the struggle is cyclical and occurs again and again. Each time the battle is won, the Sun rises again. Then the monster returns, either in the same form, as in the myth of Osiris, or in some other form, as in the story of Herakles, a solar hero often associated with Apollo. In other stories, the battle ends in defeat on the incarnate level, as in the tale of Orpheus, but results in the deification of the hero – he takes his place as a god.
  Our sense of solar specialness seems to depend on struggle. The process of development of the self in childhood arises from struggle. The ego forms through struggle. We must fight to get out of the birth canal. We must pit ourselves against our own regressive pull back into the womb. We have to fight our parents. We have to kick and scream and go through the "terrible twos". We have to struggle in order to

become someone separate. We have to struggle to assert ourselves in the world. Without this continuing struggle, there is no solar light. The two things go together. Likewise, when we express the Sun, we create struggle. By becoming ourselves, we generate the struggles which require us to become ourselves. Apollo has a lot of trouble with Plutonic figures like the Python and the Erinyes. He is always struggling with the forces of darkness. Yet he never destroys them. He creates a different balance. Because he casts so much light, he makes these chthonic creatures angry. He himself activates the struggle because he is polarised against their realm. Yet he is also part of their realm, and only exists because of them. In some mysterious way he is the product of the very thing he is battling with, because their darkness generates the necessity for light.

Apollo the curse-breaker

Audience: Can you explain that further? I am trying to understand this in relation to Sun-Pluto, or maybe Sun in Scorpio.

Liz: Perhaps we should consider it first in relation to the Sun in the 8th house. Let's start with another of Apollo's mythic functions: the breaker of curses. The Sun-god has the power to release the individual from a family curse. I think you can all understand what this might mean on a psychological level. The sense of being a unique individual with our own special destiny lessens the power that family complexes have over us, and our identification with the family psyche isn't as consuming when the Sun is shining.

We still have the same family background and the same psychic inheritance – we can't unmake that, whatever we do or become. We may still have scars, and we may still have hurts and fears with which we have to struggle. But we are not "cursed", which is to say, we don't have to keep repeating destructive family patterns. The Greek family curse is really a family complex which generates compulsive behaviour patterns generation after generation, with increasingly dire results. The Sun in the 8th house also points to a family complex which generates compulsive behaviour patterns, and sometimes reflects dramatic childhood events over which the individual appears to have no control. We might say that the Sun's destiny, when it is in the 8th, is to become conscious of these issues in order to become the "curse-breaker" for the family.

Family curses in Greek myth, like the curse of the House of Thebes or the curse of the House of Atreus, seem to doom individual members of the family. They are compelled to perform certain actions or endure certain kinds of suffering because of what their fathers and mothers and grandfathers and grandmothers did. The individual experiences a sense of impotence in the face of something that has come down through the family. One has no power over it, and one's life is completely dominated or controlled by it. Many of you may know this experience through psychotherapy – you recognise a problem, you work on it, and it just doesn't want to budge. Hillman, in *The Soul and the Underworld,* describes this as a feeling of being bound to a wheel, like Ixion in Greek myth. One goes around and around, repeating the same compulsions, feeling the same emotions. Apollo is the god to whom one turns in order to get off the wheel. He alone, in myth, has the power to stop the Erinyes or Furies, who represent the debts of the past, from destroying the object of their prey. He dispels the power of the curse because, in the moment we become truly ourselves, we aren't our family any more. We are no longer identified with that collective psyche. We have our own self, our own values. We can choose. The more conscious we are, the less power family complexes have. They may still cause suffering and conflict, but they no longer dominate one's life.

Apollo is also the god to whom one turns when one is full of grief. If we don't try to suppress grief, but instead put it into a song, a poem, or a painting, we are, in effect, offering it to the god, and he transforms it. Whatever our misery is, if we express it to the god – under whatever name we choose to give him – through a creative vessel, something happens. The very process of doing this is magical. It creates a space between oneself and one's grief without creating dissociation. Although it's still grief, it's bearable grief. It's no longer overwhelming.

Audience: Grief can be beautiful.

Liz: Some of our most powerful emotions, especially those connected with loss, are not beautiful, and Apollo does not necessarily make them beautiful. He makes them bearable. The object is not to create something pretty, but to offer one's grief to the god, naked and unashamed. This is different from wallowing in it, which is not an act of offering. Grief can be horrific, but expressing it in this way changes the way we experience it. Feelings of grief are not usually beautiful. They are more often savage and black and brutal. Nor do they necessarily become beautiful through creative expression, although some people try consciously to make them so – which is not in the least bit helpful.

But something happens when we put the sorrow inside us into an image or a piece of music as an act of offering rather than an act of control or a litany of self-pity. I would be hard-pressed to explain exactly what happens. Such things do not lend themselves to rational analysis. Think of the songs which were sung by the black slaves in America a century and a half ago, which form the basis of modern blues and jazz, and which are usually spiritually focused. This offers us a living example of the mysterious process through which creative expression makes grief bearable.

Creative speech

Let's jump around a bit, and look at the Sun in another house to see how the Sun can light up the chart. We can take the Sun in the 3rd. We have been looking at Apollo as cosmocrator – the god who keeps the system in harmony. We have also looked at his role as dragon-slayer and breaker of curses. Another of his important functions is as the guide and educator of youth. He was known as *kouros,* the divine youth, the quintessential *puer.* Apollo is always portrayed in Greco-Roman art as not quite mature. He is manly and beautiful, but with the beauty of a youth who is on the threshold of manhood, and he is always clean-shaven with long hair. Sometimes his body is almost feminine, and never heavily muscled as are the figures of Zeus or Ares.

All this is relevant to the 3rd house. Apollo's name has an earlier form: Apellon. This word is related to assemblies and elections.[8] Apollo

---

[8] The etymology of Apollo's name, Apóllôn, has defied linguistic reconstruction for a long time. Walter Burkert proposed that the Doric form of the name, Apéllôn, be connected with the noun *apéllai,* meaning a seasonally recurring festival of kinship groups. Gregory Nagy suggests it is also connected with *apeilé,* based on the concept of speech, so Apollo is the god of authoritative speech, speaking before an assembly, or speaking myths, *mûthos,* in the context of a ritual. It is also the speaking of a vow. It is clearly connected with the pronouncement of the oracle. (See *Apollo: Origins and Influences,* ed. Jon

presides over those initiation ceremonies in which the full-grown youth becomes a sharer in sacred rites, and can enter the assembly and discuss community issues. Apollo was also Phoibos of the unshorn hair, for those who were passing from childhood to manhood went to Delphi and offered their youthful long locks to the god – one of the rites of puberty. He-of-the-unshorn-hair is youth incarnate, just about to be initiated.[9]

How many of you have the Sun in the 3rd house? What does this Sun need in order to experience a sense of specialness?

Audience: Communication.

Liz: What does "communication" mean? It is one of those words, like "creativity", which we throw around a lot.

Audience: Connection.

Liz: Connection with what?

Audience: Knowledge.

Audience: It's about exchanging ideas

Liz: What is an idea?

Audience: It is a thought that you have.

Liz: Let's think of the zodiacal cycle, beginning with Aries, or, transposed onto the horoscope, the 1st house. Sometimes we need to go back and remember our basics. The first degree of Aries is the beginning of the new yearly cycle: the great cosmic cry of life, which shouts, "I'm here!" It is the eruption of cardinal fire, the first impulse of the life-force which bursts forth in the spring at the vernal equinox. The 1st house of the horoscope is the point of birth: the individual arrives in life as an

---

Solomon, University of Arizona Press, Tucson and London, 1994, "The Name of Apollo: Etymology and Essence" by Gregory Nagy.)
[9] From *Themis: A Study of the Social Origins of Greek Religion* by Jane Harrison, Merlin Press, London, 1963.

independent entity. Then we move into Taurus and the 2nd house. In Taurus, life says, "I am embodied. I exist in form. I have physical reality." The 2nd house of the horoscope is the experience of embodiment: I see, I hear, I smell, I taste, I touch. I am hungry, I am cold, I thirst. What will satisfy my needs? This feels nice, that feels horrible. This gives me pleasure, that gives me pain. I value what makes me feel good, and reject what makes me feel bad."

And then? Then we move to Gemini and the 3rd house. In Gemini, life says: "I am here, and I am embodied. Now I must learn about the world I inhabit." The 3rd house of the horoscope is the discovery of the otherness of the outer world. Hence, like the 7th and the 11th, it is a house of relationship. The world impinges in the form of siblings, who are much more "other" than parents, and through our first experiences at school, when we move beyond the family matrix. We are overwhelmed with information and must learn to process it. Therefore we must think, we must learn, we must formulate and conceptualise, we must gather information. Otherwise, how do we cope with the overwhelming flood of experiences that are hitting us at every moment of every living day?

Audience: I thought the 6th house was the house concerned with ordering the environment.

Audience: This isn't about order. I think I can understand this. In the 3rd, you are finding out what is there.

Liz: Yes. And how do we do that? We name things. We identify their characteristics and categorise them for future reference. Virgo's kind of order, the order of the 6th house, is further down the line from Gemini. Once we know the names of things and the categories to which they belong, we can then work out how they connect with each other, and which among them is useful and helps to make life better and more efficient. But the Virgoan dimension of Mercury can only operate if the Geminian dimension has first identified the nature of the world in which one lives. Virgo may want to get from Regent's College to Berkeley Square in the fastest, most efficient way. But to do that, direct Geminian experience is necessary first, which comes only from exploring every possible route, getting lost many times, and giving a name to each street once it has been identified. Virgo can then put all this knowledge together and make a map, ordering the information that has been gleaned from Gemini's experience, so that one does not have to keep getting lost again and again. Gemini is happy to meander and discover. Virgo is interested in the fact that the fastest, most efficient route is to cross the Marylebone Road, walk down Baker Street, cross Oxford Street, and make one's way down Duke Street. This would not be possible if Gemini had not first discovered a thoroughfare and called it the Marylebone Road.

Audience: So the 3rd house provides a sense of structure.

Liz: Yes, it provides mental structures. In the 3rd, we structure our environment by identifying the differences between things. We do this by creating an idea of each thing, abstracted from the thing itself. Through ideas, we categorise experiences which would otherwise be overwhelmingly muddled. Our senses cannot name and identify things for us. We simply smell, hear, see, taste, and touch them. Very young children orientate themselves by smelling, touching, and tasting things. This establishes whether the object smells, feels, and tastes good or bad. When they are old enough to form words, they point at the object and say, "Cat. Me. Dog. Pencil." The child has structured sensory experience by abstracting an idea of the object for future reference. "Now I know what dog patootey is. Next time I see some, I won't put it in my mouth. It comes out of the bottom of a dog, and it smells and tastes bad." All this is part of the 3rd house process. It involves recognising and differentiating the components of the environment.

How do we acquire this kind of knowledge? We can't develop it in a vacuum. We must make contact with the world. 9th house knowledge may arise intuitively, but 3rd house knowledge depends on interaction. How do I know this is a pen? If there is no one who can tell me, then I have to make a mess and work it out myself. Ah! it writes! And it drips black stuff all over my hands when I pull it apart! A child is forever saying to parents, siblings, teachers, "What is this called? What is it for? Why is the grass green? Why is the sky blue?" We have to interact in order to learn, either with other humans or directly with the object we want to learn about. The 3rd house is concerned with learning, and in order to learn, we must make contact. This is the house of contacts and connections, all for the purpose of expanding our mental data base. In order to feel alive, to feel there is a point to existence, a 3rd house Sun must constantly and forever go on learning. If that capacity is taken away, or the person with the Sun in the 3rd doesn't understand how profound the need is, what happens?

Audience: The light goes out.

Liz: Yes. One sinks into a very dreary, boring, soul-destroying, lifeless world. One suffocates, mentally and spiritually.

Audience: I know someone with Sun and Moon in the 3rd house, and he worked for a long time studying sleep disorders. He would stay up all night studying, and remained in college for twelve years to do this. He studied sleep disorders because he couldn't get to sleep.

Liz: The quest for knowledge, when the Sun is in the 3rd, is both a hunger and a struggle. The hunger comes from the sense that learning makes one feel more alive than anything else. The struggle comes because all the knowledge one absorbs through conventional educational channels seems somehow insufficient and incomplete. We don't start off life with the Sun already shining. There is a little glimmer that beckons, but there isn't yet an ego that can integrate it or formulate it as a goal or aspiration. In childhood we project the Sun. Although we are it, we don't yet know we are it, or even that we want to become it. We perceive it "outside", and we follow the light. We have to struggle to actually become the Sun ourselves. Very often, when the Sun is in the 3rd house, the projection lands on a sibling, who appears to be the carrier of the light. Or it may attach itself to a teacher, or a system of thought, or a set of ideas. The light seems to be out there somewhere, and we try to get it by modeling our thoughts and attitudes on "outside" sources. Then there is a tremendous ongoing struggle to find one's own light.

The lonely god

There is another thing I would like to mention. Apollo is a beloved god. He is loved by both other gods and humans. In the Homeric *Hymn to Apollo,* when he first enters the great hall of the gods on Olympus, all the other gods stand up for him. And yet he has no family, no wife or partner. He has the occasional lover, but in the main, they reject or betray him. The children that he fathers come to early bad ends. There is something that doesn't work here, something this imagery is telling us about the Sun. Apollo is a god who founds no family. There is no dynasty. All the other gods father heroic demi-gods who carry on the god's line into humanity. Zeus fathers many sons and daughters on mortal women. Aphrodite has a child, Aeneas, by the mortal Anchises, and the Julio-Claudian emperors in Roman times claimed to trace their decent from this Trojan hero. Throughout the ancient world, people claimed descent from one or another of the gods. But Apollo's children don't create dynasties. Phaëton dies in flames when he crashes the Sun-chariot. Orpheus is torn to pieces by Maenads. Aesklepios is struck down by Zeus' thunderbolt when he brings a dead man back to life. This is a family-less god. What do you think this tells us about the Sun?

Audience: That it stands alone. There is something very isolated about being entirely yourself.

Audience: Solar creativity is a solitary process.

Liz: Yes. One cannot do it with other people. The dark side of solar light is the experience of absolute aloneness. We cannot create in a committee, and we cannot make a connection to our inner *daimon* if our allegiance is given to the outer world. We cannot be ourselves if we are pouring our energy into pleasing others. There is a price to be paid, and a place of suffering which awaits us if we live the Sun. For all of Apollo's excellence in myth, he cannot have this one thing. He cannot be the vessel for the Sun and play happy families at the same time. Now, please don't take this imagery literally. I'm *not* saying that one cannot have a family or a rewarding permanent relationship in actual life. The Sun's solitude is symbolic, and is concerned with inner allegiance.

Audience: But we don't feel entirely alive if we don't live the Sun.

Liz: Yes, and there is a price to be paid for feeling entirely alive. There is an essential loneliness inherent in the Sun. We cannot have the light without paying the price.

Apollo and the Muses

Audience: What about the Muses? Aren't they connected with Apollo?

Liz: Yes. There are different versions in myth of who the Muses are. Usually they are portrayed as his companions. But they don't produce children either. They are curiously static figures, without stories of their own. They are really facets of Apollo himself. I have put their names and functions on the diagram I showed you earlier. Apollo sends them out into the world, and they visit humans with creative inspiration. The fact that they are female, like the Pythoness, is very interesting. With all of these female images connected with the Sun-god, we end up recognising that Apollo is not strictly male. He is androgynous. The Muses, as well as the Pythoness, are his female attributes.

There is something important about this image of inspiration coming to humans through female figures. The direct impact of solar power on consciousness would destroy any mortal. One doesn't hear the Ninth Symphony directly from the god. He sends a Muse, which is to say, inspiration is filtered through the feelings, the intuition, the imagination, the body's sensations. For many artists, the Muse is projected onto a real woman who serves as a conduit – an *anima* figure, as Jung put it, activating the soul and opening the gate to inspiration. But the Muse does not have to be embodied in human form, as it was for Wagner when he wrote *Tristan und Isolde*. The Muse may be nature. Wordsworth's poetry and Elgar's music were both inspired by nature.

Audience: Is the Muse always female?

Liz: The Muses are female in myth. But creative inspiration occurs in both sexes, and does not depend on an actual woman to do the inspiring. As I said, nature may provide the inspiration. A man may also serve as a Muse in a relationship with either a woman or another man. We may need to look more carefully at the way we attribute "masculine" and "feminine" qualities to the planets. What does this myth of the Muses mean? Why is creative inspiration portrayed as initiating with a male deity yet transmitting through a female one, whether it is a man or woman that is being inspired?

Audience: If you are a woman, you have to use your male side to be creative.

Liz: Creative work is a synthesis of both male and female qualities, whichever sex is doing the creating. I think this is what the juxtaposition of the Sun-god and the Muses means in myth. To write a book or paint a painting or compose a piece of music, we need both logic and imagination, structure and fluidity, forward planning and spontaneity, clear sight and the darkness of gestation. Logic without inspiration produces an instruction handbook. Inspiration without logic produces a chaotic mess, if it produces anything at all other than a fantasy of the great work that is never actually produced. Inspiration begins with the Sun but comes, not through a masculine channel, but through a feminine one, whether you are a man or a woman. What does that mean?

Audience: It's the receptive side.

Liz: Yes, its the receptive side. It is something which can be still and listen and receive. To create, we must first receive. Also, I think it has something to do with the involvement of the feelings, the body, the intuition, and the imagination. Expressing solar light in a creative way requires something more than the intellect or practical skills. It has to come from subtler faculties. It has to be felt. This is why attempts to create from an intellectual structure so often fail miserably. There are many pieces of modern music, as I mentioned earlier, which are created intellectually. People listen to them and nothing happens. They are boring and dreary, and we turn the radio off or leave the concert halfway through because there is nothing being transmitted through the feelings, through the heart, through the body. No images are invoked; no memories rise up; no inner change occurs. One might say the same about certain architectural projects. Such buildings are intellectually designed, without any feeling of what it might be like to live and work in them. They are cold and soulless, and create inner distress and alienation rather than harmony and joy. Inspiration through the Muses must come through the feminine side of both men and women.

Audience: In a way, that makes it easier for a man to create.

Liz: Why?

Audience: I'm not sure. But it seems to be the case.

Liz: Perhaps "creating" seems different from what you ordinarily do as a man. A woman working from the feminine side of herself is just being herself, so she doesn't necessarily say, "Now I'm being creative." Relating to children, putting a meal together, putting a home together, dealing with other people at work – these things require great creativity. But they are taken for granted, and not thought of as creative. I have heard so many women say, "I'm not a very creative person, because I haven't gone off and written a book or painted beautiful paintings." Yet the skill of interacting with others receptively can be a work of art. Because it is not something dramatic, not something separate from everyday life, one doesn't recognise the solar creativity in it. One doesn't see the Muse in it. To dance gracefully within the ebbs and flows of a relationship is a work of music. To dialogue creatively every day with a growing child is a work of poetry. The Muses don't limit their inspiration to the opening night performance or the gallery exhibition.

Within this mythic framework, astrology is also perceived as an art, and there is a Muse of astrology called Urania. Some classical textbooks try to make her the Muse of astronomy, but in the ancient world there was no such thing as pure astronomy. Astrology and astronomy were conjoined, and the latter was used to provide the structure for the former. The Muses are the personification of the arts.

History is an art, and so, in myth, there is a Muse of history. Yet we are led to believe that history is the study of facts. This is a naive assumption. Mehmet the Conqueror invaded Constantinople in 1453. That is an historical fact. But depending on which history book we read, Mehmet was either a redeemer or a cruel tyrant, a warrior for the True Faith or a vile heretic. Christian biographers decry the fact that he slaughtered Christians and turned the great church of Aghia Sophia into a mosque. Yet Mehmet did not tear down the church as the Christians tore down the temples of the gods in Greece and Rome, and the Church has been culpable of far more gratuitous slaughter over the centuries than Mehmet was.

Which history is true here? If you visit the Colosseum in Rome, you will see a huge plaque mounted by one of the Popes in honour of the Christian martyrs who "died for their faith". But the Romans were

Part One: The Meaning of the Natal Sun 41

not interested in persecuting those of different faiths. They were extraordinarily tolerant of diverse religious approaches and did not perceive Christianity as intrinsically wrong or threatening. They wanted obedience to the basic laws of the State, within which one could worship as one pleased. The early Christians would not acknowledge the Emperor as their ruler. That is why they died. It was political rather than religious martyrdom. Perhaps the plaque should read, "To the Christian martyrs who died for their political views." Which history is true here?

Audience: I sometimes think a lot of the history we are taught at school is a pack of lies. I was brought up in America in the 1950s, and we were taught that the Indians were violent savages and the settlers were the good guys. Now that's politically incorrect. Now we're told that the Indians were the good guys and the settlers were greedy and vicious. What is the truth?

Liz: That's what Pontius Pilate is reputed to have asked. Historical truth depends largely on which government, which religious perspective, which social ideology is in power. Earlier perspectives are overturned, books censored or burned, educational programmes rewritten. In Shakespeare's "history plays", the Tudors always come out squeaky-clean and the Platagenets, like Richard III, are always villains. Richard III wasn't a hunchback, and according to all the latest research, he didn't murder the princes in the Tower. Henry VI (who was a Tudor) probably did. But in the play, Richard is a villain. This is because Shakespeare was writing for Queen Elizabeth I, who was also a Tudor.

Those in power rewrite history, either directly or through the artists they patronise. History is a creative process. We select the facts that support our premise, weave them together, and interpret them with imagination and feeling. Then we say, "This is history." Of course the interpretation changes, and the importance of specific facts changes as well. And sometimes facts themselves can be ignored or denied. There are still Germans who claim the Holocaust never happened. They are not merely being creative with history; they are denying reality altogether. The British history of the British presence in Ireland is a very interesting exercise in creative imagination. The Irish history of the British presence in Ireland is an equally interesting creative exercise. Often they seem to bear little resemblance to each other. I think you can see the parallel with an individual's personal history, which, as any analyst can tell you, is a creative process rather than a mere recollecting of facts.

Whether by nations or by individuals, historical facts are often suppressed or doctored, and then rise to the surface a long time later, requiring a new history to be written. Our understanding of history is constantly changing. We create stories out of whatever facts are either available or palatable, depending on how we want to see another country, how we want to see our own country, how we feel about other races, how we feel about our own race – in short, how we want to see life and ourselves. Whatever our issues are, as individuals and as a collective, we create and recreate history to justify the place we want to hold in history at any given time. It is a creative process.

So, here is Apollo, Lord of the Arts, who sends his Muse of history out to inspire a creative story for a particular society, for a particular culture, for a particular historian at any given time. We keep saying, "But these are facts. These are the statistics. This is the truth." Some astrologers likewise beat their heads against a brick wall, saying, "Astrology is a science! We can prove it with statistics!" But in myth, astrology is a Muse. As astrologers, we are inspired by Apollo's Muse, Urania. What does that mean? What happens to us when Urania is sent by the god to inspire us?

Audience: We interpret the chart creatively. The symbolism speaks.

Liz: Yes, we make a story, don't we? It is a creative art to make a chart into a story which can be communicated to someone who needs to hear their story. Whether it is the "right" story depends on many things. What is the "right" story? All of you who are honest with yourselves and are not locked into a rigid system of interpretation will know that several different approaches may apply to the same chart. Every chart has different levels. Although certain fundamentals remain the same, we can interpret signs, planets, house placements, and aspects differently, depending on our particular personal slant. Yet whatever that perspective, we can put our insights together and make a story which is absolutely appropriate for that client at that moment.

If the client comes back a year later, the fundamentals may be the same, but the story might be told differently. Think of the many different film versions of a particular novel, like *Dracula, Great*

Expectations, or *Wuthering Heights.* Reading a chart in this way is an enormously creative, spontaneous, inspirational state. It is an art, and it has to come through a Muse. That means it has to be felt and intuited, not merely patched together through logic. Although we need to always keep in mind the fundamental structure of the chart and the astrological basics, which must be learned thoroughly and well, a chart can't be interpreted by the intellect alone, or it remains two-dimensional. Even if the interpretation sounds good on paper and the keywords are accurate, the client will go away without inspiration and without light, because we haven't had the Muse with us.

Now I am going to put a chart on the overhead projector, and we can use it to look at the Sun in a particular sign and house. We can go back to the mythic images for amplification.

An example chart

Creative mediumship: the Sun in the 12th house

Many of you will recognise this chart – it belongs to Tony Blair. Here's the Sun in the 12th in Taurus. Let's start thinking about the Sun-sign as well as its natal house. Keep in mind all the things we have been looking at in relation to Sun-god mythology and psychology. Let's have some interpretations, please. Try to put aside your political convictions for the moment, and view the chart as though he were any new client. This man has come to you for a chart reading. What do you say to him? How does the Sun in the 12th need to shine?

Audience: He needs to get the hidden picture.

Audience: He needs to be involved with the collective.

Liz: The 12th is one of the houses concerned with the collective. Like the 8th and the 11th, it has two rulers, one of which is an outer planet. What dimension of the collective does the 12th reflect?

Audience: The collective unconscious.

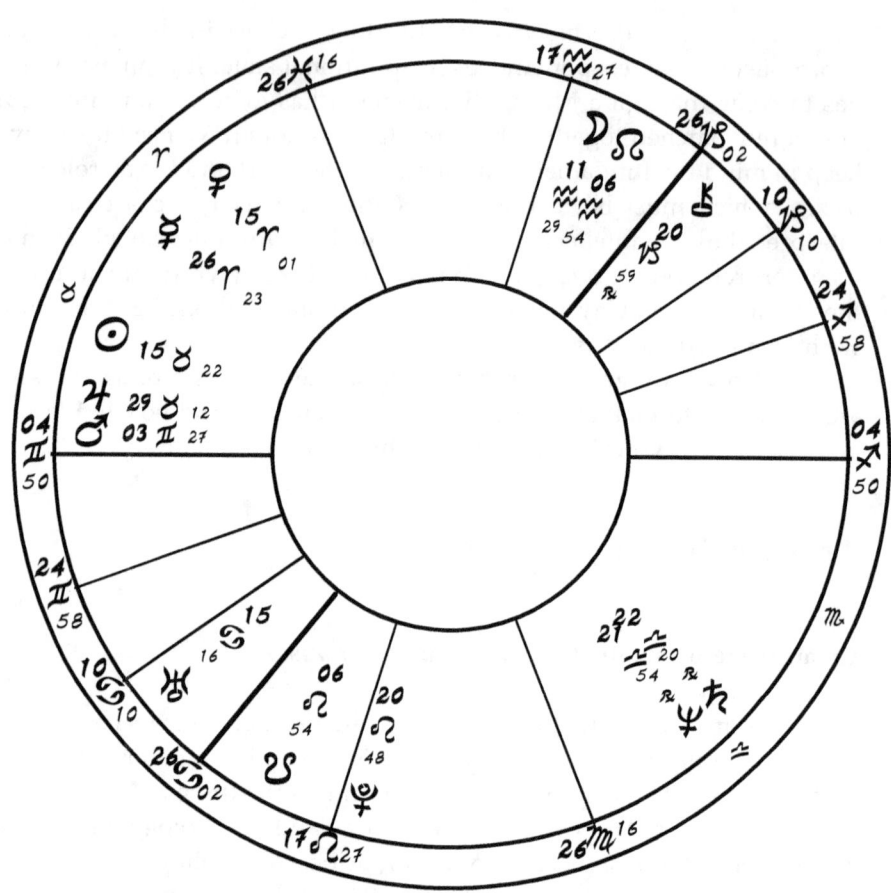

Tony Blair
6 May 1953, 6.10 am, Edinburgh

Liz: But what level, what dimension of the collective unconscious? The 8th is also concerned with collective unconscious issues – inherited family patterns of conflict, loss, and the use and abuse of power. The 12th is concerned with collective dreams, longings, and yearnings for redemption. The 8th deals with family compulsions and family "curses". The 12th is the house of the ancestors. It stretches back in time to one's social, racial, and religious roots.

Audience: It's called the house of karma.

Liz: How do you understand the word "karma"?

Audience: Old ancestral patterns that have to be worked through.

Liz: All right. Can you start making a story?

Audience: This is someone who is carrying hopes and dreams for an entire collective. He is in touch with everyone's longings. His personal goals are in the service of something much greater. Whether he can actually materialise it is another story.

Liz: Yes, that would depend on other things, not least the aspects to the Sun, and the whole balance of the chart. With the Sun in the 12th, the impulse to be a unique individual, to make an inner connection which conveys a sense of purpose and destiny, is coloured by a sense of unity with the larger collective. So the Sun cannot be entirely individual, except in the manner in which collective dreams and aspirations are expressed and given voice. This is the last of the twelve houses. It is the place where everything from the old cycle breaks down and disintegrates, and where everything is in a state of formation before a new cycle begins. It is a house of both endings and beginnings. Do any of you have the Sun in the 12th? Quite a few of you. What does this Sun need?

Audience: There is a sense of debt – needing to put something right.

Liz: That is a very astute comment. There is a sense of debt – the feeling of an obligation to the collective past. Also, the Sun placed here is a medium, a conduit. Many actors and artists have the Sun in the 12th.

Audience: It needs to give shape to the collective unconscious.

Liz: The Sun is in an earth sign, so the way in which this Sun mediates and transmits the 12th house world needs to be earthy. Something must be "made" out of the world of dreams and longings which is practical and useful to others. If it were the Sun in Pisces in the 12th, the vehicle might be more imaginative, or more inward, without the necessity of "making" anything. Or it could be through a spiritual path which other people don't get to hear about. Here, it is in an earth sign. What "thing" does it want to give shape to?

Audience: It wants to shape the immaterial realm into something Taurean. So it could have to do with material wealth or stability, or with beautiful objects, or with nature.

Liz: Yes, the collective longings to which this Sun is attuned are linked with safety, stability, and comfort in the material world. Yet despite the earthy component, this man is a visionary. All Suns in the 12th are visionaries. The Sun is always the vessel for the light, but here the vessel for the light here is shining underwater. What is it trying to light up?

Audience: What you said. The human longing for safety. Our need to feel safe in life.

Liz: Yes, I think that is the collective yearning which works through this Taurean Sun. It's a fundamental human longing going back over aeons.

Audience: The Sun in the 12th needs to bring to consciousness what is hidden.

Liz: Yes – what is unformed, what is unconscious, what is hidden. Here are all the debts and legacies from the past, the ancestors and ancestral *daimones*, the family and cultural myths. That's what it is shining light on, that's what it carries. Not easy, is it? How can one be an individual when one is so open to the collective? What happens to the individual?

Audience: He has to go through a sort of crucifixion.

Liz: There may be an element of suffering involved. 12th house myths often portray dismemberment, disintegration, drowning, purification, sacrifice, the giving up of something. For the Sun to shine in the 12th, it has to give something up.

Audience: Would he have to give up comfort? Taurus makes me think of material comfort, nice food, nice feelings. Maybe the Sun in Taurus in the 12th has to give up the pleasure of being comfortable.

Part One: The Meaning of the Natal Sun

Audience: Surely Sun in Taurus is related to the body. Maybe there needs to be some kind of sacrifice in the area of health.

Liz: Rather than interpreting the Sun-sign as the thing which has to be sacrificed, it might be more helpful to see it as the manner in which service is offered, and the kind of collective longing which is asking for embodiment. If there is sacrifice involved, it may have to do with giving up the purely personal level of solar expression. If the Sun is above the horizon, our *daimon* involves us with more than our own personal development and fulfillment. The Ascendant-Descendant axis, which is the east-west horizon, divides the houses into those concerned with personal development and those concerned with development through or with a larger humanity. Some people call the houses below the horizon personal and those above it universal. The 12th, if we use that terminology, is the last of the universal houses. This Sun has to give up its purely personal claim on Taurean values and pleasures. That doesn't mean Mr. Blair can't enjoy physical pleasure or must sacrifice his comfort. But he won't feel fulfilled unless other people are also comfortable and contented. The ghosts of past generations are always whispering in his ear. If he wishes to follow his destiny, he cannot live totally and utterly for himself. The personal expression of his solar light is blended into a greater collective need. That is the sacrifice.

With the Sun in the 12th, we need to ask, "What is this individual mediating for the collective? What is the nature of the ancestral inheritance they need to express?" Now, mediating the collective is not necessarily a good thing. Having the Sun in the 12th doesn't mediate only positive qualities in the ancestral inheritance. One can mediate the collective at times when the collective is in psychosis. And if the family inheritance is deeply disturbed, then one has to find a way to give positive shape to it. One can be a mouthpiece for a collective gone mad. "Collective" doesn't necessarily equate with goodness or spirituality. There are times in history when the collective has gone completely bonkers. Usually these times coincide with major outer planet configurations. Everything goes haywire and mass movements erupt, some of which are incredibly frightening and destructive.

The collective is not always fun to mediate. It is a sea of potentials, both dark and light, which are not yet manifested and which arise from both the past and the unformed future. A person with a 12th house Sun must struggle to be conscious, or they will be dominated by that which they are mediating. Unless the individual is able to express solar light, they may become the victim of the collective rather than a voluntary mouthpiece of expression for something in the collective. 12th house Suns are often victims because the Sun isn't shining. It is underwater and it is drowning, and then the dark side of the 12th is very much in evidence. Older textbooks don't mince about in naming these manifestations: madness, addiction, hidden enemies, and debilitating illnesses are all traditionally associated with the Sun in the 12th. So is "self-undoing", which may be more applicable in this example than we have yet seen. Yet the Sun in this house is not "malefic". There must be consciousness, because otherwise one will be crucified by one's openness to the larger psyche.

Audience: So survival depends on developing the Sun.

Liz: Yes, survival depends on developing the Sun.

Audience: Right. So although it's underwater, it is constantly trying to shine light.

Liz: Yes. The difficulty is that often the ancestral background mitigates against individuality. It's hard for the person to validate that solar need. That is the nature of the struggle when the Sun is in the 12th.

Audience: Could we say that the Sun in the 12th moves toward the Ascendant? That it wants to come out of the water?

Liz: All planets in the 12th eventually move out. They transit over the Ascendant in the early days or months of life, and the Moon moves out within a couple of days at the latest. Even if a planet is retrograde in the 12th, it will progress out by solar arc progression, or the progressing house cusps will eventually carry it into the 11th. In one sense, there is always a movement toward the light, an urge to express individuality directly and visibly. But even when a 12th house Sun progresses over the Ascendant, it always pulls the past behind it, because it begins its journey in the 12th.

Sun and Moon in square

Let's look at the Sun's aspects. The values of the Sun-sign must be part of one's life. We can't dismiss our Sun-sign, even if it's a singleton by element or seems incompatible with other important factors in the chart. The Sun-sign needs to be lived, by both element and quality, in the sphere of the house in which it is placed, even if this makes things difficult for other natal placements. But the sign and house are not, of course, the end of the story. In Tony Blair's chart, the Sun is square the Moon. It's also trine Chiron, square Pluto, and sextile Uranus. All these planets have to be included in the story of the Sun's development. None of them can be ignored, projected, or repressed. Every planet aspecting the Sun is an integral part of the Sun's story.

Of these planets aspecting the Sun, only one of them is personal – the Moon. The rest are all outer planets. How can he bring in the Moon as part of the Sun's expression? Anyone with a Sun-Moon aspect needs to include the lunar world in the solar one, but here there is a conflict. What kind of difficulty might that square portray?

Audience: Maybe there would be early problems with the mother. I think a Sun-Moon square shows a very deep split in the person's nature, and it starts with the parents.

Liz: Yes, that is one perspective. The Sun and Moon are parental significators, and the square suggests a perception of the parental relationship as a battleground. Our "inner" parents also seem to be in eternal conflict, and what we aspire to as an individual always seems to be incompatible with what we need to feel safe and emotionally secure. Usually, with a square, we favour one side and try to disown the other, often projecting it on others.

In Tony Blair's chart, I think the Moon is the stronger of the two planets, partly because it's angular and partly because the Sun in the 12th has to struggle for a long time to emerge into the light. The Moon in the 10th reflects an instinctive identification with the mother in childhood, and later on, an instinctive identification with "the public", the people "out there". The Moon in the 10th gets its emotional nourishment and sense of safety by being seen and wanted, by achieving public recognition as a means of acquiring public acceptance. This Moon needs to belong, to be needed by as many people as possible. And in Aquarius, it needs to feel part of the larger human family. The manner in which this Moon establishes its emotional connection with others is through shared ideals.

There are both dark and light sides to this, and it would be easy to highlight one or the other depending on our own personal feelings about him. There are those who say that Tony Blair's politics are the politics of expediency, motivated by the desire to be admired rather than by genuine ideals and convictions. There are also those who say that he has a real "feel" for the people and understands what they want and need because he is "one" with them. Both may be true. But Tony Blair's talents as a politician are instinctive, and spring from the 10th house Moon in Aquarius. He has a natural ability to sell himself to the public. That's not solar. If he acts from the Moon alone, and doesn't work to develop the Sun, then what do you think will happen?

Audience: He will be exploited by the collective.

Liz: Ultimately, yes. But first, he may exploit it, perhaps not always with integrity, in order to feed an unconscious solar sense of destiny. If the role of mediator for the collective psyche is unconscious and un-individualised, it moves into the terrain of the redeemer-archetype. The danger is that he will become so identified with the role of collective saviour that he loses the power of conscious decision-making. If this happens, he will become the victim of the collective, and he will be sacrificed without mercy when he fails to redeem the world as promised.

Audience: In other words, he may give people what they want, not what he really believes in, and eventually he will corner himself and be seen through.

Liz: Exactly. He may lose his allegiance to his individual inner values. If he allows this to happen, he may lose the next election as well, or be ousted by someone within his own party. Can you see how tricky this lunar square to the 12th house Sun is? As to whether or not he is expressing solar light, I leave you to work out the answer. The chart cannot tell us how he deals with this natal configuration, although it does tell us the deeper purpose that is motivating him from within. What gives his life its meaning? What gives any 12th house Sun person's life its meaning? The Sun needs to be a mouthpiece for the collective psyche – to give shape, in a highly individual way, to the dreams and longings and yearnings that are swimming around in the collective unconscious and have not yet come to birth. We can only hope that this deeper motivation, despite the emotional requirements of the 10th house Moon, is sufficiently conscious to direct his policies.

Not every 12th house Sun goes into politics, but there is a powerful pull toward involvement with the collective, and many of them do it through the arts. Another good example of a 12th house Sun in Taurus with a Gemini Ascendant is Laurence Olivier. Here is someone who chose the arts as his medium. But the need to feel special and alive by giving shape to collective dreams is just as applicable to Olivier as it is to Tony Blair.

Audience: Will Tony Blair be forced into his Saturn-Neptune conjunction?

Liz: I don't know what you mean by "forced".

Audience: I was thinking that, because of the 12th house emphasis, the Saturn-Neptune would be much stronger.

Liz: Yes, that makes sense. Saturn-Neptune reflects a deep sensitivity to the Neptunian world and a strong need to make Neptunian dreams manifest, and it echoes the theme of the 12th house Sun. But the Saturn-Neptune conjunction is not actually aspecting the Sun. I would give it a lot more weight if it were part of the solar configuration, although I'm not suggesting it's unimportant. The Sun is involved in a T-cross with the Moon and Pluto. To give shape to the Sun, Tony Blair has to deal with that T-cross. Pluto is the trickiest one for him to work with. Wherever the Sun goes, Pluto goes with it, just as the Moon does, but Pluto is an outer planet and is likely to be lot harder for him to integrate into his conscious goals and values.

The collective survival instinct, which in Leo reflects a generation group with an intensely dramatic and self-mythologising response to survival threats, has to be accommodated with the lunar need to be needed and the solar impulse to channel collective longings through practical service of some kind. If it remains unconscious because the Moon wants to be Mr. Nice Guy for the public, the power drive will be enormous, covert, and quite ruthless. Let's keep Olivier in mind. If you don't like Tony Blair, you can always say to yourself, "Well, he is an actor too."

The actor's gift

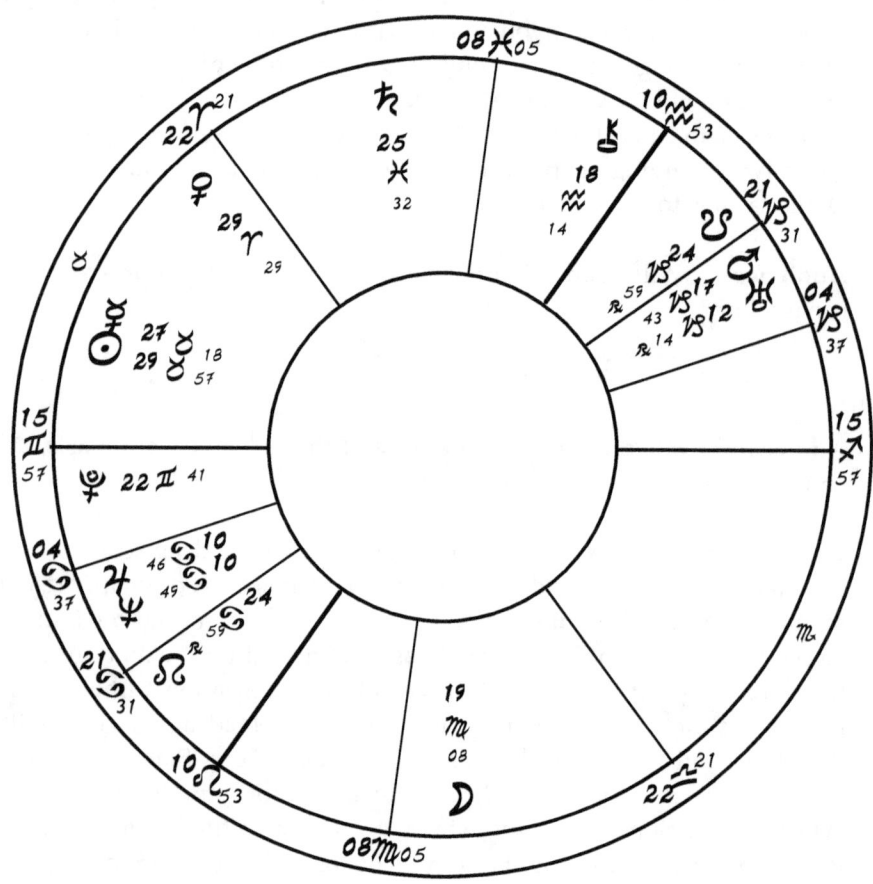

Laurence Olivier
22 May 1907, 5.00 am, Dorking, Surrey

Audience: And not as good an actor as Olivier.

Part One: The Meaning of the Natal Sun

Liz: I was about to say that, but then thought one of you would probably do it for me. If you do like him, you can still look at Olivier's chart to understand the power of a 12th house Sun. Olivier was an extraordinarily powerful actor. How much was applied skill and how much was 12th house mediumship is difficult to determine because, at the time he gave his performances, he was in touch with something the collective needed. His big break came when he played Heathcliffe in *Wuthering Heights*. The character he personified caught the collective imagination right by the short-and-curlies. Through a strange kind of psychic osmosis, he was attuned to and portrayed what the collective needed to see at the time. A 12th house Sun has the capacity to identify with the state of the collective at a particular moment, and give voice to its dreams, fears and longings.

If we look at an historical personage who mediated the collective longings of their time, we might easily think, "That person could never have been famous now." Olivier's early style of acting looks florid today. If he made *Wuthering Heights* now and overacted as he did then, hurling himself about with intense grimaces and burning eyes, people would be rolling in the aisles. The critics would have him on toast for breakfast. That style of performance is longer fashionable. But when he made *Wuthering Heights,* it was exactly what was required. That is the magic, the gift, and the necessity of a 12th house Sun. It is plugged into the currents of the collective at the time.

Audience: Olivier had an incredibly strong physical presence. That is very Taurean.

Liz: Yes, it is one dimension of Taurus, although not the only one. Olivier conveyed physical qualities which, in many ways, weren't what he was actually like in his personal life. He communicated an incredibly intense, almost brutish sensuality in the film.

Audience: I'm not sure I think of Tony Blair as brutishly sensual.

Liz: No, that isn't quite how I see him either. Certain writers in *The Times* keep referring to him as Bambi. But a lot of people find him physically attractive, however bizarre that may seem to you or me, and that has undoubtedly influenced his success. Before the days of television, people didn't really know what the Prime Minister looked like. When the time came to vote, they had to base their opinions on other qualities, such as intelligence, articulateness, and decisiveness. An unattractive Prime Minister was not hampered by his appearance. Think of Churchill. Now unprepossessing looks work against public figures, no matter how well equipped they might be to hold office. It is an inevitable product of the media age. Actors have always been required to be beautiful. Now politicians are as well.

We can see many parallels between these two Taurean Suns in the 12th. Tony Blair came to power because the collective wanted this particular mediator at this particular time. What is said and promised is always attuned to an awareness of the collective's need to hear and be given these things. Whether his popularity will sustain itself remains to be seen. The only way for him to keep the Sun shining is to maintain his integrity and his individual values in the midst of this flowing collective psychic sea. If he loses his integrity, he will, as they say in the old textbooks, invoke his own undoing. If he keeps his integrity, then he can mediate with consciousness. Of course I don't know whether he will hold his ground, or whether his integrity will be subsumed by the Plutonian power-drive or the lunar need to be loved by the public. All this remains to be seen. We are having an astrological discussion, not a political one. But that is the challenge of this Sun in the 12th.

Audience: There's a devotional element, something religious, about the way a 12th house person relates to that inner world.

Liz: Yes, although "devotional" doesn't mean giving up the sense of self. The attitude of devotion is on a feeling or intuitive rather than an intellectual level. There is a sense of participating in, and serving, something greater than oneself. Even if the Sun is in an air sign, it needs to open the gates on an intuitive and imaginative level and then translate what it mediates into concepts and ideals.

Audience: Do you think there is a danger in that kind of religious devotion? Especially if the person isn't consciously religious?

Liz: Yes, there is always a danger of this kind with the 12th. That's why the solar principle is so important – it can hold its ground and maintain personal integrity. One needs a long spoon to sup with the collective unconscious. It can rise up and swamp the personal ego without the individual realising what is happening. In effect, it's identification with the collective yearning for the light, and that means believing one is a messiah. One identifies with the light, rather than recognising that one is an ordinary stumbling human attempting to give shape to a little part of something vast and boundless. The same thing could apply to an actor, an artist, or a spiritual teacher with the Sun in the 12th.

Audience: Do you think all those planets in Tony Blair's 12th house mean he can't really enjoy a private life?

Liz: It depends on what you mean by private. The fishbowl world of the politician is not the route of every 12th house person, and many live lives which are very withdrawn and introverted. But in terms of the ability to give oneself over to one's own personal development, I think you are right – with so much emphasis in the 12th, it isn't possible for him to forget the larger unity of which he is a part. He will always be buffeted by collective currents, and may often find it hard to work out who he is because he is so open to collective needs and fantasies. I suspect he must feel a bit crazy a lot of the time. Those of you who don't like his politics will undoubtedly say that he behaves accordingly.

I have heard many 12th house people say they sometimes feel quite mad. Some do go through some kind of psychotic episode at some point. This has to do with being so open to the currents of the collective psyche. One can't differentiate between one's own feelings and the feelings of the group, especially if the group's feelings are unexpressed. This can be a problem in childhood if the family atmosphere is full of secrets and suppressed emotions. If a 12th house Sun person performs before the public as an actor or a politician, they are the audience at that moment. If the audience is hostile or unresponsive, they feel dreadful. When they have managed to give expression to the audience's feelings, there is a tremendous sense of unity. Then, when they get off the platform, they may feel dreadfully lost, confused, and empty.

Olivier suffered from terrible stage fright. It was like leaping into the sea every time. He had to open himself and let them all in. Before every performance, he experienced a moment of horror and panic. He never got over it, no matter how many performances he gave or how many accolades he received. I suspect something similar happens to Tony Blair, although we don't hear about it.

Audience: The north Node is in the 10th. That seems to require him to go before the public. He couldn't live a retired sort of 12th house life.

Liz: No, he couldn't. The nodal axis suggests that, whether he likes it or not, he has to get up in front of the public. His development, portrayed by the north Node, depends on 10th house work. The line of least resistance is portrayed by the south Node in the 4th. He might dearly like to be a private person, but he can't. The Moon's emotional needs are underlined by a sense that he *must* make his mark on the world. He can't mediate the collective in quiet ways. He has to do it in 10th house ways.

Problems with boundaries

Audience: I would like to know what I can do to help build up my Sun in the 12th. I have a big boundary problem. As you say, I sometimes can't tell what is me and what is other people.

Liz: 12th house Sun people may need to engage in slow, painstaking ego-building work in order to create a firm sense of individuality. This is certainly what I've found with those I've worked with analytically, although analysis is, of course, not the only way to do this kind of inner work. The family psyche may be experienced as overwhelmingly pervasive and powerful when the Sun is in the 12th, and this placement may indicate a family inheritance where the expression of individual identity has remained undeveloped or repressed for many generations. Boundaries, not to mention personal creative expression, may be actively discouraged by family members, and this forms the basis of the Sun's struggle to shine.

A 12th house Sun child is open to everything going on in the family unconscious. It's very difficult to be clear and say, "These are my feelings. Those are their feelings. The anger I sense in the air is not mine; it's unspoken between my parents. The monsters in my nightmares are not just my monsters; they are ancient fears that were there before I was born." Because of this buffeting by invisible undercurrents and ancestral ghosts, it may take a long time to develop physical and psychological boundaries. The Sun needs to be fully owned in order to mediate the 12th house in a positive way. Careful attention to the details of mundane life can help, as well as a conscious defining of personal values. What element is your Sun in?

Audience: Fire.

Liz: That could make it harder to establish boundaries in everyday life, since fire doesn't tend to enjoy everyday life anyway. You may need to work to define your personal tastes, likes and dislikes, and feeling responses. This may mean taking plenty of time on your own, and not rushing to give a response or make a decision if you haven't yet worked out what you really want or what the consequences are likely to be. Don't be afraid to make other people wait, even with apparently trivial things. The opposite house, the 6th, is obviously important because it represents the complement to the 12th. Think about Virgo's skills and attributes, because these can give you a focus. It's easy to say to a 12th house Sun, "Oh, just learn to express yourself." But how do you do that if you don't know what "yourself" is?

From the moment you get up in the morning, you may need to think about what kind of breakfast you like, and what rituals make you feel comfortable in the physical world. That doesn't come naturally to the fire signs. Learn to tell other people to go away if you don't want them invading your space. Get into the habit of putting yourself first. This may need to be done for a long time before you are able to express yourself without feeling guilty or confused. It may sound boring and selfish, but it is essential work. Separateness and embodiment allow a 12th house Sun to shine instead of drowning. Most importantly, you have to be able to be lonely, which 12th house Suns find very painful. Even the most withdrawn and retiring kind of 12th house Sun still wants to feel connected, although maybe not through endless partying. This is partly why there is often such a fear of separating from the family matrix.

More example charts

The eternal quest: the Sun in Sagittarius

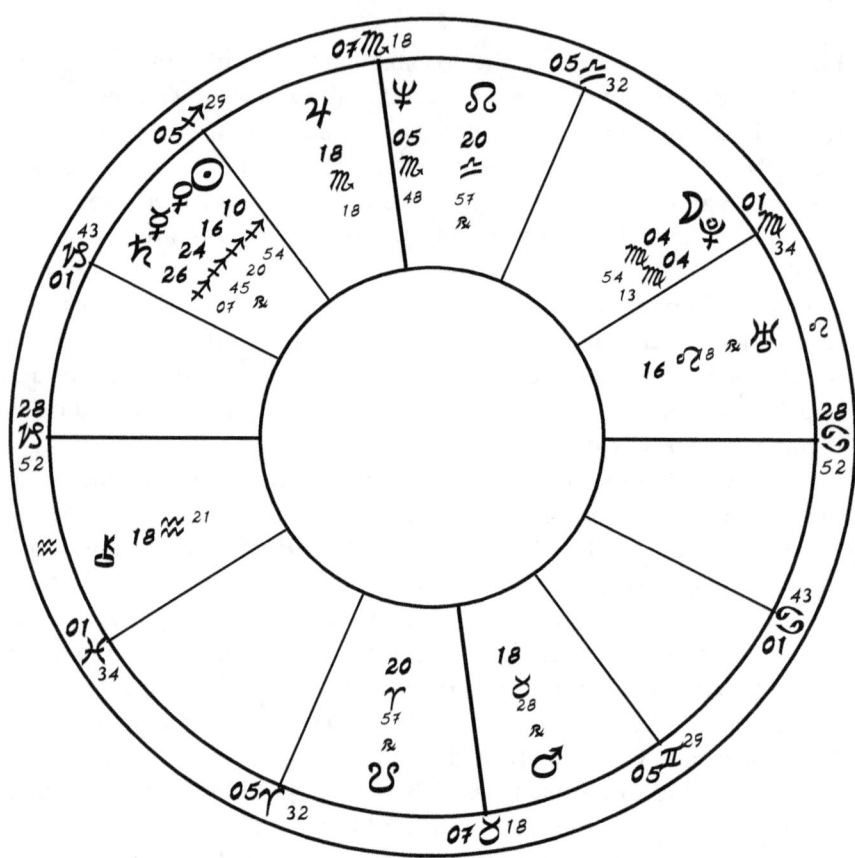

Lila
(Birth data withheld for reasons of confidentiality)

Now let's allow our beleaguered Prime Minister to rest in peace. I'll put up another chart with a different solar house placement. This chart is from Lila, who is on the seminar today. The Sun is in the 11th in Sagittarius. Let's start with the Sun-sign. What does Sagittarius want from life?

Audience: A quest.

Audience: A spaceship.

Liz: We know that the Sun in Taurus needs to embody its values in concrete form and create something solid and enduring in the world. What does the Sun in Sagittarius need?

Audience: Meaning.

Liz: And what do you mean by "meaning"?

Audience: A sense of purpose.

Liz: The Sun itself conveys a sense of individual purpose. All of the solar attributes I have been talking about have to do with a sense of purpose, a sense of personal destiny. The Sun, regardless of sign, conveys an inner conviction of specialness. Meaning, for Sagittarius, has to be expressed in a very particular way.

Audience: Sagittarius needs understanding.

Liz: Yes, but once again, in a very particular way. This sign needs a world-view, a philosophy of life, a universal context in which to place experiences so that they reveal a bigger plan. The 9th house, the sign Sagittarius, and the planetary ruler, Jupiter, all relate to the ongoing creation of a world-view. Sagittarius is not an air sign, but nevertheless understanding is important. Sagittarian understanding isn't the same as Geminian knowledge, which is based on the acquisition of information. Sagittarius seeks understanding of the whole, the big cosmic design, through intuitive revelations or realisations. The light is glimpsed through making intuitive connections. Sagittarius says, "This event has some link with what happened to me three years ago. I *know* they're connected. They're telling me something." There is a pattern, and it means something. It has a message and a teleology. There is a plan somewhere. For the light to shine, Sagittarius pursues clues which will reveal the plan. It is like looking for God's footprints – the patterns that will reveal the ultimate truth, the ultimate meaning of life. It may well turn out to be *Monty Python's Meaning of Life*, but that doesn't matter as long as it's universal. Yes, Sagittarius needs a quest.

Audience: Are Sagittarians prepared to make sacrifices to find meaning? I always think they look for the easiest route. They're opportunistic.

Liz: That sounds like a personal judgement based on an encounter with a Sagittarian that didn't work out. Being opportunistic doesn't mean there isn't a willingness to pay the full price for what is sought. Sagittarius will endure very painful sacrifices if there is a sense that the experience will make one grow, and that it will lead to something else. This touches on the mysterious issue of what we can endure, because the Sun gives us a clue as to what makes life bearable. What makes life bearable for the Sun in Taurus? Beauty is a vital ingredient. This is often overlooked in relation to Taurus, but it is a Venus-ruled sign. Taurus can bear many sacrifices if there is the possibility of finding beauty.

Audience: Or, at the least, comfort. The Sun in Taurus will buy the extra silk shirt, and maybe not even take it out of the wrapper. It's nice just to have it.

Liz: I don't believe comfort in the instinctive sense is Taurean. It's lunar. The need for a full belly and a warm place to sleep at night is not Venusian. Taurus wants more than that. The extra silk shirt which is never worn doesn't give comfort. It provides beauty and the feeling that there is something in reserve.

Audience: So Taurus isn't concerned with basic needs.

Liz: All living creatures have the same basic needs, regardless of their Sun-signs. Taurus wants things which give pleasure, a feeling of well-being, and an experience of harmony and beauty. Never underestimate the Taurean need for beauty – it is as strong as Libra's. For both Venus-ruled Sun-signs, beauty makes the difficult aspects of life bearable.

Sagittarius needs something quite different to feel that sacrifices are worth making. Fulfillment depends on the glimpse of understanding that allows one to say, "My life is leading somewhere. It's part of a bigger design. I'm a traveler, and I can see the road winding into the distance. This road has something at the end of it which will reveal the real reason why I am on it. If I look carefully, I'll find the clues. I'll find a bit of paper under that rock with a message which says, 'Sit on that bench for five minutes and wait for a leaf to drop from that tree. If the leaf falls to the left of the tree, turn left at the next crossing.'" Synchronicity always fascinates Sagittarius. "The number plate on that car has the same three digits as the last part of my boyfriend's phone number. That must mean something." Sagittarius is on a perpetual treasure hunt. The opportunism you mentioned earlier is about finding the right clue, not about mere self-gratification. It's quite delightful to watch the face of a Sagittarian when they have found a clue. "I've got it! Now I understand!" This means far more than someone saying, "I love you madly." That's very nice, but not nearly as exciting as having found a piece of the Great Puzzle.

Creative idealism: the Sun in the 11th house

Lila has Sun in the 11th house. What does this Sun need?

Audience: Groups.

Liz: Not all 11th house Suns want to be in physical groups. I've known many very introverted 11th house Sun people who intensely dislike groups, or feel very ambivalent about them.

Audience: They need to know that they have worthwhile beliefs to give the group.

Liz: I am not sure the issue is about beliefs.

Audience: I was thinking about Sagittarius.

Liz: Belief is not a characteristic of the fire signs. Sagittarians don't believe in things. They *know*. Earth believes. Fire knows intuitively.

Audience: The Sun in Sagittarius in the 11th needs to be part of a group of people who share the same ideals, who are on the same treasure hunt.

They might not be an actual group of people sitting in one room, but they are a kind of mental group.

Liz: Now you're getting it. The physical presence of a group of people may not be necessary for the Sun in Sagittarius in the 11th, but the person needs to feel part of a larger human family who are all looking for the same treasure. The individual with the Sun in the 11th needs to contribute something to human evolution. This is Aquarius' house, and Aquarius is ruled by Uranus and Saturn. The Sun placed here wants to bring Promethean fire to other people. This does not have to be done overtly, as is the case with a political leader like Bill Clinton, who has the Sun in the 11th in Leo. For an introverted person, it can be through writing or artistic work.

But there is always a message to be promulgated, and a strong desire to reform society. The 11th house is very different from the 12th, although both concern the collective. The 12th represents the sea of the collective psyche. It is Neptune's realm. The waters flow around in a circle and come back on themselves. The 12th is concerned with the ancestors, with the repository of ancestral memory. The 11th is concerned with evolution, with progress, with society moving somewhere. There are strong ideas about what could be, what potentials are possible. This Sagittarius Sun needs to feel in touch with like-minded people who also want to progress and evolve.

Lila: That's why I find it so difficult.

Liz: Difficult to find like-minded people who want to evolve?

Lila: Yes. I see the design, and I have the vision of what has to be done. But it's so difficult to match myself with people who have that same vision. I am really intense. Sometimes I feel I am the only person who can see the potential, and I have to get other people to see it. Sometimes I feel very frustrated and lonely if I can't get my ideas recognised.

Liz: You have given voice very clearly to what an 11th house Sun wants. This Sun feels that everything is bleak and pointless if there is no sense of contact with those who share a like-minded vision. The vision may not be as grand as global transformation. It might be the development of a particular sphere of knowledge, or a particular artistic path.

Sagittarius tends to be preoccupied with the global picture. But whatever the Sun-sign, there must be a sense of belonging to a larger community with whom one can get enthused, share ideas, and push things forward.

Audience: Some of the intensity she refers to must be connected with the Moon-Pluto conjunction in the 8th, and Jupiter in Scorpio.

Liz: Yes, I'm sure it is. But although we can't really look at the Sun without considering the whole chart, I would like to keep focusing on this solar placement, for the moment.

Audience: The new technology is making it possible to find that community more easily, without having to be in a particular place.

Liz: Yes, the internet and all its possibilities are a great gift to 11th house Suns, especially the more introverted ones who don't want to have a lot of people in their physical lives. Knowledge is instantly available, and contact with anyone anywhere is possible without any physical meeting ever taking place. An 11th house community doesn't have to be a physical community. I don't think a Sagittarius Sun is likely to be particularly introverted, unless there is an angular Pluto or Saturn and many planets in more reflective signs.

In Lila's chart, Aquarius is rising, with its ruler, Uranus, in the 7th in trine to a Sun-Venus conjunction in the 11th, so I would expect a more extraverted nature. The Sun in the 11th in Capricorn, Virgo, or Scorpio may find the proximity of a physical group uncomfortable. Yet one needs to feel part of a vanguard, even if one never meets the people physically. Even if they died five hundred years ago, the 11th house Sun reads the book or sees the play and says, "Yes! That's the same vision I have!" One is part of the group on a non-corporeal level, part of a body of ideas which has been alive and developing for many centuries. One may be working alone, but one is part of a continuum of human pioneers, so one feels one is in good company. An introverted 11th house Sun can operate on that basis.

Do you know why you can't find people you can share ideas with?

Lila: I think it is partly because I come from a different culture, and I am really passionate about my ideas. I get an idea and I jump into it and get excited. If I don't have a project, I am dead. It is partly a problem of culture. I don't know how to be reserved and understated if I am enthusiastic about something. It has taken me a long time to understand how English people work. When you are with creative people in Latin America, they are normally very passionate about creativity. I don't know if this is really my place. My husband is here. He is English. I am thinking of going back to Brazil. For a while I was looking for a job, and I went to hundreds of interviews. They almost loved me, and they almost hired me immediately, but then I never heard from them again.

I realised that maybe my purpose was not to work with other people. I started working for myself and created my own media company, trying to approach people with a service. I created a name: "Creative Punch". Then people told me, "That's too threatening for the English!" I didn't understand, and I thought I had to change the name. Then I said, "No, I am going with Creative Punch, because that's what I am and that's what New Media is." So I am in the process of developing that. I don't know if it is going to work, but I am going to give it all I have got, because I have nothing more to lose.

Liz: You had an important insight into what the Sun in the 11th needs when you finally realised you had to do it yourself. The Sun must shine alone, even when serving the public. An 11th house Sun is not the same as an 11th house Moon. The solar sense of contributing to a community can't be achieved merely by being a member of the community. In other words, you can't go and get a job with a group. You have to create your own group. If the Sun is projected and you see the light in the group, you don't get to experience your own light.

It is the same kind of paradox as the person with the Sun in the 12th, who mediates the collective unconscious but must be an individual in order to mediate rather than be swallowed up by it. An 11th house Sun must make an individual contribution to the collective. I think you have found the right formula for your Sun. The need for self-sufficiency is underlined by Saturn being placed in the 11th as well. As long as you are looking for a group to give you a home, you are likely to feel disappointed and frustrated.

Lila: I have suffered so much in this country!

Liz: With all due respect, and I am not apologising for the English, I don't think your difficulties are entirely because of your nationality. Of course there are cultural differences in the way emotions are expressed. Yet you married an Englishman, so the notorious British reserve can't be entirely unattractive to you. There is a deeper issue here, connected with your Sun in the 11th. The Sun must struggle to shine its light, and you must create your own vehicle. Wherever you had gone, you would have met obstacles. If you had stayed in Brazil, the obstacles might have taken a different form, but they would still have blocked your efforts to find your solar light in others. For you to be what you are, you must run your own show. The Sun must always run its own show, and it must always struggle. One cannot rely on something outside to provide the light.

A 2nd house Sun cannot rely on other people to provide the resources, and sometimes this is a painful lesson. 2nd house Suns are sometimes born into money, or they marry or inherit money. Then something goes wrong and they have to develop their own talents in order to build security in the world. A good example of a 7th house Sun's struggle is Princess Diana. 7th house Suns usually start off looking for the light in a partner. Then something goes wrong, and they have to recognise that, even if others are the most important thing in their lives, they must find their purpose within. They cannot go with cap in hand, begging the partner to give them their sense of meaning and worth.

The Sun needs to shine and give generously, but it must first discover an inner, individual light. The light can't be borrowed. An 11th house Sun cannot go to the group and say, "Love me. Validate me. Make me feel I have a reason to be alive." It must create its own light and then offer it to the group. At certain points in life there is usually a terrible struggle around the house in which the Sun is placed, when we realise that we have to do it ourselves. As I mentioned earlier, Apollo is a lonely god.

Collective rejection of the Sun

Audience: I also have an 11th house Sun, like Lila. I spent many years by myself. I travelled all over the world. I worked as an engineer because my parents wouldn't allow me to study biology while I was at school. I was only allowed to study engineering, and I made a great success of that, but I wasn't actually happy. I am now working with animals, and I am trying to publish my insights into their behaviour. I am finding it extremely difficult. It is like having to start all over again. But at least I am doing what I want.

Liz: The person with the Sun in the 11th needs to offer something to the collective for the betterment of the larger human family. But the stages between what you have discovered – that you must follow your own heart – and what you actually end up offering may take you through many levels of compromise and reshaping. The 11th is a collective house, like the 12th. What you are now creating does need to be offered in some form. But that may not be the form it is in at the moment.

Audience: It feels as if it is being offered, but not recognised or noticed.

Liz: There is a certain inevitability about this. Initially, it feels as if one's offering will not be valued. It may, indeed, be rejected. There aren't any easy answers to this dilemma. For some people, the way through is compromise. For other people, it is sheer persistence. I don't know what the right way is for you. But both you and Lila sound as if you have hit the same road barrier. You realise you must do it yourself, and you have given up trying to find a sense of meaning and purpose by pleasing the crowd. You have created something of your own, and nobody seems to want it. That is part of the dragon fight. The Sun sinks down into the darkness and has to fight the dragon of depression and hopelessness. The feeling that nobody wants what you have created is part of the process.

Audience: What you have created is also something with which you identify. A rejection of that is a rejection of you.

Liz: Yes. This is one of the most difficult things about developing the Sun. If one creates solely in order to please other people, what emerges has no life in it. It's not authentic. If one creates to please oneself, or one's Self, it is a rejection of the collective, and the collective retaliates. People say, "We don't like that. It isn't what we're used to. It's too individualistic. Too elitist." There is a kind of archetypal inevitability about this at a certain stage. One has to find a way through it. A lot of people give up at this point. It's too painful and too lonely.

Lila: One friend told me, "Well, if these people think Creative Punch is threatening, then you don't want to work with them." I said, "That's right." These people tried to convince me to do something else. I struggled with the confusion of whether to go with what I feel or with what others accept. Finally I said, "I am going to go for what I want, because that is the only thing that gives me the power and energy to keep on struggling."

Audience: I am very interested in people like Mozart, who seemed to really live the Sun. He created in dire poverty. That says something to me about a risk or gamble. What you are creating could be worth something to others, but it might not be worth anything.

Liz: Yes, it's a gamble. There is no guarantee of collective acceptance. When we make the effort to live the Sun, we can't take rewards for granted. There might not be any reward. We might not ever get the message which says, "We love you. Your work is appreciated." Like Apollo, you may get rejected. Daphne preferred to become a laurel tree rather than submit to the god's embraces. There is no guarantee that the light will be welcome. But the pleasure of a reward isn't why the Sun shines.

Audience: Surely, if you believe in yourself, the outer world will reward you.

Liz: Well, that sounds really nice when you say it. But expressing the Sun with the assumption of a worldly reward is contradictory to the nature of the Sun. It just doesn't work like that. Can't you see the paradox? The act of devotion necessary for creative work requires a relinquishing of ego-control, which means, among other things, a relinquishing of the expectation that goodies will follow.

It's rather like religious devotion, and is perhaps even identical. There is a sacrifice involved. If you're good in the hope that God will reward you, it's tantamount to making a deal, and you're missing the whole point of both goodness and God. Also, you are implying that life is always fair, and that the good guys always win the prize. That happens in Walt Disney films. But here on this planet, the good guys sometimes lose, and it isn't because they aren't talented. Also, belief in oneself is not always easy to come by. It is extremely frightening to walk out on a limb and say, "I am going to commit my heart and soul to this project, or this ideal, or this way of life." Deep insecurities and hurts may make it quite impossible. If it is possible, one's contribution may or may not be rewarded. One does not do it for the reward. One does it because one must. Life was not fair to Mozart. He died in poverty and was thrown into a pauper's grave. We are the ones who have been rewarded by his music.

Audience: Where would music be if he had given up?

Liz: Quite. But he didn't give up, because he was living from the Sun and not for the reward. Most of us are not Mozart, and we don't have the capacity to directly transcribe the Music of the Spheres. We lumber along and get a little glimpse of something shining. It is harder to believe in oneself when one gets only the odd glimpse. It is easier if the music is pouring through and one is transcribing madly to catch up with it.

There is no value in crying, "Shame on me! I have given up! I am a failure!" We all give up at some point, and then we have to try again. This is the Sun's process. Many times in life, in large and small ways, we get frightened and betray the Sun. Then we rally, and the next time maybe we have more courage. Then we give up again, and we pick ourselves up and try again. The Sun always goes down into the dark and struggles with the serpent and then rises again. Giving up is not a statement of cowardice or failure. But we need to know when and why we've had enough, and when we need to conserve our energy or work to heal something until we are ready to try again. It's only if we give up permanently that we may wind up in bad trouble, because then we may be opening the door to many kinds of illness, physical or psychological. If we give up too early in life and give up for good, we may pay a terrible price. If we remain loyal, we may suffer for it, and we may never get the recognition we deserve. But we have to keep trying.

Audience: In most charts, the Sun aspects other planets. Isn't there some compromise required?

Liz: Yes, of course. I'm not implying that everything else in the chart must be sacrificed to solar needs and goals. Any planetary aspect to the Sun requires one's solar light to be integrated with the needs of the other planet. And all the other planets, regardless of whether or not they aspect the Sun, need to be expressed somewhere in life. This includes the Moon, which finds its contentment in belonging. But it is possible to express lunar needs without betraying the essential integrity of the Sun.

Lila: It's very difficult to know how much you have to compromise.

Liz: The degree of compromise is a very individual issue. No one can tell us how much is acceptable and how much is unacceptable. And it may change, depending on age, circumstances, and the kind of transits and progressions operative at any given time. The 11th and 12th houses require an ongoing relationship with the collective. The issue of compromise is particularly important when the Sun is in either of these two houses. Ultimately one must ask, "Where does compromise end and selling out begin?" For the Sun, selling out is death. Every person has to discover where the line needs to be drawn, and one will inevitably make many mistakes. That is part of the solar journey.

Creative serpent-slaying: the Sun in the 8th house

Audience: Could you say more about the Sun in the 8th? I have it there, and I'm still finding it difficult to grasp.

Liz: All right. What does this Sun need?

Audience: To fight the serpent.

Audience: Turmoil.

Liz: This house is governed by both an inner and an outer planet. It is above the horizon. That means it is concerned with a dynamic between self and not-self, Self and Other. What kind of Other is represented by the 8th house?

Audience: Powerful partnerships.

Liz: I don't think the 8th is concerned with partnerships in the external sense. That's the 7th house. The 8th is subtler.

Audience: Power in relationships.

Liz: Let's have some basic house interpretations. The 8th house is opposite from the 2nd. What does that mean?

Audience: Other people's money.

Audience: Joint interests.

Liz: Yes, this house has something to do with substance which is ours but not wholly ours – substance which we share with others. We can "own" physical substance, and we can "own" talents which are uniquely ours. What sort of substance do we partake of which cannot be "owned"?

Audience: Psychic substance. The life force. We can't own that.

Liz: No. We have an individual consciousness and an individual body, but we are also participants in a much deeper life with its own patterns and intentions. What happens when we encounter the 8th house realm?

Audience: We change.

Liz: Yes. We die, and we come back different. Discovering that we are not separate after all, but live on a thin surface beneath which an invisible world teems, changes us. In the 2nd house, what is ours cannot be taken away from us. We build it, we accrue it, we possess it. In the 8th we are at the mercy of that which is greater than ourselves, which cannot be built or accrued or possessed through individual effort or consciousness. In the 8th, what we think is ours can be taken away from us. What we believe to be ourselves can be dominated or even destroyed by what is more than ourselves. In the 2nd, we have power through the development of personal resources. In the 8th, we discover that we are powerless.

The unconscious dimension of life is alien to the individual ego. It is Other in the most profound sense. Sometimes we say, "Oh, that slip of the tongue was my unconscious at work," but there is no such thing as *my* unconscious, only *the* unconscious. We do not own the unconscious. It underpins conscious life, and by coming into contact

Part One: The Meaning of the Natal Sun

with it, we are forced to change. We are broken open and have to recognise an invisible domain which has its own objective life. The 8th is not others on a physical level. It is the reality of the psyche. It is the underworld, the inner world, the invisible world. This is Pluto's realm. It reveals family complexes, compulsions, hidden patterns, mysteries – everything that comes up from the depths that we didn't know was ourselves because it isn't entirely ourselves. When we confront this realm, we are subjected to a process of breaking down. The ego has to recognise that it is no longer in power. The 8th is concerned with power, but it isn't one's own power. One is not controlling the show. The 8th often reveals itself through crises – near-death experiences, the death of others, wrenching separations, the eruption of illness, losses and sudden turns of the Wheel of Fortune, madness, night hauntings, sexual compulsions. These are things we cannot control, and they reveal deeper, more mysterious dimensions of life.

When the Sun is in the 8th, we usually discover this realm very early and are forced to recognise, often unwillingly, that we are not in control of life. We can't avoid this realm, so we must learn to live with it, make a relationship with it, and give creative expression to it. But to do that, we have to follow an 8th house process. In the 12th we have to build an individual vessel which can remain open to and give expression to collective history and collective dreams. In the 11th we have to contribute something to a human evolutionary process. In the 8th, what do we have to do?

Audience: We have to be prepared to let go, to die, to be changed.

Liz: Yes. We have to hold what we think is ours with loose hands. We need to be prepared to be changed by what we encounter in life. We have to say, "I can't fight this any more. I give up. I am defeated. I relinquish my power." In our defeat we make a connection with something. In our death we come alive. In our crisis we discover an unexpected serenity. In our loss we find something. Struggle is not inappropriate with the Sun in the 8th, but arrogance is, and so is superficiality.

Lila: My relocated Sun is in the 8th!

Liz: You can't win, can you?

Audience: Could it attract the person to others with psychological problems? Or indicate that someone in the family has this kind of problem? You can't control it, but you have to deal with it somehow. The Sun in the 8th might feel, "Here's this person who's crazy, and I have to handle it and find meaning in it. But I can't control the fact that they are out of control."

Liz: Yes, there is often a pattern of this kind. 8th house relationship encounters tend to reveal hidden dimensions of life that require bringing light into very dark places. Sometimes it's the 8th house Sun person who suffers the breakdown or the serious psychological problem. Sometimes it's someone in the immediate family. But this doesn't mean the Sun in the 8th is itself malefic. These things are teleological. They lead the individual into the depths, which is where he or she belongs. Since we do not usually go into the depths voluntarily, we are often initially dragged down involuntarily.

Sometimes there is a refusal to acknowledge Pluto's realm, even when it knocks loudly on the door. Then an 8th house Sun can get into trouble. Problems can also arise when there is a desperate attempt to control life, because anything in the 8th is always subjected to a breaking down process. If the ego is too rigid and one says, "I refuse to acknowledge anything beyond material reality," or, "I'm going to control all these emotions and compulsions," then one may go through the meat-grinder. It is by trying to understand and co-operate rather than control that the Sun begins to shine in the 8th. It is the recognition of the Other, the invisible underpinnings of life. It is not wise to say, "Do it my way!" when one is dealing with Pluto. It is more sensible to say, "Grant me the wisdom to fight when I must and relinquish when necessity demands it." This is an acknowledgement of and a relationship with fate.

The 8th house and fate

In myth, Apollo, alone among the gods, cheats the Fates. He only manages it once, but once is better than never. He makes the Fates drunk in order to save the life of his friend, a mortal called Admetus. Even the Sun-god can't cheat them indefinitely or make Admetus an immortal. But he succeeds in prolonging his friend's life. In the end we are still circumscribed by the laws of mortal existence, but there is perhaps more flexibility in the way our lives unfold than we might realise. We have to live in the belief that we are free. We will discover quickly enough when we have overstepped our boundaries. If we struggle against the "fate" imposed by family complexes and compulsions, we may get more leeway than we expected. But when we confront the inevitable, we are up against the ancient weaving and spinning of life-thread patterns. We only discover these by struggling against them and failing. Then we have established a relationship with the source of something deep, dark, and life-sustaining as well as life-destroying.

In myth this is also portrayed by Apollo's relationship with the Python. He battles with this giant chthonic creature and manages to establish his shrine in the Python's former lair. But his oracular powers depend on the co-operation of the underworld, so he creates the Pythoness, a human female who serves as the mouthpiece for his oracles. Her wisdom is only partly derived from the god. It also emerges from the underworld. The Pythoness is a blend of solar light and Plutonian darkness. She sits over a chasm and breathes the noxious vapours rising from the depths, which put her into a trance-state. Then she receives inspiration from the god, and pronounces an oracle which prophesies the destiny of individuals and nations. Prophetic wisdom, which perceives both past debts and future purpose, emerges from this interaction between solar god and underworld. Do any of you with 8th house Suns want to comment on that?

Audience: No.

Liz: Have I been unclear in what I am describing?

Audience: No. But it isn't easy to articulate a reply.

Audience: I have a friend with an 8th house Sun. He is studying film-making. He has a morbid fascination with violence and death. All his scripts are about shootings and rapes and murders, which is surprising if you know him. He is a very quiet person with a very strong presence. He is not morbid as a personality, but what comes out of his imagination is.

Liz: That word "morbid" is interesting. From the 8th house perspective, death and violence are not morbid subjects. They are simply part of life. The 8th house Sun looks at life and always sees the potential pit into which one could fall. One knows that there are shootings and rapes and murders. It is perfectly acceptable to talk and write about such things. But if you don't have an 8th house Sun, it can seem morbid. If you say this to your friend, he may well look at you and think, "How naive."

Audience: He also has the Sun in Sagittarius. He's looking for signs and omens all the time.

Audience: I have a colleague with an 8th house Sun in Aries. If you sit with her and try to have an ordinary conversation, she can't talk to you. It is like a tennis game – she doesn't quite return the balls. We both work clinically with people who can't express themselves, and this woman is particularly good with clients who are very disturbed. If I ever want to get any information from a difficult, silent client, I ask this woman for help. I may never get anywhere with the client, but she always seems to get amazing communication from them. I am always so astonished. I can't really have a conversation with her. But she can get to the heart of an emotionally difficult client. I don't know how she does it.

Liz: The Sun in the 8th may develop healing gifts, particularly in the sphere of psychological illness. Because they have found light in their own darkness, they often know instinctively how to shine light into others' darkness.

The Sun in the 11th or 12th faces the paradox of developing individuality while remaining open to the collective. The Sun in the 8th does the same. The sense of self develops through that which is not oneself. All three of these houses are ruled by outer planets which symbolise collective energies inimical to the nature of the Sun. If the Sun is in one of these houses or aspects Uranus, Neptune, or Pluto, one has to live with this paradox. Finding the right compromise may take a long time, so one shouldn't be in too great a hurry. The Sun does not wish to relinquish its specialness. When it confronts the 8th house realm it must give up its sense of individual power. It regains power, but the power is shared. When the Sun is in the 11th, it must relinquish its sense of individual specialness. It regains this specialness through service to the group. When it is in the 12th, it must relinquish its feeling of individual destiny, but regains it through an awareness of history and the unity of life.

This paradox creates constant tension, and the tension is perhaps greatest with the Sun in the 8th. Life is often simpler for those with other Sun placements. This doesn't mean it's better – just simpler. If one has the Sun in the 2nd, one will still have to struggle to live it, and what one creates may be of equal value. But there is not the same profound paradox as with the Sun in the 8th. There are many Egyptian wall paintings and bas-reliefs which portray the god Ra in his Sun-boat, journeying into the underworld and fighting the serpent. He must descend and fight every night, and he is all but destroyed. But he refuses to be vanquished, and he rises again the next morning. If he didn't fight, the world would descend into darkness and life would cease. The struggle with the serpent generates creative energy for an 8th house Sun. It is more complicated to live like that than to live the Sun in the less paradoxical houses of the chart.

Audience: People with the Sun in other houses don't know what they are missing.

Liz: Probably not. The house in which the Sun is placed is where the individuality can shine. As astrologers, we are privileged to get glimpses of other people's realities. We can get a little peek at what the Sun in other houses feels like. There's a strange thing that happens. If the Sun is shining, whatever its house, one can honestly say, "No, it isn't easy sometimes, but I would rather be myself than anyone else."

When the Sun doesn't shine

Father and Sun

Now I would like to look at some of the things that give the Sun a hard time. Why does the Sun have trouble shining in some people? Why does it seem harder or take longer? This is also the right time to talk about issues connected with father, because father and father-surrogates are the means by which the archetypal image of the Sun is first mediated into our awareness.

This is why we need fathers. They don't have to be our biological fathers, and there is a school of thought which argues that they do not even have to be male. But we need someone who can act as a mediator for the archetypal father-principle in early childhood. Someone must embody solar energy so the child can see it, touch it, feel it, admire it, and internalise it in human form. "When I grow up I want to be like/marry someone like Daddy!" says the child, or, "I don't want to be like/marry someone like Daddy!" which is equally powerful and just as psychologically valid. When there is no mediating principle, no human who can act as a hook for the projection of the solar principle in light or dark forms, the solar archetype remains on a mythic level. It is very difficult to translate this into everyday human terms, and it may remain unexpressed. Later it may get projected onto other individuals. We fall in love with them because we are still seeking the Sun. We worship them and believe they will provide the light. And we may also hate them because we haven't internalised the solar principle and remain deeply envious of those who have.

An unaspected Sun

An unaspected Sun in the birth chart can suggest that it will take longer to find the Sun inside, because the relationship with the father may not be solid enough to allow the archetype to be embodied. Father as a real person does not have to be perfect. He just needs to be human enough for the child to glimpse the Sun in him, have it mirrored back, and say, "This is what I admire," or, "This is the opposite of what I want to be." We all begin life projecting the Sun. Children do this because the ego is not sufficiently formed to say, "I myself am these things." What is outside and what is inside are indistinguishable. In early life, the Sun within us needs an outside hook, and this is usually provided by the father. In some cases it may be projected onto a brother, uncle, or stepfather. Sometimes the mother is more solar and the father more lunar, and the Sun is accordingly projected onto the mother.

In a single-parent family where the mother raises the child alone, both Sun and Moon may be projected onto her. This places a tremendous burden on the single parent. The burden is not necessarily a bad thing for either mother or child. But it is a burden nonetheless. When the mother carries the projection of both Sun and Moon, the child cannot move psychologically from one to the other as children can when there are two parents. Two parents provide alternative realities and can be played one against the other, and that allows the child psychic breathing space. When everything is perceived in one parent, that parent becomes incredibly powerful, and there is no escape from her (or, less commonly, him). Are any of you here single parents? Do you understand what I am saying? You have to carry both solar and lunar principles for your child, and that can be a heavy weight for both you and the child unless there is someone around who can play the other luminary.

Audience: He is around, but not very much.

Liz: "Not very much" may be enough to provide breathing space.

Audience: Even if the father is cold and rejecting?

Liz: Yes. I'm not saying this because of any preconceived notion of so-called "normal" family life being a "good" thing. There are endless statistics which try to demonstrate that children are "better off" with two parents who are married to each other, but what does "better off" mean? Some marriages are so pathological and miserable that the child would be far happier and healthier with a single happy and healthy parent, and some gay relationships, although not deemed "normal", can provide a very good balance for the child. Single parenting, although it can create many problems, can also lead to immensely creative developments in the child's psyche. But we would be stupid and naive to ignore the psychological consequences of single parenting, however positive its potential outcome in any individual case.

Even if the father is distant, disappointing, cold, rejecting, or frequently absent, there is a human being the child can get to know. Dislike and hurt can be as much of a stimulus to the Sun's humanisation as love and admiration. The relevant factor is a human being on whom solar qualities can be projected in positive or negative form. This is why it is not a good idea for a woman to deny her child knowledge and experience of the father, even if she feels great resentment toward the man. The child still needs to know that there is a real person named Fred or Luigi who fathered him or her. This person may one day be contacted or, in the case of the father's death, known through letters, photographs, or others' direct experience of him. And even if the mother is full of anger and hatred, the child may feel differently, and has the right to experience positive feelings even if the mother can't. If there is no knowledge of father, there is a psychic vacuum, and the solar archetype remains on a mythic level or is indistinguishable from the Moon in the same parent.

An unaspected Sun doesn't indicate that there is no father. But it can describe a certain absence of contact. When the relationship with the father is tenuous, the solar principle cannot be mediated easily, and it is difficult for the Sun to be internalised and rooted in everyday life. It may seem so impossibly distant that one feels one will never reach it. It may be expressed in an extreme, mythic form which has little integration with the rest of life, or it may be completely unlived and projected on others. Or it may generate physical or psychological symptoms because it is blocked.

The Sun aspecting the outer planets

There are other chart placements which may suggest difficulties with the Sun. In fact, I doubt there is a chart without some solar difficulty implied. There is no such thing as a perfect birth chart. The question is not, "Is there a difficulty?" but rather, "What is the nature of the difficulty? What process does the Sun needs to undergo in order to shine?" I have already mentioned the paradox of the Sun in the three houses naturally ruled by outer planets. This can slow up the Sun's ability to shine in an uncomplicated way. It often takes a long time before the individual feels, "I know who I am and what I want to do in life," because there is always something pulling them away from individual development.

Audience: Could you say something about Sun-Neptune aspects? Is it similar to the Sun in the 12th?

Liz: There is a similarity. The same conflict between individual and collective is suggested, and it is very important to find a compromise which honours both. If we identify only with Neptune, we are swallowed up by collective longings, and can find no joy in life and no reason to be incarnated as an individual. If we identify only with the Sun, we become insensitive to the suffering of those more vulnerable than we are. And perhaps we also cut ourselves off from subtler or higher dimensions of life which might provide solace for the pain of mortal existence. Neptune then creeps up on us from the outer world, and we wind up marrying it or meeting it in our children. Or it surfaces in the body through illness, or in the psyche through phobias and addictions. Or we meet it in the collective and are threatened by those elements in society which habitually swim in Neptune's waters.

Audience: That's very true.

Liz: With any planet aspecting the Sun, it isn't very helpful to farm out the planet because it always comes back home again. It belongs to oneself. Struggle is essential in order to find a point of compromise. This is especially true of solar aspects to the outer planets.

Audience: It seems that many younger people with the Sun aspecting an outer planet don't want to do anything with their lives.

Liz: Perhaps we aren't sufficiently understanding of young people with the Sun aspecting the outer planets or placed in outer planet houses. If we lack such aspects ourselves, we may be inappropriately judgemental, which is not a helpful quality in an astrologer. These people can sometimes take a long time to form individual boundaries. They may make some bad mistakes before the Sun really begins to shine. The young Sun-Neptune or 12th house Sun person may be on drugs for a while, or drift along doing nothing, or play the victim in a destructive relationship. Sun-Uranus and Sun in the 11th may display distinctly anarchic behaviour, and Sun-Pluto and Sun in the 8th may be the "identified patient" in a dysfunctional family, acting out the depression or rage which others refuse to acknowledge in themselves. It may look as if, at nineteen or twenty, the person is getting nowhere, and they may exhibit some very serious problems.

I am not suggesting that the problems will just magically "go away" when the time is right. Sometimes therapeutic help is needed. Nor am I implying that the individual has no choice. Equally, when we see such chart placements, it doesn't mean that the Sun will never be able to shine. But the journey may be convoluted. Outer planet energies can be overwhelming unless the ego is solid enough to mediate them. The wise parent will cultivate patience and understanding, as well as the recognition that the world may have to catch up with the individual rather than the other way around.

The person with Sun-Neptune may pass through a long period of languishing in Never-never-land before the Sun rises up and says, "Pull your finger out and get a life." The Sun-Uranus person may spend many years smashing everything in sight until the Sun finds its own voice and says, "Who are you when you're not spouting polemics and throwing rocks at the police?" The person with Sun-Pluto may go through long phases of depression, isolation, or anti-social behaviour, or pursue a chain of difficult relationships which involve destructive power-battles, before there is enough light for the Sun to say, "I want to be an individual with choices, not just a bundle of burning compulsions or a helpless victim of patterns that were formed long before I was born." Outer planet aspects do slow up the Sun's development. And when the Sun isn't shining, depression may be one of the first by-products.

The narcissistic wound

There are many different kinds of depression and many different clinical ways of defining and diagnosing it. There is a particular kind of depression which has to do with feeling empty and unreal. We don't feel we exist, and unless other people keep reminding us that we exist, there is a horrible feeling of sinking into a bottomless pit. Then life seems utterly pointless. This may be linked with an unexpressed Sun. If we don't feel real, we must get our reality mirrored back to us by other people. This can lead to many distortions of the personality because of the overwhelming dependency on others' love and affirmation.

This psychological dynamic is called narcissism. A narcissistic wound means that there is no sense of independent self. There is a sort of hole in the middle, like a Polo Mint. The only time that we feel alive and worthwhile is when someone else is mirroring back to us their belief in us as a worthwhile, lovable person. If they go away, we fall into the hole again. Yet even if we surround ourselves with those who are willing to provide constant positive mirroring, the person with a narcissistic wound doesn't really believe them. Gnawing away inside is the conviction of being a fake, although this is often unconscious. If one's emptiness, one's unworthiness, is discovered, one will be rejected. Various manipulative methods must then be employed, some of them very destructive, to ensure that others do not discover the terrible truth which one believes about oneself.

We all suffer from some degree of narcissism. It is very much the *malaise* of the modern era. But some suffer more than others. There is a book you all might be interested in by Alexander Lowen, called *Narcissism: Denial of the True Self*.[10] Lowen writes from a Reichian perspective rather than a Jungian or Freudian one[11]. Those of you who are psychoanalytically inclined might not be aware of this book, which was first published many years ago. Lowen suggests that psychological as well as physical illnesses are characteristic of the culture of the time. In Freud's Vienna at the end of the 19th century, hysteria was the "norm" in terms of psychological illness. It was the product of a certain kind of suppression of certain aspects of human nature, and the symptoms reflected the culture and psychology of the prevailing *Zeitgeist*. Freud's psychological theories on hysteria were also appropriate for the time, although they might seem less appropriate now. Lowen then goes on to say that, since World War Two, narcissistic disorders are on the increase in Western society. They are endemic now. We might not have encountered that many instances of narcissistic personality disorder a hundred years ago. But now they are everywhere, and Lowen presents various ideas about why this should be.

Narcissicism, viewed astrologically, is a solar wound. In psychoanalytic circles it is viewed causally, and is attributed to having had insufficient mirroring in infancy. This leads to a lack of ego-formation and an inability to separate from the mother. The child is required to mirror the mother rather than being mirrored by her, and is therefore unable to experience himself or herself as a separate being. Certain birth chart configurations can suggest an inherent reluctance to form as an individual. The same configurations may also reflect an innate gift of sensitivity – a talent for mirroring which may then be exploited by a needy parent. The usual suspects are involved, most

---

[10] Alexander Lowen, *Narcissism: Denial of the True Self*, Touchstone Books, 1997.
[11] A Jungian approach to narcissism can be found in Nathan Schwartz-Salant, *Narcissism and Character Transformation: The Psychology of Narcissistic Character Disorders*, Inner City Books, 1982.

commonly Neptune and the 12th house.[12] Behavioural psychology doesn't recognise an inherent personality pattern. Genetic studies imply that the personality pattern is not only inherent but unalterable. Astrology presents us with a more holistic picture. The right chemical mix must occur between environmental conditions and inner predisposition, and the birth chart can give us insight into both. The parental figures in the chart are both objective and subjective. But we can never know from the chart how the actual parents have handled the archetypal patterns which the chart portrays and which the child experiences in and through mother and father. Some parents handle these patterns very badly indeed.

We become self-aware in infancy through mirroring and feedback. We become real to ourselves if our identity is reflected back to us by our mother. If no mirroring is given, we flounder around without a clear sense of being anyone at all. This usually involves having a mother who is not enough of an individual to offer a mirror to her child. She is a psychological child herself, and therefore, instead of responding to her child, she wants the child to respond to her and provide her with a sense of reality and value. Sometimes we speak of having to mother one's mother, which is another way of putting it. The mother requires constant emotional mirroring because she is so needy, so the child does not get the response he or she needs in order to form a sense of independent identity. This is a solar wound which is passed down from one generation to the next. I am sure you can see why it runs in families. The mother who cannot mirror her child has herself probably not received mirroring from her own mother. When an "inherited" pattern is described in this way, the usual astrological suspects tend to dominate, in one form or another, in most if not all of the family charts.

Do you all know the myth of Narcissus? When he was born, his mother, anxious to know his fate, consulted the blind prophet Teiresias. "Will he live into old age?" she asked. The prophet replied: "As long as he does not know himself." Narcissus' mother took this literally, and never allowed him to see his own reflection. Thus he had no opportunity to view himself objectively and critically. This made him callous and unfeeling toward others. When he eventually saw the reflection of his own face in a pool of water, he fell in love with it. He was so infatuated with his own image that he became obsessed with it.

---

[12] See *The Astrological Neptune and the Quest for Redemption, op. cit.,* Note 3.

To lack a mirror of one's developing identity in childhood may mean that, in adulthood, the individual is self-obsessed, constantly needing to see himself or herself reflected in the eyes of others.

Audience: Is this similar to what Alice Miller writes about?

Liz: Yes. Alice Miller writes from a Freudian perspective. But she and Lowen are talking about the same thing.[13]

Audience: You said there are patterns in the birth chart that can point to narcissism, and the usual suspects are involved. Can you say what these patterns look like?

Liz: There are a number of patterns which can point to a sense of existing only to mirror the mother. But I want to stress that these patterns in themselves do not mean the person suffers from narcissistic personality disorder. The outer environment is extremely important, and without the right – or wrong – kind of mother, the pattern may describe great sensitivity to the needs of others without suggesting a narcissistic wound. As I said, Neptune is usually involved, as is the 12th house. This isn't surprising, since a powerful Neptune can describe both great sensitivity to the feelings of others and a deep reluctance to suffer the loneliness of a separate existence. I would also look carefully at the 10th house as well as aspects to the Moon, and I would pay attention to combinations such as Sun or Venus in the 10th with Moon aspecting Neptune, or Neptune in the 10th with Moon-Uranus or Moon-Saturn or Moon-Chiron in the 12th, or Moon in the 10th with problematic aspects to outer planets.

Audience: Tony Blair has Sun in the 12th and Moon in the 10th opposite Pluto. Do you think he is narcissistic?

Liz: Yes, I would say so. He does so much need to be loved, and image appears to dominate over substance. But do you think there is any political leader in power at the moment who *isn't* narcissistic?

---

[13] See Alice Miller, *The Drama of the Gifted Child: The Search for the True Self,* Basic Books, 1996, and *For Your Own Good: Hidden Cruelty in Child-Rearing and the Roots of Violence,* Noonday Press, 1990.

I would also keep an eye on an angular Jupiter, or a preponderance of planets in the element of fire in combination with the configurations I have just mentioned. This is because fiery children, as well as those with a strong Jupiter, are naturally self-expressive and expect and need an audience. If the parental audience is a psychological child who appropriates her actual child's imaginative gifts for her own greater glory, the child may learn to perceive his or her talents solely as a means of acquiring love, rather than as a source of inner joy and sustenance.

All these combinations, which are only a few of many possible ones, present the mother in an ambivalent way, powerful yet helpless, rejecting yet needy. They also present an inherent temperament which is both highly imaginative and deeply dependent. Neither of these qualities is pathological, but both are vulnerable to unconscious parental exploitation. We need to see more than one planetary significator to get a sense of severe disturbance in the early relationship. And I don't think we can come to any conclusion without meeting the individual and getting a look at what he or she has done with these natal ingredients. Neptune does seem to be implicated a lot in narcissistic problems because the child needs so badly to merge with the mother, and is so vulnerable to being turned into mother's redeemer.

It's also important to remember that intense self-centredness, of the kind sometimes described by Sun conjunct Moon or lots of planets in Leo, usually doesn't suggest narcissism in the clinical sense. It's just ordinary, garden-variety self-absorption, and may suggest that one has a hard time recognising the reality of others or the effect of one's behaviour on others' feelings. But a Sun-Moon conjunction combined with the other configurations I've mentioned may suggest more than mere insensitivity.

The formation of the ego

Audience: So the idea is that the child, instead of being able to play like a child, has to parent the parent. The ability to play is taken away.

Liz: Yes, exactly. Play requires the ability to trust and let go. If one is constantly attuned to mother and required to tend to her needs, there is no room to enter one's private inner world. The process by which the

Sun develops in early life involves struggle against the mother. Remember the myth of Marduk and Tiamat? The child needs to be mirrored and then, having acquired a sufficient sense of self through this mirroring, he or she must struggle to complete the process of developing an independent identity. That is facilitated by play, which allows the child to enter an independent imaginal world.

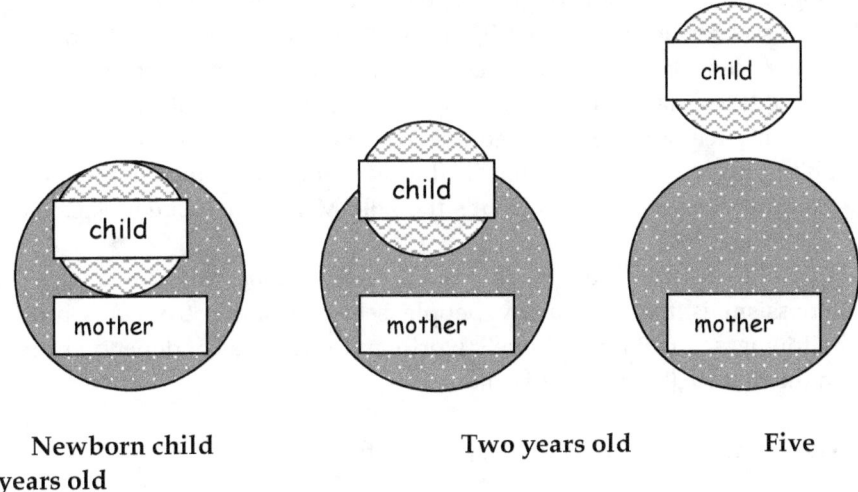

Newborn child   **Two years old**   **Five years old**

    Here is a very simple diagram, which I am sure many of you have seen me use before. I've adapted it from Edward Edinger's book, *Ego and Archetype*.[14] Edinger uses the diagram to describe the changing relationship between ego and Self, but it serves very well as a portrayal of the changing relationship between mother and child. You can see that, in early infancy, the psyche of the child is enclosed within the psyche of the mother. The child is not a separate entity. The Sun is only a potential, because there is no conscious ego. Gradually, as the child gets older, separation begins to occur. The period known as the "terrible twos" is an important staging post in this process. This is the time of the first Mars return, and aggression and anger help the Sun to emerge. Eventually the child becomes a separate individual. At least, that is what happens in drawings like this one. Between infancy and five years old, however, a lot of things can happen which may make the reality different from the map.

---

[14] Edward Edinger, *Ego and Archetype*, Penguin Books, 1973.

The process of separation needs some acceptance and encouragement from the mother. At the very least, it needs indifference. But sometimes there is active refusal on the part of the mother to allow the child any separateness at all. If, like Narcissus, the child is not allowed to see his or her own face, the separation process can be delayed, and if the child's own temperament colludes, it may be blocked altogether. If we are brought up to mirror our mother and are merely the vessel for her unfulfilled life rather than being acknowledged as an independent individual, we may only feel real when mirroring others. This is the situation of many people in the helping professions. Or we may only feel real when an audience reflects back to us an identity we can't experience inside. This is the situation of many people in the entertainment professions. That's the Polo Mint. When one looks inside, it is empty.

I believe that what Lowen says about the prevalence of narcissism is true. So many people seem to suffer from a sense of hollowness, a feeling that one's worth and one's reality depend entirely on the feedback and love of others.

Audience: Some people live happily with it.

Liz: They appear to live happily with it until they experience an unwilling separation from someone or something with whom, as with mother, they are psychologically fused. One can indeed live in a state of Sunless unconsciousness and be quite content until the children grow up and leave, or until one's husband or wife or lover has an affair, or until one's mother dies, or until the acting roles dry up and there isn't an audience any more. People can remain asleep for many years, until life changes and something happens that demands inner resources. Then the sky falls. I am not suggesting we grab people off the street and shout, "You are asleep! You have to become conscious of the Sun!" Life tends to do this for everyone sooner or later. When an individual in distress consults an astrologer, it often is because a separation has happened and they have been forcibly kicked out of the womb. Suddenly they realise they are like a Polo Mint and there is nobody at the centre. Why are you laughing?

Audience: I'm laughing at the Polo Mint. It's a wonderful analogy. I will remember that one when I have a client sitting in front of me. They are a Polo Mint. Better fill it up.

Liz: Many people consult an astrologer because they have discovered with horror that they don't know who they are. Life has dealt them some kind of blow. They look inside for resources and there aren't any to be found, because the Sun is not shining and there is no sense of individual identity. As you say, people can remain happily unconscious and unformed for a very long time. But sooner or later a challenging transit or progressed aspect will come along, and undeveloped dimensions of the psyche are constellated. This may coincide with an external crisis, but sometimes the panic arises with no apparent cause. At such times depression and anxiety can be very severe because there isn't a solar sense of individuality. That is often when people arrive on the astrologer's doorstep.

Narcissistic wounding down the generations

The reasons why the Sun remains undeveloped are many and varied. On the external level, part of the problem often lies with parents who are themselves undeveloped as individuals, and therefore they have no idea at all how to be parents. They may know how to change nappies, cook meals, wrap Christmas presents, and go to work to pay the mortgage and the electricity bill. But their understanding of parenting is gleaned primarily from a sorry mixture of *Coronation Street* and their own unformed parents, and inwardly they lack the resources to mediate the solar and lunar archetypes for their children. I don't think blame is very helpful here. It's just how things are. It would never occur to many people that good parenting may need to be taught, and that it is not an inherent ability which everyone automatically possesses. If it ever was, modern society has put paid to that. Many parents are psychological children because they weren't parented, and their parents couldn't parent them because they themselves weren't parented.

This is what Lowen writes about. He points out that, during the First World War, a whole generation of men was lost. There were many women left with young children but no husbands, brothers, or fathers. These women endured extreme states of anxiety, and many had to go out to work against their wishes. They couldn't stay home with the children, but they couldn't afford a dependable child-minder. The children born during this time – when Pluto entered Cancer and Saturn conjuncted first Pluto in Cancer and then Neptune in Leo – spent their childhoods in a psychic atmosphere of desperation and loss.

These children in turn married and had their own children, just in time for the horror of the Second World War. Another generation of young men was lost, and another generation of women endured great suffering and anxiety. And another generation of children, this time born with Pluto in Leo and Saturn conjunct first Uranus in Taurus and Gemini and then Pluto in Leo, were never truly parented. How could they parent their own children? Lack of real parenting tends to propel people into early marriages, because there is so much hidden anxiety and so much need for comfort and security. Often they have children too soon, and those children in turn have no feeling of being parented. I don't think I need to go on. You can see how there has been a passing down of this wound through virtually all the generation groups in the 20th century. It is a vast problem which extends beyond the personal failings of any particular mother or father. It should be obvious that blame is inappropriate unless we wish to blame the entire human race, which is not an especially helpful attitude.

Lowen is not an astrologer. He doesn't mention the astrological Sun. But the issue of narcissistic wounding is bound up with the lack of a central sense of identity, and it is very much a solar issue. The nature of the society we live in is making it increasingly difficult for us to get the kind of mirroring we need in order to develop the Sun. Therefore we must learn to give this mirroring to ourselves, because no one else is going to give it to us.

Audience: Would you conclude that, if a person has been working to develop a sense of self and then has a child, the child might not have the same difficult aspects in the chart that the parent does? You said that aspect patterns repeat in families. Do difficult aspects that repeat over generations become easy ones, or disappear from the family charts, if a person works to change things?

Liz: I don't think it's quite that literal. And a "difficult" aspect can be just as positive and creative as an "easy" one, depending on the attitude and consciousness of the person. Particular signs and planetary combinations, including those involving the Sun, do repeat in families. But the efforts of individuals don't make a challenging aspect "disappear". What changes is the way in which an archetypal pattern is handled and expressed. For example, there may be a Moon-Uranus pattern repeating in your family. Whether the two planets are in trine, sextile, square, semisquare, conjunction, or opposition, this constitutes a family *daimon*. A need for emotional breathing space and a resistance to too much domestic closeness – qualities typical of Moon-Uranus people – will be evident in many family members.

This fundamental need will be dealt with according to each individual's level of awareness. Sometimes it will be dealt with creatively and sometimes destructively, and sometimes both. Greater consciousness can certainly help the next generation cope more constructively with the planetary combination. But it isn't "better" to have a trine than a square. One can't say, "Oh, look, I've got a trine between Moon and Uranus. My mum had them in opposition. That means she must have worked on it, and I have got the benefit." Repeating aspects are part of the family inheritance. Every generation can do something different with them. The birth chart won't say whether the previous generation got it right or wrong. All it says is, "This is a family *daimon*. It has come down through the paternal or maternal line. Do your best with it."

Let's say that you have a Sun-Neptune opposition. That is an archetypal pattern inherited through the paternal line. Individual expression needs to be allied with an openness to, and creative expression of, the imaginal world. Your father may have handled his Neptunian qualities in a very positive way. Your opposition is not a statement that he failed. His father probably also had a receptivity to Neptune's world, and so did his grandfather and his great-grandfather. Any one of them might have been a wonderful artist or poet with a kind, compassionate nature. The next generation still has the option of making a complete balls-up of that same Neptunian *daimon,* even if the preceding one handled it really well. Your Sun-Neptune opposition suggests a particular kind of inheritance from the father. You have the option of making a mess of it. If you make something beautiful out of it, that is a wonderful gift to give your own children. But there is no guarantee they will value the gift.

Audience: Are you saying I have the option of making a mess of my Sun-Neptune trine?

Liz: Of course you can make a mess of your Sun-Neptune trine. We can all make a complete balls-up of anything in the chart, including trines. All we have to do is identify completely with them, allow our innate abilities to make us lazy, convince ourselves that we are always entitled to a free lunch, and repress all the squares and oppositions in the chart. Then we have made a mess of our trines. Trines can be very manipulative and good at maneuvering other people, and we can misuse our talents if we lack integrity. Trines say nothing except that the ego finds it easy to combine the planetary energies. Trines make no other statement. The really relevant statement is made by the individual.

The Sun in aspect to any planet means there is another god allied with Apollo, or a Muse who is in some way conjoined with Apollo. This story has come down through the father's line, and we need to develop it ourselves in our own way. If the father lived his story badly, we can learn from his mistakes. We can say, "He couldn't find a way to express Neptune's world positively. He didn't have enough confidence, enough of an inner solar centre, to develop his creative talent. He couldn't bear separateness. So he became an alcoholic. He couldn't maintain the Sun's light against the flood of Neptune's longing to go home." Or we can say, "He was utterly anti-Neptune. He hated hippies, socialists, mystics, and anything that reminded him of his own secret yearnings. He projected his Neptune on me, and always made me feel like a failure." We can learn from that kind of mistake too. Both kinds of fathers can teach us how to deal better with our inheritance, which was their inheritance as well.

Audience: He could also be a doctor who is so busy treating other people that he never notices his own child.

Liz: Yes, he could be a doctor who is never at home because he is always saving other people. He may project his Neptune onto all his suffering patients. But in that case, at least he is making some kind of positive contribution to life.

Audience: I suppose it's a bit better than `an alcoholic father, although if he had drunk himself silly he might have been at home more.

Liz: Your anger at your Neptunian father may not be entirely appropriate. He did try to make an individual contribution to a suffering community. As a personal father he may have been a disappointment. But in fact he wasn't a bad model of a creative use of Sun-Neptune.

Audience: Did I say I was angry?

Liz: No. But it was oozing out a bit between your words. "A bit better than an alcoholic father"? Your father did mediate Sun-Neptune for you. You may feel he didn't do a very good job of parenting on a personal level. I can't comment on that, although often a child's wish to have a beloved father entirely to herself can make it seem as though he was a "bad" father when in fact he wasn't. In any event, he did give you a positive model of how to balance Sun and Neptune – how to be individual and special yet also serve the collective. This may not be the way you wish to live your Sun-Neptune, but he demonstrated that it could be lived in a human and constructive way. He may have given you a greater gift than you are yet able to realise. Whatever our personal feelings toward father, and however justified they may be, we need to look beyond them to whether the father provided us with any positive model of the planetary aspect described in our own chart. It's often quite surprising how much we can see, understand, and forgive if we are willing to view things this way.

The father and the solar spirit

Audience: It feels like both my parents were the Sun.

Liz: That can happen, especially if one parent carries the light side of the Sun and the other the dark.

Audience: I am not sure I understand what you mean when you link the father-archetype with something beyond earth life, something outside personal experience.

Liz: Until the latter part of the 20th century, father generally went to work, while mother looked after the children – often more children than she could cope with. Obviously there have always been exceptions to this rule. But throughout history, children have seen relatively little of their fathers, and have spent their formative years in the company of their mothers. That is a purely pragmatic answer to your question. Mother is what we are used to, but father appears and disappears according to his own laws. The advent of easily obtainable birth control methods, the increasing availability of good educational and professional possibilities for women, the legalisation of abortion, and the social changes effected by the feminist movement have certainly shifted the rigidity of this ancient apportionment of roles. Yet we continue, in dreams and in outer life, to link solar qualities with the father. There is something subtler than concrete experience involved in this symbolic equation of father with spirit. A child may certainly project the Sun on the mother if the mother is obviously solar, or if she is the only parent. Yet these are not common situations.

Audience: I have got the Sun trine Neptune. My mother is a musician, and I feel she is solar.

Liz: You may be one of the exceptions to the rule. Despite the changes occurring in male and female roles in society, there is still a mystery around father on the archetypal level. In myth, the god fertilises a mortal woman and then makes his exit. The most typical of these mythic divine fathers is Zeus, but there are many others. Apollo enacts the same pattern with his own lovers – he fertilises them and then vanishes. He doesn't take them home to Olympus to meet his parents. I believe this mythic motif is saying something about the fact that we don't have a direct physical experience of coming out of father's body. He is alien. We have come out of mother's body and we know that body intimately, albeit unconsciously. We have a direct, ineradicable knowledge of it because, before birth, we shared her bloodstream and heartbeat, and during birth, we struggled for life in the blood and fluid of her birth canal and issued our first desperate cry when the cord connecting us to her was cut.

But father is a stranger. That is reflected in the archetypal image of the invisible creative spirit. Unlike the ancient Greeks, we know all about how a sperm fertilises an egg, and we have DNA tests to prove paternity. But our bodies remember, not through theory but through experience. Ultimately, even though society is changing radically, we

Part One: The Meaning of the Natal Sun

still continue to project the Sun on our father and the Moon on our mother. Our lunar responses are based on physical familiarity. Our solar goals and ideals are based on what we have not yet become. We are not there yet. Who we are physically is known from our pre-birth state. Who we are inwardly can only be guessed at, because we have no corporeal identity with father. We don't have a sense of connection with his body.

Audience: So he comes from "outside".

Liz: Yes. Although many women are now going to work and many men are staying at home and looking after the children, or at least sharing domestic responsibilities that were once the sole domain of women, we still cannot alter the biological fact that it is not possible for a man to give birth to a child. That may come one day, but it hasn't happened yet. We come from father's seed, but we don't know his body. That is what constellates the solar image of the divine. We sense intuitively that this is where our secret origins lie, but our bodies have no knowledge of it. A human father, however flawed, mediates that spiritual mystery and gives us something against which we can bounce our projections. Without this humanisation, solar attributes remain in the mythic realm. At the present time, Britain has the highest number of single mothers in Europe. This will undoubtedly have far-reaching effects over the coming generations. I have no doubt that some of these effects may be highly positive, but some will be highly negative. We may not live to see the full consequences of such profound social changes, which may take many generations to unfold.

The Sun aspecting Saturn or Chiron

Aspects from Saturn or Chiron – any aspect, not just the hard ones – can also give the Sun trouble. In the case of outer planets aspecting the Sun, we must find a compromise between individual and collective – a place where we can maintain our personal ego-ground but at the same time give expression to the dreams, inspirations, and needs of the greater whole. This can slow down solar development. Something rather different happens when Saturn or Chiron aspects the Sun. Our shining solar sense of individual potential is dampened by worldly limits and an awareness of human suffering, and we may find it very hard to maintain faith in our specialness and creative power.

With Sun-Saturn and Sun-Chiron a compromise is required, just as it is with an outer planet aspecting the Sun. But this particular compromise can be painfully slow to achieve because the light of the Sun is overshadowed by the immovable boundaries of reality and the fundamental unfairness of life. The recognition of one's flaws and imperfections, as well as the feelings of victimisation characteristic of Chiron, can make it hard to believe in future possibilities. Naturally the paternal inheritance is relevant. Sun-Chiron may portray a father who has been wounded by life and has given up hope, or who wounds his child's self-esteem because of his own pain. Sun-Saturn may portray a father whose creative spark has been crushed by worldly responsibilities, or whose inability to cope with the mundane world has resulted in chronic material problems. These configurations don't necessarily mean that the father was a failure in any general sense. But the person with Sun-Saturn or Sun-Chiron usually feels the relationship has failed in some way. This could be because the father couldn't deal with the challenges of the Saturn or Chiron archetype and became withdrawn, negative, over-critical, or unable to respond to his child. Or he may have had to leave, perhaps through no choice of his own, or because the parental marriage failed. The compromise required between Sun and Saturn or Chiron becomes more difficult if the father could not provide a positive model.

These aspects do not say, "Father made a total mess of it." Nor do they say, "You are too damaged to be creative and fulfilled." They merely state that Apollo will always be accompanied by Saturn or Chiron as he carries the solar chariot across the heavens. Solar light must be lived within worldly limits, with an acceptance of imperfection and a respect for how things actually are. The Sun must be able to shine within that burdensome structure, that flawed and mortal flesh. It needs to go on shining in spite of the fact that it casts its light within a kind of a prison. If we can achieve this, we transform the prison, although it will always seem like a prison from the perspective of the spirit. But if we give up, depression, rage, negativity, self-pity, and hopelessness can be the results. It is very important for Sun-Saturn and Sun-Chiron people to go on struggling, even through very hard times. Feeling sorry for oneself, and demanding that others compensate for one's real or imagined difficulties, is not especially helpful. Struggle energises the

Sun and gives it strength and hope. If the struggle is abandoned, feelings of powerlessness and inferiority may be projected, and this can form the basis for the scapegoating of others. Or we may project these feelings on our own children and become envious and hypercritical, thus perpetuating the problem and passing it down to the next generation.

These solar aspects are extremely challenging and require self-honesty and integrity. Complaining about the lack of a free lunch does nothing to improve the situation. Sun-Saturn and Sun-Chiron make a flat statement: "Your solar light has to be grounded in the real world. Stop whining and get on with it. The rewards are commensurate with the difficulties." This will never be a perfect light, but it can be a strong and enduring light which gives warmth and healing in this world rather than illuminating some transcendent vision that lies beyond mortal reach. If the light is not embodied within worldly limits it may be too fragile, lacking strength and tenacity, and easily defeated by everyday mundane challenges.

With Sun-Jupiter aspects, there is often a feeling that one can accomplish anything. There is no sense of limitation. With Sun-Saturn or Sun-Chiron, one may feel, "Who am I to think I am anything special?" The sense of limitation is sometimes overwhelming. If these feelings are conscious, it is painful, but it's possible to struggle and preserve an enduring flame. If the feelings are unconscious, they can produce very destructive results. With Sun-Saturn and Sun-Chiron, one must accept that the god's vessels are not always perfectly shaped and without flaw. Sometimes they have been damaged, dropped and broken, and then patched up. But they are sufficient to hold the light. They may generate an indestructible light which cannot be extinguished by life's disappointments. The Sun, tempered by the limits of reality, keeps on shining because there is no expectation that life is like Disneyland.

Audience: What is the difference between Chiron and Saturn?

Liz: The nature of the limits is different. Both may require a painful compromise. But Chiron's wounds are rooted in a sense that human nature hasn't improved much in the last three millennia. Chiron symbolises difficulties much bigger than any individual family. With Saturn, one has the sense that there was something lacking in the family, something one badly needed but didn't get. If conscious, this can generate strength and self-sufficiency: "No one is going to give me this thing. To hell with them. I am going to go out and build it for myself." With Chiron, one is more likely to think, "My family couldn't provide this thing that matters so much to me. But no family can. It's just the nature of the society we live in. Human beings are in a mess." Chiron's wounds can't be fixed through hard work. Although effort is important, Chiron also demands acceptance of what cannot be healed, while Saturn demands a willingness to do the work oneself.[15]

Audience: You said earlier that the Sun grows through separation. If someone is in the grip of an outer planet, can we know from the chart whether or not they will find their solar consciousness?

Liz: We don't know whether they will. We hope they will. The chart can't tell us about an individual's willingness to do the necessary work or make the necessary sacrifice. It also can't tell us when environmental or genetic issues are stacked against the person. When we meet a client in this situation, we can make positive suggestions. But we don't know if the person will listen. A young person with a powerful outer planet contact to the Sun is always buffeted by collective currents. They may feel very small and impotent and frightened, or they may identify completely with the collective and be quite unaware of themselves as individuals. The outer planets remind us of our unimportance. The Sun in a young person may not have enough light to struggle against this.

The faith that others have in us matters enormously here. When we are young, we need someone who says, "I know it's taking you a long time to find your feet. I know you are confused. But I also know you are someone very special. I can see your potential, and I believe that one day you will get there." Ideally, the parents should be able to offer this kind of individual affirmation. It doesn't require a lot. Sadly, they often make things worse by reminding the child how selfish he or she is. A teacher might provide the right support. But in Britain we don't educate our teachers psychologically, and they are often ignorant of their own problems and unable to help their students. Or they are so

---

[15] For a more thorough exploration of the differences between Saturn and Chiron, see Liz Greene, *Barriers and Boundaries: The Horoscope and the Defences of the Personality,* CPA Press, London, 1996.

determined to inculcate their political ideology that they aggravate the difficulty.

We hope that a young person in this situation will reach the point where they can say, "The world is huge and full of problems, and I can't redeem it. No individual can. But I am going to try to sort out my small corner and make a positive individual contribution. And I intend to enjoy life at the same time." As astrologers, we can give insight to a young person who is drifting. Some will listen and some won't. Some will never make it, and there's nothing we can do about that. Many of you here have the Sun aspecting an outer planet. Perhaps you could give us some feedback.

Sun-Pluto aspects

Audience: I have the Sun square Pluto. That certainly applies to me. I had a terrible time when I was young.

Liz: Did you have to journey powerless through the dark for a long time?

Audience: Yes.

Liz: And do you feel you have come out, at least occasionally?

Audience: It has become more conscious. I spent years in a kind of dark tunnel. I may never entirely come out, but now I have a sense of what I'm dealing with, and it doesn't look so dark. That makes it much easier.

Liz: If the Sun aspects Pluto, life will always have periods in the tunnel. But the Sun can bring light into the tunnel, rather than being overwhelmed by darkness. With Sun-Pluto aspects, Apollo and Hades are inextricably bound. The Sun-god can spend time in the upper regions, but he is always called back to the underworld again. I don't think the object is to permanently get out of the tunnel. It is to work toward an alliance between the two gods. The Sun can light up Pluto and bring the riches of his realm into consciousness. Pluto can give the Sun depth and substance, and the capacity to survive in the world.

Audience: Naturally, what you do at first is try to get out of the tunnel. When you become conscious of the fact that the tunnel won't go away, you say, "Okay. I live in a tunnel. How am I going to make the most of it?" But it took me a long time to work that one out.

More solar themes

Liz: How many of you have a Sun-Neptune aspect? There seem to be a lot of you here today. Did any of you go through an aimless time when you were younger? Yes? No? You mean it is still ahead of you?

Audience: I'm still in it!

The Sun in a grand cross

Liz: I would like to put another chart from the group on the overhead projector. You can see that the Sun is in Taurus, opposition Neptune in Scorpio. It's also square Uranus and square the Moon, so it is part of a grand cross configuration. The Sun is on the cusp of the 3rd house. Can we hear something of your story, Lucy?

Lucy: Which part of the story? About my father?

Liz: Not specifically, although no doubt that will come up. I would be more interested in how you perceive your creative potentials. How do you understand the Sun-Neptune opposition?

Lucy: It feels dangerous to me. Sometimes I have a sense of terrible isolation, as if there is nobody else in the world. Just me. It is really frightening. It's hard to believe people who say, "Oh, your poetry is so beautiful, you should have it published." I always feel it's a load of rubbish. Whatever I am, I feel I should be different. I'm too self-centred or too closed. I should be more in tune with something bigger. The other thing is that it feels like I should be there for everybody. If I am just being myself, I'm convinced I'm totally selfish and unfeeling.

Part One: The Meaning of the Natal Sun

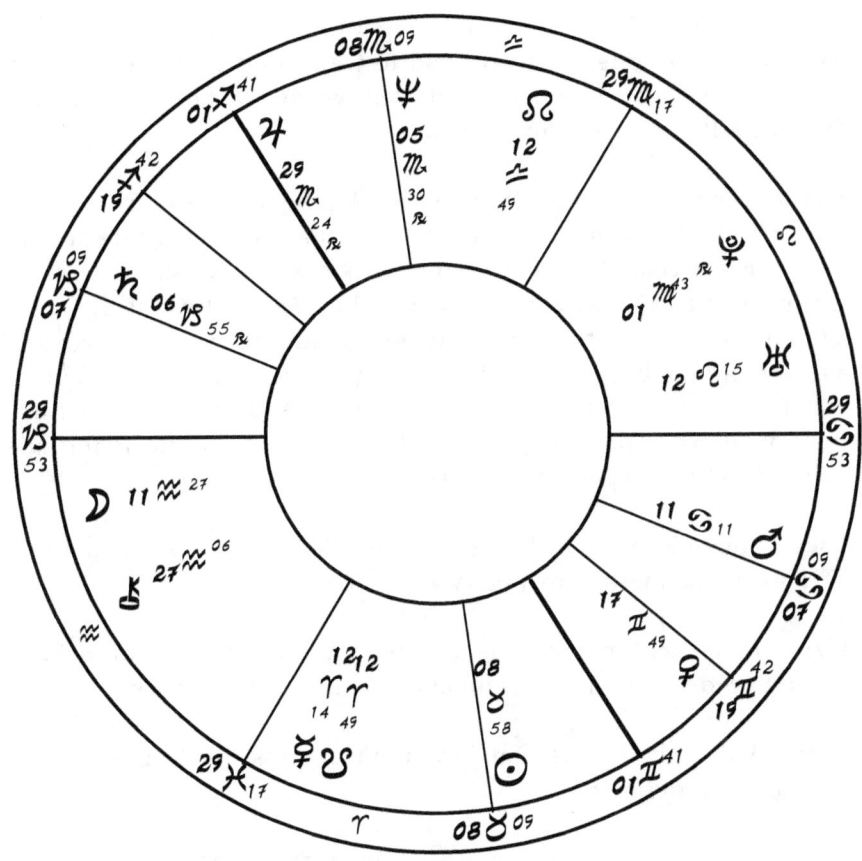

Lucy
[Birth data withheld for reasons of confidentiality]

Liz: So you are pummeled by Neptunian collective needs which say, "Give us everything. Don't give anything to yourself. Sacrifice yourself."

Lucy: Yes. I am now in a relationship with a man who has the same birthday as me, with the same Sun-Neptune opposition. Both of us have to work really hard to say, "Just a minute, that's my limit. That's my boundary." I know I have difficulty with ordinary communication. I joined a theatre group because I knew there was a problem. I thought it would help me to express myself. I do love it. But at first I didn't feel I had anything to offer. I always had to wait to be invited before I said anything. I have a real problem with self-worth. Maybe that's something to do with the Sun being in Taurus.

Liz: A Taurus Sun shines through developing a sense of worth, which comes through developing innate talents and resources. There are other things in the chart that may also have a bearing on the issue of self-worth, such as Chiron in the 1st house, but we can look at that a little later. It is interesting that you write poetry, and that you are involved in a theatre group, because both these things are expressions of a 3rd house Sun and also Sun-Neptune. Do you know what drives you to get up in front of people to perform? What makes you want to write, to formulate in words what you perceive and feel?

Lucy: I don't know. I hadn't thought much about the Sun being in the 3rd. I always connected my poetry with Moon-Neptune.

Liz: Moon-Neptune feelings are poetic. But Moon-Neptune alone doesn't need a voice. It's the Sun in the 3rd that needs a voice.

Lucy: I thought it was that I couldn't express my feelings through anything except poetry.

Liz: That may be true. But the need to express them, to communicate them, is solar. Perhaps it isn't easy for you connect with the Sun. But it's the Sun that's driving you to give shape to Neptune. The Moon is not impelled to express itself. The Moon feels. The Sun expresses itself. Moon-Neptune isn't concerned with expressing Neptunian feelings. It wants to feel Neptunian feelings, to be immersed in Neptune's embrace. But the Sun in the 3rd in Taurus says, "That's not enough. I need to express these things in concrete form." The moment we need to express something, we know the Sun is pushing to come out. Your poetry is a Sun-Neptune vehicle. Neptune is in the 8th in Scorpio. The Sun gives a voice to Neptune's secret, complex emotional world.

The problem of perfectionism

Lucy: Is the Sun concerned with perfection? I always think there is some perfection that I can't quite reach. I feel as if my Sun gives up and says, "I know there is a perfect way to express Neptune." But I haven't got there yet, so I am never satisfied.

Liz: The Sun square Uranus may reflect your constant striving for perfection. But that is Uranus bringing its vision into the equation. The Sun is not a perfectionist. Apollo's world is one of harmony, not of perfection. Above the entrance gate at Delphi was carved in stone the famous Apollonian dictum, "Nothing in excess. Everything in measure." The Sun strives toward a harmonious organism in which all things have a place. Uranus comes in and says, "But it's not perfect. It doesn't fit my concept of an ideal work of art." Sun-Uranus aspects can make it hard for the Sun to shine through an ordinary human vessel. No actual creative work ever lives up to the idea of the perfect creative work.

Audience: What is the difference between harmony and perfection?

Liz: Harmony is inclusive. Perfection is exclusive. When we are with an individual who is living from the centre, we instinctively sense that they are a whole person. Of course we can pick out all the imperfections. Yet the person's life has integrity. We have to acknowledge this, even if we don't personally like them or approve of their values. It is like a fine piece of music. There may be discords from time to time, and it may not be entirely to our taste, but when we listen to the whole piece we recognise its integrity. Imperfection is entirely acceptable in Apollo's world, provided it is contained within the integrity of the whole and serves the Sun at the centre. This can make the difference between a difficult chart aspect acting out in a destructive way, or expressing as a problematic but valid and necessary part of the personality.

There are some very gifted people around who never produce anything with their talents because they know that what they produce won't be perfect. They have an image of perfection in their mind, and unless they can achieve it they give up or won't even begin. So the book sits half-finished in the desk drawer, and the painting is visualised but never attempted. The Uranian idea of perfection dooms creative children to the underworld, never to be born, which is precisely what the god Ouranos does to his children in myth.

The Sun says, "I know this novel is not perfect. But I've done my best with it. It has integrity. I can't keep rewriting it forever. I'll send it off to the publisher now and start thinking about the next one." Many films have this kind of integrity. We can pick out isolated elements and say, "This bit of dialogue is banal. That characterisation doesn't work." But the film moves us because it has its own integrity. It shines. There is a huge difference between perfectionism and integrity. The former can make us destructively self-critical. The latter allows us to be confident. A shining Sun is confident but not arrogant. An arrogant Sun is an insecure Sun, unsure of its light. The Sun says, "I'm human. I have many flaws. But I'm doing the best I can with what I've got. I will keep trying to become more of what I know I can be. But I don't wish I was somebody else." We respond to people like this. They may not be "enlightened", but they are real and they are generous-hearted.

Sun square Uranus may also say something about your father-image, Lucy. He is Uranian as well as Neptunian, and an internalised Uranian father-figure can be highly critical and demanding of an impossible level of perfection. Consciousness of this inner image and its links with your family past can help you to maintain a high standard of creative work. But if it sabotages you unconsciously, and you let it beat up the Sun with its impossible expectations, it can take away the joy which could come from your Neptunian expression of poetry.

Audience: It is interesting that, if you break down a perfect note into its component harmonics, they are not always harmonious. But when they are put together, they make a perfect sound.

Liz: That's a nice analogy, applicable to every horoscope. Some charts are obviously harder than others. Over the years a practising astrologer will see many permutations of human fortune. We may think sadly, "That's a tough chart," or enviously, "It's all right for some." It would be stupid to pretend that every birth chart is equal in terms of ease or difficulty. The gods are not communists, and we are not all dealt the same hand of cards. But fulfillment is not dependent on easy aspects, nor is the sense of a worthwhile life. Sometimes those lovely, easy charts are not what they seem. Some time, have a look at the chart of Josef

Mengele,[16] which is full of beautiful aspects. Would you like to be remembered that way?

Having Chiron in the 1st may not always feel like a bundle of joy, Lucy. Your vulnerability and feeling of being an outsider may never go away. But with Aquarius on the Ascendant and Uranus square the Sun, there is an innate tendency to dissociate when the going gets rough. The 1st house Chiron humanises that Uranian propensity by making you aware of individual suffering, your own and others'. When we look deeply at any birth chart, we begin to realise that configurations we assume to be negative always provide a creative balance to configurations which might otherwise be too much of a good thing.

The whole chart tells an integrated story, even though particular components, when viewed in isolation, may seem rather thorny. Every chart has something in it that is not very pretty. We could say, "Damn! I have got whatnot square thingey! What a terrible aspect! If only it weren't there I would be happy!" On one level, that might be true. But if we look at the chart as a whole, which we can do only do if, like the Sun, we are standing at the centre of it, we will see that it tells a coherent story. It is in harmony within itself, although it may not match some childlike ideal of perfection or unending bliss.

The acceptance of limits

Audience: I have both Saturn and Chiron in aspect to the Sun. Could you say something about that?

Liz: With both planets aspecting the Sun, it is important to recognise and accept your limits but not be defeated by them. Many of the limits represented by these planets seem, and often are, unfair. Yet it is important to maintain faith in oneself and one's individual values. We can react to limits in many different ways. We can pretend they aren't there and get enraged when we run up against them, trying to smash through them and hurting others as well as ourselves in the process. We can feel utterly defeated by them and say, "What's the point? My life is

---

[16] Josef Mengele, b. 16 March 1911, 11.45 am, Günzburg, Germany. Particularly striking is the grand trine between Sun and Mercury in Pisces, Neptune on the Ascendant in Cancer, and Jupiter in Scorpio.

hopeless." Or we can struggle with them and make a relationship with them. All the time we need to push the light as far as it can go, but when we know it can't go any further, we need to avoid becoming bitter.

It is quite an education to work with someone who has a severe physical handicap, because this is a tangible limit that cannot be attributed to one's subjective attitude. Of course the majority of people with Sun-Saturn or Sun-Chiron have no actual physical handicap. But there is often an unconscious feeling of being inwardly handicapped, and sometimes this is projected onto the circumstances of outer life. Then there is a strong sense of victimisation. One can meet many people who feel bitter because they are not particularly beautiful, talented, or wealthy. They resent anyone who seems to have more than they have, and they complain endlessly about their bad luck and others' lack of sympathy. Yet the real source of the bitterness is the awareness that they cannot be exactly what they wish to be, and must live within their human limits and work for what they have. Instead of living the Sun through conscious effort, they want solar light handed to them on a plate like a child's birthday gift.

Some years ago I went to a concert in Birmingham given by the Israeli violinist, Itzhak Perlman. This man was crippled by polio when he was four years old. He has to use metal support frames to get about because he can't walk properly. He staggered onstage with great difficulty, and then proceeded to play. He is the most exquisite musician. From what people who know him say, he is an extremely kind, charming, and very loving person, without any bitterness in him. I watched him performing and thought to myself, "This morning I had a Sun-Saturn client who, all her life, has made a huge meal out of the fact that her father was cold to her when she was a child. She could learn something from Perlman, whose suffering is irrevocable and unending." He is a wonderful example of someone who, despite severe limits, still maintains his faith in life and his commitment to creating something of beauty to offer others. I have no birth time for Perlman so I have no idea of the Sun's house placement, but he was born on 31 August 1945, and has the Sun in exact semisquare to Saturn. Perlman expresses the most positive face of Sun-Saturn. Fortunately most people's limits are not as severe as his. Unfortunately many people don't deal with their limits as graciously as he does.

We all have to accept our limits. But Sun-Saturn and Sun-Chiron people feel their limits more. They are more sensitive to the limits in life and in themselves, and they must struggle to maintain hope and confidence within those limits. If they become bitter, the light of the Sun is dimmed and their potentials are spoiled by their resentment. We have many options in terms of how we deal with our limits. But whatever we do, we need to respect those limits without being defeated by them. It is a great challenge. One may have to swing between *hubris* and bitterness for a while. It is probably appropriate to kick against one's limits and then give up, and then get up and try again, until a balance of some kind is achieved. The Sun aspecting Saturn or Chiron always carries a certain degree of sadness. Sun-Saturn and Sun-Chiron people tend to be robbed of their innocence long before they realise what they have lost. Father Christmas, the Easter Bunny, and the Tooth Fairy rarely have much appeal, even in early childhood, because these children know too much about life. Accepting the sadness without becoming chronically depressed is the greatest challenge of these solar aspects.

Audience: So, for example, Saturn in 12th square the Sun in the 8th means the person senses what is happening on a collective psychic level.

Liz: Yes. There is often a deep sense of the sorrow in life and the inevitability of human loneliness. There may also be a difficult family inheritance of a collective kind, involving experiences like persecution, scapegoating, or the ravages of war. There are plenty of places in the world where the collective displays its less attractive features rather floridly, and perhaps there is no place entirely free of these things.

Audience: Then the struggle, for the Sun in the 8th in Virgo, could be more of a mental struggle

Liz: Virgo is not a "mental" sign in the same way Gemini is, although both are Mercury-ruled. Virgo is more concerned with ordering and refining the mundane world through the application of knowledge. Virgo is earthy, not airy, and it is also concerned with service and usefulness. All the earth signs have the need to do something useful. The Sun in the 8th in Virgo needs to express itself through applying knowledge and practical skills to the invisible and often darker dimensions of life. I would expect a person with this solar placement to be attracted to some sphere of the helping professions, or some area of work which helps to order, improve, or clean up the environment. With

Saturn in the 12th square a Virgo Sun in the 8th, there is no escape from the hidden side of life. But there is a powerful desire to use the experience of the underworld to contribute something useful and improve the quality of life.

Audience: Also to avoid depression.

Liz: Yes. Being useful, for the Sun in earth, is the route out of the dark. The earth signs, when they fall into depression, find their confidence again by feeling they are contributing something useful to life. The route out for water is to relate, to make contact emotionally. The route out for air is to learn, to understand why, and the route out for fire is to tap the imagination and give expression to it. These are four basic ways of dealing with the kind of depression linked with the 8th house.

Audience: I had an encounter with a person who has a Sun-Saturn conjunction in Pisces, and her Saturn is exactly conjunct my Moon. I was always being blamed for rejecting her, but I felt she was doing this to me. I feel I normally express my Moon quite well. But she was somehow crushing my Moon.

Liz: She probably projected her Saturn onto you, perhaps because she identifies with you – her Sun conjuncts your Moon – but can't live the Piscean qualities easily because Saturn is sitting on her Sun. She tried to block your Moon because you reminded her rather painfully of what she wants so badly to express herself. Your empathy probably touched her deeply, but she couldn't handle it. Saturn or Chiron aspecting the Sun often get projected onto other people, who are then blamed for the problem. If you are the recipient, it is not a lot of fun. But sooner or later a transit will come along to trigger her Sun-Saturn, and she may have to face her inner issue.

Envy

The last solar theme I want to talk about is envy, and it is connected with the mythic motif of Apollo's loneliness. It is one of the chief reasons why people find it difficult to express the Sun – they fear the envy of others. Often this problem starts in the family background. A parent may be envious of their child. This is an extremely common situation. It goes hand in hand with the narcissistic wound which I talked about earlier. If we don't have a sense of individual value, and we are hoping that our child will provide a mirror and give us a reason to live, and the child then begins to display an individuality rather than co-operating with these expectations, the parent may feel great envy. Envious parents can also be loving parents. They are not mutually exclusive, and often go together. The envy is unconscious and the love is conscious and expressed, but the envy seethes away underneath, always ready to find covert outlets which undermine the child's confidence.

A child who is the recipient of parental envy may learn to stifle the Sun because it is extremely painful to have an envious attack coming from a parent whom one loves and needs. One learns to hide the light in order to avoid being the recipient of envy. The problem is that we may then reach adulthood being eaten up by envy ourselves. If we aren't showing our light, we may resent those people – including our own children – who are able to show theirs. We may project our Sun on them and want to be around them to get a bit of that light vicariously, but at the same time we may try to hurt them because we are so envious of them. Thus the cycle of envy moves down through the generations.

There are a number of configurations in the birth chart which can hint at this issue. Usually there are planets in parental houses. Sometimes Venus is implicated. A woman with Venus in the 10th, or a man with Venus in the 4th, may have to face the issue of envy with the parent of the same sex. Sometimes Chiron can be very envious, and so can Saturn and Pluto. When we see these planets in the 10th or 4th, we may need to think about the issue of an envious parent. Envy may not always look like envy, especially when it is unconscious. It may appear as constant criticism and disapproval, or studied disinterest, or a powerful negative mood. The child subject to an envious attack from a parent usually comes away feeling inferior and inadequate, and never realises that behind the criticism, rejection, or bad atmosphere lies envy.

I have sometimes raised this point with clients who have suffered from feeling they weren't good enough. Lurking in the background is often a highly critical parent whom the person has internalised as an inner judge. Saturn is often in one of the parental houses in such cases, or there may be a Moon-Saturn aspect, or Sun-Saturn if the father is involved. The client may say, "My father was so critical of me," and I reply, "Maybe he was secretly envious of you." The client then says in astonishment, "Envious? Why should he possibly have been envious of me? I was only a child."

Of course any parent frustrated in their solar potential can be afflicted by envy of their child. Saturnian parents are not the only ones. We need to think about how disturbing and deeply hurtful parental envy can be to a child, who expresses the Sun in an unconscious way. The child is playing and says to the parent, "Look at me! Look at my drawings! Aren't they good?" Children don't suffer from the social etiquette which muzzles adults and makes it impossible for them to ask for praise. The envious parent looks, frowns, and says, "Not bad. But you've used the wrong colour here, and that part is very blurred, and this doesn't look like a tree at all." Behind these words is the implicit statement: "You're not as special as you think. Stop showing off." That is the form the critical attack takes. But the parent doesn't really believe the child is not good enough. The parent is actually unconsciously thinking: "I wish I had that talent. But I don't have it and never will. And even if I did, it's too late for me." There may also be envy of the child's childhood: "As a child I was never allowed to play. And I certainly can't be self-centred and irresponsible and joyful now. I have a family to look after. Why should my son/daughter get what I missed out on?"

This is the shape of ordinary, garden-variety human envy. Teachers as well as parents can exhibit it, especially toward the gifted child. Our educational establishment is riddled with people who have become teachers not because they love teaching, but because they have failed to develop their own solar light. They may be terribly destructive toward a child who displays special abilities. This is usually cloaked under the guise of political ideology. No elitism must be shown, even if it means a talented child is undermined or denied much-deserved encouragement. If we have been subjected to envy in childhood, there is a high likelihood that we will fear it. And if we fear it, we will avoid being special because someone else might envy us, display their envy with hostility, and evoke our childhood pain and rejection all over again.

That may be the deeper issue behind the statement, "This book isn't good enough to be published. I won't bother to finish it." Or, "I'll never be a really good painter. I won't bother." Sometimes this is no more than the unvarnished truth. Not everyone has a marketable creative talent. But if something gives us joy, why refrain from doing it just because it isn't going to win a prize? And sometimes such anxieties are not always a realistic assessment of talent. They may reflect a fear of being special. The fear of being special is one of the commonest of human fears, because if we are special we won't be loved by everyone. A lot of people will resent us because they are envious, and they are envious because their own Suns have been squashed by parents who couldn't live *their* Suns. Under the aegis of Uranus and Neptune in Aquarius, needing to be special is now called something else. If we wish to be special, we are deemed to be elitist. Envy has recently acquired a politically correct demeanour, and lots of people are being fooled by it.

Audience: Could this be connected with the kind of violence which is so common in families? Can envy breed violence toward a child?

Liz: Sometimes an envious parent may become overtly destructive. But this is not due to a frustrated Sun. Other factors, especially problematic Mars, Chiron, and Pluto placements – in the parent's chart or involving cross-chart aspects – need to be involved in order for real hatred and violence to become part of the package. Envy toward a child's Sun emanating from a frustrated parental Sun is usually expressed more subtly, and is often, if not always, accompanied by genuine love and appreciation. Apollo is a much-loved god. He doesn't tend to attract, or display, consuming hatred, although like all the gods he can be vengeful if he is not honoured. Although we may not get family approval for shining our solar light, it is unlikely that a parent's stifled solar needs will display the kind of relentless animosity toward a child's Sun that an angry Pluto or thwarted Mars may do. The Sun, even when unconscious, is not innately violent. It simply wants to shine.

Audience: If I go more into my Sun, and if I am not with people of like mind...

Liz: ...Then you will sometimes feel lonely. The people around you might envy or dislike you, and you may find that painful. You may have to make new friends. There is a price for living the Sun, but the price is higher if we don't live it. That price might be more than we can afford. The Sun's price tag is affordable – perhaps uncomfortable, but it costs far more to betray our own soul.

Envy is not a psychopathology. Yet it is incredibly pervasive and can conceal itself in many disguises. It can hide beneath the guise of ideology or concealed beneath idealisation of another individual. It can be deeply destructive on a personal as well as a collective level. Envy is the most common solar problem in a relatively stable person whose Sun is not shining. Severe clinical depression is an extreme response to a Sunless life, but envy is not deemed to be something that merits treatment. It is just envy. But if we can get enough people to join us in our envy, then we can win elections and pass laws. And we can make it extremely difficult for anything to be expressed which is different from that which threatens to make us feel envious. Then we are back to *Amadeus,* a film which is worth watching more than once.

Audience: The play has reopened.

Liz: I have only seen the film, but it is very much to the point. The name Amadeus means "Beloved of God." Salieri is horrified by the fact that God has chosen such a coarse, undeserving vessel. Why was Salieri himself not chosen to be God's vessel? This is ordinary, garden-variety envy taken to a lethal extreme. Of course Salieri was also God's vessel. We all are, in the solar sense – we all have a unique destiny, a *daimon* which needs to be expressed through the Sun in the birth chart. But Salieri wanted to be more than an individual writing individual music. He wanted to be the Chosen, which is how people tend to perceive genius when they encounter it. He was not content to enjoy the light of his own Sun shining. Perhaps his Sun wasn't shining enough. Maybe he didn't develop his musical gift sufficiently because he was too concerned with earning a living and maintaining a good social position. Comparing oneself to genius, and resenting the inevitable conclusion, is a kind of inflation which reflects deep personal insecurities and wounds. We need to think about these issues, because I doubt that any human being is immune to some degree of envy at times, even if the Sun is shining. But when the Sun is not shining, envy breeds in the darkness, and it may be envy not just of genius, but of anyone whose light is visible.

Encouraging the Sun to shine is not a recipe for total self-absorption. By emphasising the Sun in this seminar, I am not endorsing Alistair Crowley, who declared, "'Do what thou wilt' be the whole of the law." Apollo does not try to take over Olympus. He is not the king of the gods, nor does he wish to be; he serves Zeus. But he is excellent in himself. Solar expression is not synonymous with insensitivity, ruthlessness, brutalising of other people, or megalomania. The Sun serves that for which it is a vessel. Solar expression means having a sense that there is something inside us worth developing, and offering it with as much loyalty as we can. If it invokes disapproval from the family, we must learn to put up with that. If it means that some of our friends turn out to be a bit spiteful, we must let them go and find friends who are confident enough themselves to value our specialness. But living the Sun doesn't mean trampling over others. The Sun is not oblivious to the rest of life. It is a vessel for the whole of life, and ultimately serves something greater than the ego.

Audience: One of the things that occurs to me is that people who are solar are people who really live their lives. You would never think of saying to them, "Get a life!" But if living the Sun means living your life with joy, why do so many great artists suffer a miserable life of anger and unhappiness?

Liz: It might be helpful for you to read Adolf Guggenbühl-Craig's essay, called "Creativity, Spontaneity, Independence: Three Children of the Devil".[17] He is very careful to differentiate between ordinary human creativity and genius. Genius often pays a bitter price because, as in the case of Mozart, the *daimon* demands expression without restraint, and the individual personality – and the individual Sun – are often subsumed in the process. Ordinary human creativity is not mutually exclusive of personal happiness, although it requires the acceptance of some loneliness. Genius is not a solar issue. It is something that lies beyond the domain of astrology. There is nothing in Mozart's chart that will tell you the extent of his gift – only the likely lines of its expression. Whatever genius is, it works through a chart, but it is not portrayed in the chart. And it can trample over the ordinary human needs which the chart indicates. As Guggenbühl-Craig says, we should get down on our knees and thank the gods that we are not geniuses.

---

[17] This essay is included in *From the Wrong Side: A Paradoxical Approach to Psychology* by Adolf Guggenbühl-Craig, trans. Gary V. Hartman, Spring Publications, 1995. It was also published in Issue 1 of *Apollon: The Journal of Psychological Astrology*, CPA Press, October, 1998.

Audience: But I keep getting the idea that, if I could express my Sun properly, maybe I could write symphonies.

Liz: Perhaps you could. But perhaps not. If you could, I suspect you would have been doing so by now because you would not be able to help it. By developing the Sun, you will not become Mozart. I'm sorry about that. All you will become is yourself, and because you are not Mozart, you will not have to pay Mozart's price. Mozart's genius wasn't an expression of solar creativity alone. In some mysterious way the ordinary humanness of the true genius is swallowed up by something greater. A priceless gift is given to the collective, but the vessel is sometimes smashed in the process. It is very rare that such people come along. Creativity in the solar sense is a human affair. It is not possession by the god. It is inspiration, but within ordinary human limits, and I don't think it is mutually exclusive with joy. Joy may not be there every day, but it will be there sometimes. The tragic early death of the genius is mythic, and not something the Sun itself describes. Apollo is not dismembered. He is just lonely.

Inner choices

Audience: I'm still trying to come to terms with the source of problems with the Sun. Are they environmental, or are they mapped out in the chart? Do they come from inside or outside?

Liz: I'm not sure there is such a clear distinction between "inside" and "outside". Nor do I have a definitive answer to your question. Some solar problems clearly arise in the family, and some arise from the chart itself and how the Sun is placed in it. If the Sun is a singleton in fire and the main weight of the chart is in earth, the Sun will have a hard time because it has to work harder. The attitudes and perceptions which feel most natural to the person contradict the values which mean the most in terms of inner aspiration and commitment. In the end, no single factor in the horoscope or the family background is going to give us a clear "reason" why the Sun might be in trouble. It is usually a complex chemical mix. If one accepts the idea of reincarnation, one could assume the problems arise from a former life. That might or might not be a factor in the equation. Many solar difficulties stem partly from the society one is brought up in. They may have to do with early environment, with gender, and with the culture into which was born. These are all factors over which we have no conscious control.

There are invariably several elements, any of which, taken alone, would not create such difficulty but, when added to the sum of all the others, serves as the proverbial straw that breaks the camel's back. In psychiatry this is known as "overdetermination". There are so many factors pointing in one direction that there is a kind of inevitability involved.

Let's say that a man has the Sun in Cancer as the only planet in water in an airy chart. The Sun is placed in the 12th house and it's square Saturn or Chiron. His father left his mother when he was two years old, and his mother had to do menial jobs to support the family, leaving him with a succession of well-meaning but incompetent caretakers. He is a black man living in a white neighbourhood in the American South. If all these things are added together, then it is probable that this man is going to have a hell of a job finding the light of the Sun. Any one of the factors I described is not enough, in itself, to explain the difficulty. Some factors are "outer" and some are "inner". And there may also be an issue of choice, although the choice may not be fully conscious.

Some of us choose not to go through the solar struggle. It is more comfortable to identify with one's collective and have one's sense of who one is provided on a plate. It may also be easier to blame the outer world for one's problem. If we can get away with that, great. But if we have got away with it, we probably wouldn't be studying psychological astrology. I doubt if any of you here have got away with it, although some of you may have tried.

Audience: Oh, yes, I tried.

Audience: How does the concept of *logos* fit in with the Sun, in your opinion?

Liz: There are several ways to interpret the word *logos*. In Platonic thought, *logos* is solar because it is the creative will of God, the creative "Mind" – the intent of the One. But in some psychological circles *logos* is equated with intellect and is polarised with *eros*. *Logos* is sometimes deemed "masculine" and *eros* "feminine". I don't think this interpretation is very helpful to us.

The Sun does not symbolise intellect as opposed to heart. And the images of the Sun in myth are both male and female, as we have seen, suggesting that there is a unity or synthesis of mind and heart, of intellect and feeling, of reason and vision. Prophecy is not an intellectual function, nor is music. These are Apollo's main attributes. For Plato, the Divine Mind isn't something purely intellectual, and the "intelligible realm" is not a place of abstract ideas. It is the creative vision of *cosmos*, generated by the One, which underpins all manifestation. *Logos* in Platonic and Neoplatonic, representing the creative will of the divine, may indeed tell us something about the most profound dimension of the astrological Sun.

I think we have reached the end of the seminar now. The Sun is going down. Thank you all for coming.

Bibliography

Campbell, Joseph, *Oriental Mythology,* Penguin Books, New York, 1982.

Campion, Nicholas, *Astrology, History and Apocalypse,* CPA Press, London, 2000.

Edinger, Edward, *Ego and Archetype,* Penguin Books, 1973.

Greene, Liz, *The Astrological Neptune and the Quest for Redemption,* Part One, Samuel Weiser Inc, York Beach, ME, 1996.

Greene, Liz, *Barriers and Boundaries: The Horoscope and the Defences of the Personality,* CPA Press, London, 1996.

Guggenbühl-Craig, Adolf, *From the Wrong Side: A Paradoxical Approach to Psychology,* trans. Gary V. Hartman, Spring Publications, 1995.

Harrison, Jane, *Themis: A Study of the Social Origins of Greek Religion,* Merlin Press, London, 1963.

Heath, Robin, *Sun, Moon and Stonehenge,* Bluestone Press, Cardigan, Wales, 1998.

Lowen, Alexander, *Narcissism: Denial of the True Self*, Touchstone Books, 1997.

Miller, Alice, *For Your Own Good: Hidden Cruelty in Child-Rearing and the Roots of Violence*, Noonday Press, 1990.

Miller, Alice, *The Drama of the Gifted Child: The Search for the True Self*, Basic Books, 1996.

Schwartz-Salant, Nathan, *Narcissism and Character Transformation: The Psychology of Narcissistic Character Disorders*, Inner City Books, 1982.

Solomon, Jon, ed., *Apollo: Origins and Influences*, University of Arizona Press, Tucson and London, 1994.

Taylor, Thomas, trans., *Collected Writings on the Gods and the World*, Prometheus Trust, Frome, Somerset, 1994.

West, M. L., *The Orphic Poems*, Oxford University Press, 1983.

Part Two: The Sun, Creativity, and Vocation

This seminar was given on 8 November 1998 at Regents College, London as part of the Autumn Term of the seminar programme of the Centre for Psychological Astrology.

The Sun and the creative process

Welcome to the second part of our two-part exploration of the Sun. We don't have such lovely weather this time, but perhaps that's better for sitting indoors and concentrating on a seminar. As I promised last week, I want to focus today on the complex issue of creativity – which, as you will see, is likely to become the proverbial can of worms before we are finished. From there, once we have done what we can with the Sun's relationship to the creative process and looked at the many problems which the term "creativity" invokes for so many people, we can move on to an associated area of solar concern – what we call vocation. These two themes are very closely linked. Then, later on in the day, I want to look at the meaning of transits to, and progressions of or to, the Sun, and see whether these can give us some insights into the issues of creativity and vocation. That's the rough plan for the day, which we might or might not be able to adhere to.

The nature of creativity

It might be useful to start off with some simple questions. How many of you feel you are creative? Lots of hands up. Good. How many of you feel you are not creative? Quite a few hands up. Those of you who feel you are not creative: What does this mean to you? Why do you feel you are not creative? What do creative people do that you don't?

Audience: I associate creativity with artistic talent, and I don't think I have any of that.

Liz: How would you define "artistic talent"?

Part Two: The Sun, Creativity and Vocation

Audience: I suppose I mean someone who could paint a beautiful painting, or compose a beautiful piece of music, or write beautifully.

Liz: So being creative equals being artistic, which equals producing something beautiful. I could go on to ask you how you define beauty, but others have their hands up, and it's worthwhile to hear a number of responses.

Audience: I also feel I am not creative because I am not an artist. I think of someone like Beethoven when I think of creative people.

Liz: This issue of not being an artist seems to be a problem for some of you. Evidently you don't consider that there might be other forms of creativity besides obvious artistic work. Let's hear more from those of you who don't feel you are creative.

Audience: I am not an initiator. I am a critic.

Liz: So you take other people's creative products and assess them, rather than creating something of your own.

Audience: Yes.

Liz: Do you feel this as a lack? Does it trouble you?

Audience: Yes.

Liz: All right, we will come back to this point, which is an important one – whether assessment and interpretation are themselves a valid form of creativity. Anyone else?

Audience: I know I have imagination, but I don't seem to have any way of expressing it. I don't do anything with it.

Liz: So your feeling of not being creative has to do with knowing you are imaginative, but being unable to find a vehicle for the imagination. That, to you, means you are not creative. These are two quite different things, aren't they? – imagination, and the capacity to express imagination. Anyone else?

Audience: I see being creative as bringing something new to things.

Liz: Can you tell us more about what you mean by "something new"?

Audience: Coming up with a new idea, something inventive, something no one else has thought of. It isn't just painting a bowl of fruit. It means coming up with a new way of painting a bowl of fruit.

Liz: Do you feel you can do this?

Audience: No. That's why I don't think I am creative. I have some artistic talent, but that's not enough.

Liz: So you believe you aren't creative because you are not living up to your particular ideal of creativity. That's another very important issue we will have to come back to.
    I have another question. Those of you who did put your hands up and do feel that you are creative, whatever that means to you: When you are being creative, what does it do for you? What happens to you?

Audience: I lose all sense of time. I get taken out of myself.

Audience: I feel really alive.

Audience: I always feel as if I am trying to give birth to something. It's a very painful process. Sometimes it feels like a miscarriage. Even when it doesn't, I get depressed when I've finished, because I never feel it's good enough.

Liz: What kind of creative work do you do?

Audience: I am a painter.

Liz: Some of you feel energised when being creative. One of you finds it quite a painful business. Several of you feel frustrated because you have an image of what you could do or should do or want to do and you are not doing it, so you feel uncreative or blocked. We could spend all day asking everyone how they define creativity. At the end of the day we will have as many answers as there are people here.

Audience: When I am being creative, I feel as though I am more myself than at any other time.

Liz: Can you tell us more?

Audience: I think it's about losing self-consciousness. I am totally immersed, but I don't lose myself. I just lose the sense of worrying about anything outside myself.

Liz: Three of you have described what we might term an altered state of consciousness – some kind of experience beyond the ego's usual awareness. You have described feeling more alive, feeling more yourself, losing the sense of time, losing self-consciousness.

Audience: I definitely feel it is an altered state. I feel connected with some kind of life energy. When I am blocked, I feel terrible.

Audience: We still don't really have a definition of creativity.

Liz: I did say that we would get as many definitions as there are people here today. In spite of all the interesting responses you have given, I don't think we are going to get an acceptable universal definition of creativity. All we can do is listen to individual experiences. I have no quarrel with anything anyone has said – how could I? – and all these different viewpoints and experiences are important and valid. But it is like attempting to interpret the Sun itself – we will not get very far if we try to find a nice keyword which fits for everyone.

Now I am going to play around a bit with some of the symbolism and mythology of creativity, since this might help us to see more clearly what we are dealing with.

The divine child

Playing and reality

One of the most powerful images associated with the Sun is the divine child. In myth, as we saw last week, Apollo is the guardian of children and youths, and is himself a divine child. We can see the image of the divine child in many versions of the card of the Sun in the Major Arcana of the Tarot – the Waite deck is a good example. In astrology, we associate the Sun with the 5th house, and we associate the 5th house with children. This house is the house of the child. We don't always ask ourselves why we make this association. Why should the Sun be given rulership over the child or children, and what do we mean by the "house of children"? Do we mean that the 5th house shows if a person will or won't have biological children? Or does it mean something else? We also call this the house of creativity, so in astrology we make an equation between creativity and children.

Now, we all know that children play. We expect them to play, and we get worried when they don't. Playing is the quintessential child activity. When adults play, they feel vaguely uncomfortable unless they are working strenuously to be playful. Play isn't a word we associate with adulthood. What does it mean to play?

Audience: Does playing make you feel happy?

Liz: Happy? Well, try answering that one yourself.

Audience: I'm free and happy when I play. There is no script.

Liz: Well put – there is no script. Now, if there is no script, what do we do when we are playing?

Audience: We make it up.

Liz: Yes – whatever it is, we make it up as we go along. If we are going to cook something, and we decide we are going to play, we don't open a recipe book. What do we do instead?

Audience: Make a mess!

Liz: Yes, or we poison our dinner guests. Try to be conscious of what happens, even though it is a contradiction in terms. When we put the recipe book away, what are we doing?

Audience: Experimenting.

Part Two: The Sun, Creativity and Vocation

Audience: Exploring.

Liz: We are exploring without expecting to find anything. There is no preconception of where we will end up, just the clues offered by the journey itself. Receptivity, experimentation, exploration, throwing away the script – these are all adjuncts of play.

Audience: This also has something to do with not being in control.

Liz: That is very important. When we play, we are not attempting to control what happens. But if we are not in control, who or what is in control? If the ego abdicates its seat of power, where does the inspiration come from?

Audience: From fantasy.

Liz: Many people equate the ability to fantasise with creativity. Once again, we need to examine the words we are using. Imagination and fantasy are not necessarily the same. And fantasy can be controlled or uncontrolled, depending on how much the ego interferes. Fantasies may reveal our complexes, but they may also simply reflect our wishes. When we play, we may be giving shape to a fantasy which develops according to some invisible inspiration rather than reflecting the story we started out with.

Audience: We are inventing when we are playing.

Liz: And what do you mean by "we"? Who is doing the inventing?

Audience: What about games?

Liz: Well, the word "game" is difficult because it has many different connotations. In Britain, we refer to a football match. In America, it is a football game. The word "game" is often misused because some games are deadly serious, especially when big money is involved or when one is carted off the playing field with broken bones. Play, in the solar sense, does not involve winning or losing, nor does it involve remuneration. From a solar perspective, many games are not really playful. Playing, in the sense that children play games, and playing a game in the world of sport, are not the same thing. When there is a serious intent to win, we are talking about competition rather than playing, and we are looking at Mars rather than the Sun.

Audience: Games are sometimes like warfare. The Olympic Games are like a played-out war. Two sides are fighting it out. That seems to me much more to do with Mars.

Liz: Competitive games may be played with flair and creativity by a particular individual, but they are not play in the sense we are discussing. Children may also attempt to win in a game, but this motive is secondary to the playing itself. Playful games take a brutal reality and make it symbolic. Children often play games with deadly themes. "Bang! you're dead. I'm the Lone Ranger and you're Tonto. I'm Buffy and you're the vampire." Reality is brutal and stark, but when it is made into play, we enter an "as if" world. This term is used a lot in psychological texts. If I point a water pistol at you, it is "as if" I were really threatening you with a gun. We are taking something difficult and painful, removing it from the plane of reality, and acting it out in a playful way. This is the substance of fairy tales, which do the same thing. We take intolerable human situations – suffering, warfare, death – and we turn them into an "as if" situation where they become not only more bearable, but also more meaningful. And we can laugh at them.

Then there is the word "play" in the sense of theatre: "I went to see a play last night." An actor, in Shakespeare's time, was known as a player. These multiple meanings in the same word are very suggestive. "I am going to *play at* being an altruist – I shall *act as if* I am deeply concerned for humanity." What does this mean? The word in Greek for an actor is *hypokrites,* and from it we get the word "hypocrite". So we play-act; we express ourselves *as if* we feel something, *as if* we are Oedipus or Hamlet or Medea. We play at being astrologers, we play at being priests, we play at being psychotherapists. We play-act the roles of our lives.

Play makes reality into an "as if" world. We are able to cope with reality because we have translated it into a symbolic state. And the moment we do this, we can make things up and transform reality. Once we have made something up, we have changed the way we experience it "out there". We are no longer the passive victims of life. We have created our own version of reality. The whole business of play is really all about creating realities. These creations may take their initial cue from what is "out there", but they make it into something different. If we play at cooking and we are not following a recipe, we are creating an "as if" reality. "What if I try throwing in a bit more chocolate? What will it taste like if I cut this piece of pineapple in half and put marmalade in it?" We are moving away from the "given wisdom" as offered by a recipe book, and we are making something up which is an alternative reality.

The mythic creator-gods

This takes us straight into the realm of the creator-god, who is the mythic prototype of the artist. To play is to be an artist, a creator-god. When we look at all the myths of creator-gods, we may well wonder why they do what they do. The myth merely says, "And God created the firmament," or, "Ra brought forth all the other gods." Every creator-god brings forth something. Yet there appears to be no reason for it. Our Western religious heritage tells us that God created the world. Why on earth did he bother? What was going on up there? Was he playing?

There is no reason why we play. We simply do it because it is a natural, spontaneous, and inevitable thing to do. As a rule, children play naturally and spontaneously. Yet there are many children who are unable to play. What stops an individual from playing? One of the most beautiful descriptions I have read of the act of play is in Hindu philosophy, where the creation of the universe is a playful act. The world of Maya, the world of illusion, is pure theatre. It is a dance, a performance, all pyrotechnics and fireworks. There is a tremendous sense of humour in it, although it may not be very funny when we are trapped in it. This portrayal of a playful divinity creating manifest reality is not conveyed in the Judeo-Christian world-view. God would appear to have lost his sense of humour. That humour, which is of a subtle and profound kind, is very much in evidence when we read the Hindu portrayal of the creation of worlds, the creation of universes, the creation of the gods. There is a constant process of making things up. There is joy in it. So, why do some people lose their capacity to play, or have never been able to play?

Audience: They become too serious.

Liz: But why?

Audience: Everything is a survival threat.

Liz: Yes, that is an important factor. When we are preoccupied with survival, we cannot play. We have lost our trust. When we were talking about what it feels like to be creative, one of you mentioned the experience of not being bound by time and space – being "taken out of yourself". This describes a state where we have to trust absolutely. Paying too much attention to what time it is or where we are physically blocks the state of play. When we are playing, we are not watchful. If we are watchful, we cannot play. Trust is a very important issue in solar expression, which has to do with playfulness and making things up.

Audience: When you're playing, you're not attached to the outcome.

Liz: That's a good way of putting it. What does "attached" mean? It is connected with self-definition through identification with an external object, situation, or result. When we talk about the Sun's creative expression, we are talking about an experience of being non-attached, of not being watchful, of not having an investment in the outcome.

Audience: Is it to do with giving up the will?

Liz: I am not sure that it is about giving up the will itself. "Will" in the solar sense is not the same as self-will or desire. It is devotion to something at the centre, something we are trying to serve and give shape to. But it may be about giving up the attachments which we use to define ourselves. We tend to direct our will toward these attachments, rather than directing it toward the centre.

Audience: When you play, you are alone.

Liz: Yes, even if we are playing in the company of others. Children play together, but they are alone in the imagination at the same time. That is paradoxical, but it shows us that the Sun is not "anti-social". Solar creativity can work with others. But it cannot work for others.

Solar selfishness

Now, what kinds of things might prohibit our entry into this world of play? Many people try to avoid losing themselves in it because they fear being overwhelmed. They don't trust that they will emerge from the chaos of the imaginal world. They exercise too much control, too much watchfulness. This is a Saturnian problem. Others fear being lonely and worry that, when they come out, the loving caretaker will be angry or will no longer be there waiting. This is a fear of separation, and it is a Neptunian problem.

Audience: There is such a sense of being limitless in that world. You have no limits. You can be anything.

Liz: Yes, that is a fundamental gift of the playful world of the Sun: we are no longer limited. In other words, we are no longer mortal. When we play, we lose our sense of limitation. When we interact in ordinary life, we are always aware of limits and boundaries. We are reminded of our mortality all the time.

Audience: There is also something about no longer being responsible for others. You can be selfish.

Liz: Yes, selfishness is the essence of play. Our responsibility to others no longer exists. It is part of losing our sense of "out there", because "out there" is other people. Other people remind us of our responsibilities and our fear of their criticism. Our bonds with others prohibit us from being purely selfish. This has both positive and negative connotations.

Audience: It isn't any fun to feel selfish. When I feel selfish, I feel I am a bad person.

Liz: All right. Now we are picking up one of the threads which leads back to the issue of why people feel creatively blocked.

Audience: Is this connected with the negative side of Saturn? I thought it might have to do with that judge inside which says one is a bad person because one is doing something against the rules.

Liz: Yes, it is connected, in part, with the negative side of Saturn. The issue of selfishness is bound up with the feeling that we are responsible for others. A sense of responsibility is required in order to create and live in a coherent, structured, civilised society. There must be laws which protect us from each other and from the chaotic side of ourselves. If we play, we are irresponsible, and if we are irresponsible we may hurt people. And if we hurt people, we are not only selfish – we may actually threaten the fabric of society.

Audience: There is also a moral component, or maybe a religious component. Being selfish is not very Christian.

Liz: Yes, our Judeo-Christian religious ideals demand that we sacrifice selfish wishes and desires, not only for the sake of society, but because God demands it. We are taught that we will not be permitted entry into heaven if we are selfish. We will be punished. Entry into heaven and acceptance by society are very close cousins. Both imply that we will not be separate and alone. We will be loved and welcomed into a larger unity.

Audience: This makes me think of all the times in childhood when I was told I was selfish. Maybe the real fear is, "I'm going to lose my parents' love, and then they won't take care of me." Parents are always telling their children not to be selfish.

Liz: Yes, it is a word used a lot to keep children in line. Wielding the word "selfish" is like wielding a club, and it constitutes a form of control. In this context the word really means, "You are not giving me what I want." It's rather like Ambrose Bierce's definition of an egotist in *The Devil's Dictionary*: someone who has the audacity to think they are more important than I am. The word "selfish" is regularly used in families in order to get a child or a spouse to do what we want them to do or be what we want them to be. It is also used in a socio-political context and is often combined with unconscious envy – hence the frequency of the word on the lips of those who try to convince us to "do good" by giving them what we have, rather than working for it themselves. In adulthood we still react with guilt and fear when the selfish-button is pushed. The word implies that we are doing something

Part Two: The Sun, Creativity and Vocation

against others. And if we do something against others, or against the caretaker-parent, they may turn on us and reject or even destroy us.

Many of you will be familiar with the work of D. W. Winnicott, who wrote a number of very insightful books on the issue of play and why some children seem to be incapable of playing.[18] Winnicott calls playing a transitional state, a borderland between the child's complete identification with mother and the state of being a separate individual. Play is an "as if" world which forms an imaginative bridge between unformed fusion and separateness. Psychoanalytic jargon is sometimes exceedingly clumsy and irritating, but it is worth trying to understand how the transitional borderland of play is related to the Sun, individual creativity, and individual ego formation.

The "transitional object"

Are you all familiar with the term "transitional object"? For those of you who aren't, a transitional object is something which stands at the interface between the state of psychological fusion with mother and the state of independent psychological existence. The teddy bear is undoubtedly the British National Transitional Object, and the Barbie-Doll would appear to be the American National Transitional Object. Any soft toy can be a transitional object. Perhaps some of you remember the "Peanuts" cartoons. Linus' blanket is a transitional object. You would probably all be horrified or, hopefully, amused, to discover how many transitional objects we still carry in adulthood. The ubiquitous mobile phone can be a transitional object because one is in constant contact with others. One isn't alone any more. How many of our mobile telephone calls are really urgent and justify the cost of the subscription? Perhaps one per cent. But we need the feeling that we can be reached by, and can reach, others at any time, anywhere.

Audience: I had a Barbie Doll that I used to hit and kick whenever I was angry with my mother.

---

[18] The following books by D. W. Winnicott are recommended: *Playing and Reality*, Routledge, 1992; *Home Is Where We Start From*, W. W. Norton & Co., 1990; *The Child, the Family, and the Outside World*, Perseus Press, 1992.

Liz: That is one of the functions of a transitional object. It allows the expression of rage without putting the child in the dangerous position of alienating the caretaker.

Audience: When I got my anger out, I used to hug the doll and make up.

Liz: A transitional object allows the child to move in and out of fusion and separateness according to the needs of the moment. It provides a halfway house which alleviates the terrible anxiety and loneliness of being separate, while at the same time offering refuge from the threat of being swallowed up by one's psychological dependency on mother. Emotions which would feel too frightening to express directly, such as rage or overwhelming need, are contained by the transitional object This is why children create fantasies around transitional objects.

Audience: Can family pets be transitional objects?

Liz: Certainly. Young children are not yet able to perceive the animal as a separate living entity with its own needs and nature. Unfortunately family pets may be the recipients of a child's sadistic fantasies, because feelings of rage toward the parents are directed at the animal. If this occurs, it is extremely important to try to understand the source of the anger – including the parent's own possible culpability – and encourage the child to deal more directly with it. Cruelty in an older child may reflect some very unpleasant but unconscious emotional patterns in the family, of which the parents may be unaware until a family pet is hurt.

It may be disturbing to realise that our lovers, our partners, our children, even our astrology, can serve as transitional objects. That does not mean such expressions are pathological. The imaginal world of the transitional object allows us to cope with reality better by minimising anxiety. In small doses, this is necessary for all of us at critical times. Only when one is totally addicted to the fantasy and cannot cope with reality at all can we justifiably speak of pathology. Transitional objects allow us to step away from the psychological pressures of a too-painful reality and find an "as if" place where we can replenish our resources. In this "as if" place we can make things up and recreate reality. A transitional object may be material, but it may also exist only in fantasy. The world of fantasy is a transitional place.

Part Two: The Sun, Creativity and Vocation

Every child needs to have the space to enter into this transitional place, with either an actual object or an imaginary one. The transitional world is essential for the gradual formation of a separate ego. But in order to do this, the child must feel enough trust and freedom to take the risk. The transitional world, although less frightening than reality, is still a risky place because one is no longer identified with mother. There is already a distancing. The distancing may not be complete separateness. But the moment the child enters the world of the imagination, there is already a gap between the child and the caretaker who embodies the mysterious, ego-less, Neptunian place of origin.

Bear in mind that this place of origin may also be seen as a spiritual source. We can take this whole discussion, which is psychoanalytic in its perspective, and transpose it to the spiritual realm. The only real difference is in the language. When we look at our religious rites and rituals with an objective eye, we can see that these are transitional objects. We feel separate from God, separate from the source. So we wear a little silver crucifix or appeal to the statue of a saint. We worship in a church whose cruciform architecture symbolises the body of Christ. We go to pray in a mosque whose exquisite patterns of tiles and mosaics portray God through geometry. We seize any transitional object we can find that allows us to feel we are connected with God yet still alive and on this earth. We don't want to die, but we want to feel we are not completely separate from our source. Both the child's teddy bear and the sacred talismans of the world's religions are relevant to the Sun, because the Sun is as much bound up with our image of God as it is with our capacity to play.

The transitional object is fundamental to our capacity to be creative. We need to have something we can invest with our images and fantasies – an "as if" world in which we can be alone and yet feel connected. Sadly, many children are not given permission to enter this transitional place. The mother may be too anxious and possessive, and cannot bear the child moving away from her into the inner world. She may interrupt constantly, demanding that the child's attention is always focused on her. She may unconsciously retaliate through punishment of an overt or subtle kind, or through the inflicting of guilt. And the child may be too fearful because of his or her own basic character. If both mother and child collude in prohibiting the "as if" world, then the child will not be able to complete the separating process which the transitional world facilitates. Then one can't get access to the Sun, because playing is frightening. And then the door closes on creative expression, which depends on the capacity to play.

Audience: The very term, "transitional object", is a cheat. You can be stuck with a transitional object and never find the Sun. Surely the object is to experience the Sun directly, and not through symbols?

Liz: That is an interesting question. I am not sure whether the transitional object is a cheat. It may be that it is the closest we can get to something which is too bright for us to see. A painter creates transitional objects, and so does a composer and a novelist. The term "transitional object" is awkward and clumsy, but we need to understand that it does not always apply to something infantile. I could even suggest that all symbols are transitional objects, because they stand between our ordinary perceptions and those subtler realms to which we have no direct access.

There are transitional objects which are self-destructive, such as heroin. There are transitional objects which can go both ways, such as food – a delight for the gourmet and a destroyer for the obese compulsive eater. There are transitional objects which we experience as uplifting, such as a great painting or piece of music. Whenever we invest anything or anyone with our fantasies of what could be, what might be, what it would be beautiful to be – whenever our imagination encrusts something "out there" with our "as if" world – we have entered the solar realm of the transitional. Apollo himself is a transitional image, because he carries the Sun and is its vessel. He is not the Sun itself.

The transitional object may be a cheat if an adult is still carrying around a teddy bear at the age of forty-five. But then, who is to say? If that person then sat down and wrote a book called *Winnie the Pooh,* we would say they created a timeless work of art. I am a bit cautious about the use of the word "cheat" because it implies that something in us has got arrested. There is an idea in certain esoteric circles that, if we pass through the transitional world and come out the other side, we will be enlightened. The place on the other side of the transitional realm is a place of selfness which is absolute.

Part Two: The Sun, Creativity and Vocation 131

Audience: That is what I mean. Why are we talking about transitional objects? We should be striving for enlightenment.

Liz: I am not suggesting you shouldn't strive for enlightenment. If you are looking at life with a particular spiritual doctrine in mind, then it is relevant for you to aspire to that place of absolute selfness. But not everyone shares your particular spiritual doctrine. And I reserve the right to question whether enlightenment as you are defining it is always a viable human objective, particularly when a great many people – including some very spiritual ones – can't even get into the transitional place, let alone out the other side, because they still haven't said goodbye to mother. I might even risk offending you by suggesting that, for many aspirants, the spiritual realm they envisage, the disciplines they follow to get there, and the gurus to whom they offer allegiance, are themselves transitional objects.

Audience: Could you say more about what you called the "place of absolute selfness"?

Liz: I may be unknowingly misrepresenting certain schools of spiritual thought. But the experience of enlightenment involves a realisation of the solar light without contamination. This is why the Buddha is a solar figure. This place of absolute selfness means not only freedom from the contamination of material reality, but also freedom from the contamination of thought and imagination. It is what is beyond Maya, beyond the illusion of worldly existence. I am not suggesting this is not a possibility or an ideal to which an individual could aspire. As I am not enlightened, I really have no idea. Nor have I ever met anyone who could, as it were, enlighten me on the subject, although I have met plenty of people who have claimed to be enlightened. In terms of astrological work with clients, we meet people all the time who feel they are creatively blocked. They want desperately to express something of their inner world, but they are too frightened to cross the threshold. Telling such people they should try to become enlightened rather than expressing what they want to express seems to me a dangerously dogmatic and narrow-minded way to deal with a client. It is not our job to tell people what they should believe in. Pursuing a "give-up-the-ego" path before a person has even discovered how to play may also mean that person is sidestepping something. If someone feels he or she is creatively blocked, but wishes to reach Buddha status without dealing with the issue, I would question just where the real cheat lies.

Creativity and embodiment

Audience: Are Apollo's Muses transitional objects?

Liz: The Muses seem to portray the means by which we utilise transitional objects to create. They symbolise the process of incarnating the images of the inner realm. The urge to bring things into form is part of the process of creativity. Anything we bring forth in the realm of matter has to be born from a womb, although not necessarily a corporeal one. The Muses have something to do with embodying transitional images in form, which is another way of portraying the process of creating art. When we embody or incarnate an image, we are experiencing what the Greeks envisaged as inspiration by a Muse. But the Muses are often projected onto other people whom we feel inspire us.

Audience: Does this imply that it's only men, or gay women, who are creative because they experience the Muses through women? What about a heterosexual woman's creativity? Can't she be inspired by a man?

Liz: I don't think you need to be quite so literal. The Muses represent an incarnating process which begins with inspiration and ends in art. It is the process itself which is portrayed as "feminine" in myth, because it involves something being born. We often project the source of our inspiration onto another person, and relationships are a common trigger for creativity. But the "hook" for the projection might be a man as well as a woman. I may be a female artist inspired by a man I am in love with. The Muse is really an image of my own creative process.

Audience: So a man could project the Sun onto a woman?

Liz: We can all project the Sun, men included. And the Sun may not always be projected on a human being, male or female. Sometimes it is projected on a philosophy, on science, on a place or an institution, on an ideology, or on a religion or spiritual path. We need to get away from the assumption that images that bear masculine faces in myth are always going to hook onto men, and images that bear feminine faces in myth are always going to hook onto women. I don't think it works like that. It isn't so literal or so simple. Try to move beyond the assumption that, when we project a particular psychic component, we must have one sex or the other to project it onto. If a woman has a very solar or Martial chart, her male partner may project much of his own Sun or Mars onto her. That is not necessary a pathological thing. She may simply embody these principles more vividly and expressively than he is able to do, and therefore he sees them outside himself. And she may, by carrying this projection, inspire him to develop his own creativity.

It is the same with parents. If a child needs to project the Sun somewhere and the mother is very solar – or if there is no father around – the child's Sun will be projected on her. It isn't necessary to confuse the issue by saying, "Well, it's actually mother's animus that's carrying the projection." We all carry both masculine and feminine projections for other people, depending on our own natures and how able we are to embody those particular archetypal images.

Audience: So can a woman have an anima?

Liz: If you use the term "anima" in the broadest sense – a bridging function which connects the individual psyche to the larger collective psyche and translates the images of the latter to the former through the imagination – then yes, a woman has an anima as well as an animus. In the same way, a man has an animus, if we understand "animus" to reflect a bridging function which connects the individual psyche to the larger collective psyche and translates the ideas and visions of the latter to the former through inspired thought. We should be careful of trying to make one symbolic system fit precisely into another, and astrology and Jungian psychology, although they overlap and illuminate each other in many areas, are not identical. It may be that Jung's more formal concept of anima and animus was completely appropriate for the time and culture in which he was writing. Sexual and biological roles were more rigidly defined then. But we are more homogeneous now, and the greater fluidity of astrological symbolism, amplified by the subtleties of myth, can help us to understand our timeless potential as well as our position in a specific society in a specific epoch.

The Sun-god in myth is not only male but also female – hence the images of the Muses and the Pythoness who accompany him. In some early cultures, such as the Teutonic, the Sun was perceived as feminine rather than masculine, and it is for this reason that the Sun, in German, is *die Sonne*. Every astrological symbol has many facets, and we may project some of these facets and express others as aspects of our own personalities. We may identify with Apollo and experience inspiration through a Muse who appears "outside". We may identify with a Muse and experience the focusing of our creative abilities through an Apollo who appears "outside". These "outside" people may be male or female. We may project the whole lot. Or we may consciously work with them as inner attributes – perhaps not under the ego's control, but nevertheless able to be related to. We are still largely shaped by our biology and a society which has changed considerably in the last few decades but is still heavily influenced by the past. It may be that, at present as in the past, children more often or more easily project the Sun on men than on women. But I have seen many exceptions, and it is possible that a time will come – maybe not in our lifetimes, but in the not too distant future – when our capacity to live a full individuality restricts this kind of role apportionment to the purely biological realm.

The artist and the magician

Audience: I'm very interested in the connection between consciousness and creativity. The hardest thing, it seems to me, is to relinquish enough control to allow the expression of something without losing your awareness of self. I think it involves some kind of altered state of consciousness.

Liz: Yes, I agree. When some of you spoke earlier about how it feels when you are being creative, your comments clearly pointed toward some kind of altered state of awareness. When we relinquish ego-control (which is not the same thing as relinquishing the ego itself); when we have sufficient trust; when fear of loneliness is not so great that it prevents us from entering the "as if" world; when our sense of limitation is not so crippling that it undermines our confidence; when we are not too frightened of being selfish – these are the conditions that allow us to act as a vessel for something deeper which needs to be expressed through us. We have lots of nice words for this "something". We call it the unconscious, whatever that is, or we call it the imagination, whatever that is. We have no idea what it really is. But it is indeed an altered state, and it allows us to participate in the magical experience of making something out of nothing.

In myth, this is the function of the creator-gods. They are magicians. They make worlds out of nothing. They don't recycle substance from earlier efforts. There is a profound sense of mystery around the creation of something out of nothing, because we don't understand how it happens. That is the essential experience of being creative, on however small a level. Whatever it is that works through us, we cannot grasp its source. It appears to have come from nothing. It is a very peculiar experience because, although we cannot understand it, it connects us with a sense of meaning, a glimpse of destiny, a feeling of joy, an experience of timelessness. In the moment when we give ourselves over to creating, we are free of mortal limits. Afterward, of course, we lose it and are plunged back into human incarnation.

Post-partum depression does not apply only to the time following the birth of a child. It also follows any creative birth. It may not always be severe, although some artists suffer terribly from it. When we lose our connection with that "something", it is as if the Sun has sunk beneath the sea and the darkness comes. We sometimes use the term "anti-climax" to describe this. It may not be the florid state of the artist who has finished the great work and then sinks into a profound depression. It can also be the sense of flatness after the delightful dinner party when we have created a really stunning meal. The guests all enjoyed themselves immensely and then they go home. And we feel like champagne that has lost its bubbles, because the connection to that place of joy is gone. This is inevitable, because it seems we cannot stay in that place indefinitely. We are back to the mythology of the Sun, which has to set each night. It can't stay up in the sky forever. Otherwise the world would burn up.

Audience: It is episodic.

Liz: Yes, episodic is a good word. Or we might say that it is cyclical, as is the path of the Sun as seen from the Earth. From our geocentric perspective, the Sun has to go down into the dark. Our unique situation as human beings living on the Earth demands that we experience the Sun's light as cyclical.

The sustenance of the Sun

Audience: Could you use the word "sustenance" in relation to what the Sun's creativity gives us?

Liz: Yes, it gives us a sense of being sustained. It is a kind of umbilical cord, and through it we receive a nourishment which takes some of the sting out of what is essentially an existential place of aloneness for us all. If we didn't have access to the "as if" world of the solar child, we would probably all kill ourselves. If we look with brutal clarity at the destiny of mortal life, what do we have? We are extremely vulnerable creatures who, at any moment, could be injured or destroyed, from within by physical or psychological illness or from without by cars, aeroplanes, other people, environmental poisons, or natural disasters. The human being is incredibly fragile and always in danger. Also, the human being is always alone, and the process of aging and dying is not a pretty one, although we may find meaning and grace in it. We have a finite life span. We are here only for a very little while.

Without that solar sustenance, why should we bother? What would be the point? We may feel love is the point, and our relationships give our lives meaning. But even the most enduring of relationships ends one day with someone's death. If the Sun's light goes out and we lose our ability to create an inner reality which has light in it, what remains except a death sentence which is inevitable and irrevocable? We don't know when or how death will come. We are now told we are doomed by our genes. If there are certain illnesses in our family, we are told we will eventually get them. As we grow older, what do we have to look forward to? Our friends start dying. Our relatives start dying. Our children move away. Our pensions no longer cover inflation. Our bodies no longer do what they are told, and bits start dropping off. Our religious beliefs are sorely tested by scandal, hypocrisy, and corruption in our organised religious institutions. If we lose the "as if" world of play and joy, we would not bother. I'm not really trying to depress you all. I am taking an extreme point of view to illustrate how important the solar world is for us.

Audience: Would you have a bread knife handy? Or a plastic bag and an elastic band?

Liz: I'm sure it can be arranged. But seriously, I hope you can understand the depressed and sometimes suicidal nature of the place at which people arrive when they have lost their solar connection, or have never really found it and have only been able to glimpse it through another person. Many people become suicidal at the breakup of a relationship. We may encounter such a person and think to ourselves, "All right, it's painful, but why kill yourself? Surely you will meet someone else one day."

But if the beloved is the transitional object and carries the light of the Sun, and that beloved goes away, there is not much left except the bread knife or the plastic bag. The picture I am painting is very dreary and bleak. We are no more than ashes to ashes and dust to dust, as our cheerful Christian service over the grave pronounces. I am painting this picture so that you can get a glimpse of the internal world of the severely depressed person. It is a Sunless world.

Audience: I've heard it said that the brain cells associated with anxiety die out as we get older. It is always something I have held onto.

Liz: Whether or not it's because our brains start to die, it is true that many people feel more trust in life as they get older. When we look at solar progressions and transits later in the day, we may get a sense of why this should be. With some people, trust is eroded, but this is usually because there wasn't any real trust to begin with, and over time the person's defences get stripped away.

Audience: So with age, the light of the Sun grows stronger.

Liz: In an ideal world, that is what happens. But the world is not ideal, particularly in childhood. The issue of creative play is fundamental to our capacity to feel hope. Those of you who said earlier, "I am not creative," may need to think hard about what you mean by this. If you are not an artist, that makes no difference whatsoever in terms of the Sun. Solar creativity is not exclusively about creating art. But if you are unable to play – if you are frightened to enter that imaginal world – then there may be an inner issue that needs addressing, because the inability to play may rob you of the capacity to feel hope.

It may be important to start by looking at childhood issues. Separation anxiety afflicts many people. The causes may not always be parental. There are particular generation groups who suffer a great deal from this anxiety – for example, people born during World War One or World War Two. If the whole of one's world is under threat because one is born in a country which is being bombed, or one's father is off fighting and one's mother is in a state of panic because she doesn't know how she is going to survive and look after the family, then naturally there will be little sense that it is safe enough to move into the inner world of play.

Entire generations in the 20th century have been injured in this way, and in such conditions only the strong are able to retain enough trust to play despite what is going on around them. The birth chart usually reflects such strength through powerful aspects to the Sun. Anxiety in the family is poison for the process of play, and this is often the hidden issue behind an individual's belief that he or she cannot be creative.

In many therapeutic approaches, the client or patient is encouraged to put their feelings into some kind of imaginative shape through painting, writing, sculpture, or dance. This encourages the act of play, the creation of an "as if" world which can provide a transitional place between difficult feelings and external reality. The act of play allows separation and detachment. Many people describe feelings of anxiety when they sit down and try to express imaginatively what they are experiencing. They simply can't do it. They don't know how. They leave the therapeutic session thinking, "Yes, what a good idea." They go home and sit down with some crayons or paints and the anxiety starts bubbling up, and then suddenly they remember they haven't done the shopping and the dog needs feeding, and all the rationalisations crop up for why they cannot enter the transitional world. Sometimes they don't even know that it is anxiety that is interfering, because the reasons for avoiding the inner world always sound very sensible. Usually it's, "I just don't have time."

We defend ourselves from this great anxiety because the transitional world is a place of separation. If we have not felt safe enough in early life, and have not been able to internalise a safe mother sufficiently to psychologically separate from her, we are not going to feel safe enough to play. Then we may feel blocked and stuck, too fearful to risk leaving her to enter the "as if" world.

Audience: Sometimes, when I'm being creative, I get the idea that play is really very close to death.

Liz: Can you tell us more about what you mean?

Audience: It's something to do with letting go. I think it must be a similar thing to let go at the moment of death and trust whatever lies beyond. It requires the same kind of trust.

Liz: Like trusting that the Sun will always rise in the morning. Jung wrote about a tribe of Native American Indians who believe that, if they do not perform the appropriate prayers and rituals each morning, the Sun will not rise. This must be incredibly stressful. But there may also be some truth in it, because we need to perpetually renew our link with the Sun. We can never take it for granted. We always have to struggle to reconnect with its light.

Audience: Can you say more about the link between creativity and immortality? I think I get it, but I'm not sure.

Liz: The "as if" place, the place of transition, is a place of immortality. We are not bound by time and space. We live forever, which is why the divine child is divine and not mortal. This inner child doesn't grow up and die. If we have a connection with this inner reality, death is not so frightening. The fear of death is connected with the fear of life, which is synonymous with a lack of trust in life, which prevents the child from playing. The connection with that transitional place gives us a sense of immortality, even if we know the body will die. Death will have no dominion, as Dylan Thomas said. There is no sense of threat attached to it, no terror of extinction, if we are able to play in the sunlight.

Audience: What about actual children? Where do they come into this? The 5th house in the chart is associated with both children and creativity. I find it hard to see what the link is between the two, other than biologically.

Liz: If we want to understand the 5th house, we need to consider what we project onto our children. We may feel we have managed to grab hold of eternal life because we invest our children with the "as if" world of the Sun. This is a common experience for many people – the birth of a child conveys the sense that we will have continuity for ever and ever, through the passing down of our genes if not through our own bodily immortality. It is, of course, a totally irrational experience, because our children too will die one day. But we assume they will outlive us, and we cannot bear to contemplate their mortality.

This is one of the reasons why it is so deeply shocking when a parent outlives his or her child. We feel it is somehow against the natural order – although in reality children are more physically vulnerable than adults, and in earlier centuries many children did not survive infancy. Yet we want to know that we can face death in the knowledge that our line will continue. For people who do not have children, the Sun cannot be projected in this way, and the psyche demands that the sense of immortality be found within. Many people who are not really temperamentally suited to be parents still insist on having children, not because they really want them, but because they need something on which to project a solar sense of meaning and purpose.

Inevitably and naturally, we project the divine child onto our children. The impetus to have children may not always be because one actually likes children or feels emotionally mature enough to raise a child. We need to believe we are immortal, and for many people it is the only way immortality can be achieved. Through children we make a connection with our own divine child. If we observe parents' progressions and transits at the time a child is born, it becomes apparent that some people have children at a time when it is not a child they are actually wanting, but rather, some connection with an experience of immortality.

We might reasonably expect important lunar transits and progressions at such a time, yet often we see solar movements instead. The emotional and instinctual link with the actual child may not be present at all. This is where the 5th house comes in. It is our inner divine child that is described by the 5th house. This house portrays our individual "as if" world. If we cannot enter this world, we project it on our children, who then have to carry what is in our 5th house.

Audience: You're saying that people feel different things about their children, and that the impulse to have a child can come from many different places.

Liz: Certainly. Every planet has its own expression of love and can be active in the chart at the time one falls in love. Likewise, every planet can be active at the time of childbirth and can portray how we feel about that child. A child can be perceived through Saturn or the 10th house as a responsibility or even a burden. Or the parent may project worldly goals on the child, imagining that this son or daughter will fulfil all the ambitions the parent failed to achieve. The child can be experienced through Venus or the 7th house as beautiful and beloved, even as a surrogate husband or wife. Every planet and house can be the significator for a child. When 5th house solar energy is connected with the child, the child is carrying the inner image of solar light.

Audience: So if I have Mars in the 5th house in Leo, that means that I'm really the one who needs to be passionate about creating? I can't expect to have a creative, innovative child?

Liz: You might. There is often a correspondence or synchronicity between our inner child and the children we produce in the world because children, like the children of our imagination, come through us and are linked with our ability to act as vessels and facilitate the incarnation of the life-force. But if you do nothing with your 5th house Mars, your child will have to carry the whole archetype – your share as well as theirs. Then the child might become difficult, aggressive, or hostile because of the immense psychic pressure this would place on them. The more you expect the child to carry your Mars, the angrier the child will become. Like planets in the 7th house, planets in the 5th need to be owned, even if there is also a mirroring of inner and outer.

The Sun at work

Creativity and the 5th house

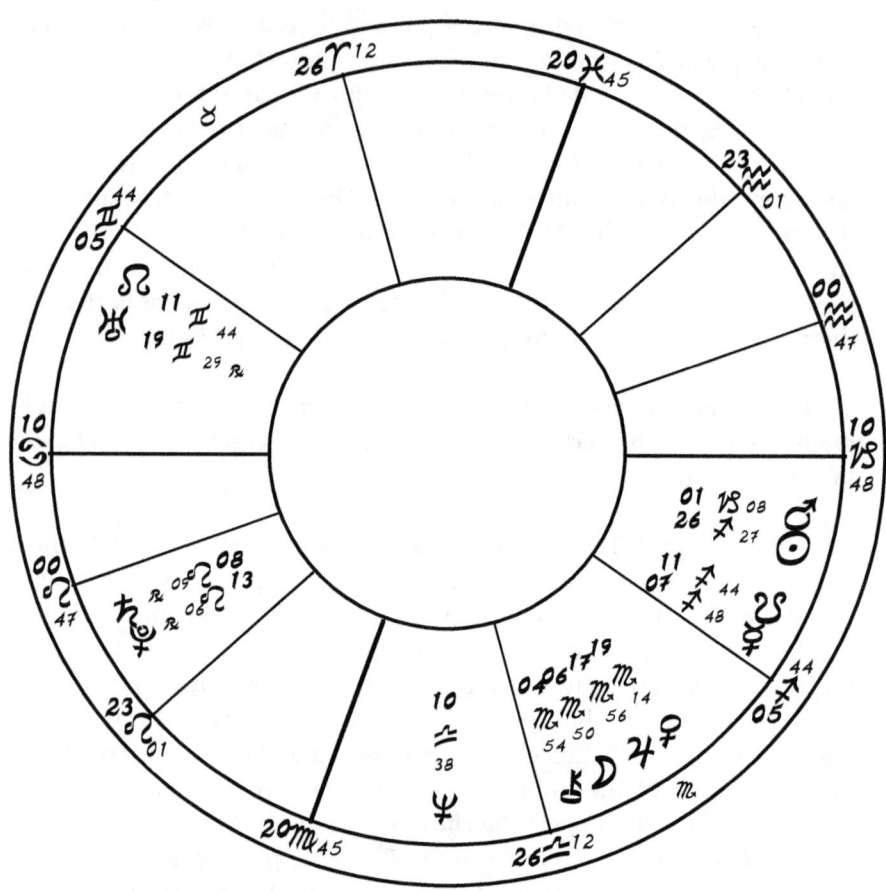

Steven Spielberg
18 December 1946, 6.16 pm, Cincinnati, Ohio, USA

Here is the chart of a man. I would like you to try to see whether there are any clues which might suggest what kind of inner world this man carries. What kind of medium might provide an outlet for his creative expression? What sort of inner child does he have? Start with the 5th house. Chiron is there, conjunct the Moon, and Jupiter conjuncts Venus. All of them are in Scorpio. The Sun is in Sagittarius in the 6th, conjunct Mars and opposition Uranus. The Sun makes one minor aspect, a sesquiquadrate to Pluto. Let's say he came to you as a client and said, "What am I good at? What creative work should I be doing?"

Audience: Romance.

Audience: Passion.

Liz: Yes, he needs to live passionate, romantic stories, either literally or imaginatively. You have touched on another area which is traditionally connected with the 5th house – romance and love. What is romantic love? Why do we say, "They are romantically involved," or "It's a romance," rather than "It's a relationship"?

Audience: We say that when people are wrapped up in fantasy. They are in love. That's a place of fantasy.

Liz: Some people would say that sounds cynical. When one is in love, it seems more real than what others call reality. But the world of being in love is an "as if" world. That doesn't mean it's false or mutually exclusive of a more substantial relationship bond. Love, like God, has many different faces. When it wears a 5th house face, what is its nature?

Audience: Playful. It's love as play.

Liz: What are its qualities?

Audience: Free.

Audience: Creative.

Audience: Boundless.

Liz: When we are in love, we reinvent and recreate ourselves and the object of our love as we go along. It is very different from being with someone for twenty years, by which time we know everything about them and they know everything about us. We may feel deep love, but we are not reinventing ourselves or our partner. Romance implies that there is at least some element of fantasy involved. There may also be some perception of the real person, depending on how much or how little Neptune is included. Like a work of art, the state of romantic love is a process of creation. Our beloved is not only a flesh-and-blood person. They are also a symbol of a light which is within, but which we perceive outside. The world of romantic love is a bigger-than-life world, an "as if" world. It makes us aware of our potentials and our dreams. We experience ourselves in a new and more positive and hopeful way.

We are conditioned, in Western culture, to associate certain objects and rituals with romantic love. We take someone out for a candlelit meal, we drink a bottle of really good wine, and we have a romantic conversation. What is a romantic conversation? Obviously we don't say, "Sorry I keep shifting my feet, but I have a corn on my right little toe. Do you know a really good make of corn pad?" Nor is it as simple as saying, "I love you."

Audience: Romantic conversations always explore possibilities. There's always an element of anticipation, or hinting at things that might happen.

Liz: Yes, romantic conversations explore possibilities. We could become anything. Suddenly the limits are removed. We no longer have a Saturn or a Chiron. We are better and brighter and more beautiful than we thought, with so many potentials still to be explored. We see ourselves through what we believe to be the beloved's eyes, but actually we are seeing ourselves through the eyes of a solar child within us who has unlimited possibilities. Even if these possibilities aren't articulated, they provide the undertow of the conversation. That is why it is so exciting. If this need to explore unlimited possibilities, to create a romantic story, is strong in us – and it clearly is in this chart, with four planets in the 5th including the ruler of the 5th and the chart ruler – then it is not just a pleasure. It is a necessity. If it is blocked, no prizes are awarded for working out what will happen.

Audience: He would probably become severely depressed.

Liz: Yes.

Audience: Could he become addicted to that world?

Liz: Addiction and vocation are close cousins, and they may also overlap, but they are not the same thing. For some people, the "as if" world becomes an addiction. They don't wish to retain any link with reality. Then the inner world is no longer transitional. It becomes a cut-off place without any movement. It is a womb with a lock on it, in which one incarcerates oneself. The "as if" world needs a formed ego, made up of a good mixture of Sun and Saturn, to prevent it from swallowing the individual. The Saturn-Pluto conjunction in the 2nd house, squaring the Scorpio planets, suggests that, although this man may be unable to live without his transitional world, an urgent need to make things manifest in the material world will keep him from closing in on himself in a self-destructive addiction. Also, although Neptune sextiles the Sun and is widely square Mars, Neptune does not dominate this chart. He would be likely to make the 5th house a materially productive vocation. But I am sure this involves a considerable ongoing struggle.

The creativity of Sun-Uranus

Let's talk about the Sun-Uranus opposition. Planets that aspect the Sun tell us what kind of characters inhabit the inner world and romp about on the interior playing field. Any planet that aspects the Sun tells us where inspiration comes from. With Sun opposition Uranus, what kind of Muse inspires this man? What is the nature of Uranian play? Because it is the centre of the individual's world, the Sun has to contain and carry any planet aspecting it. If this man expresses Uranus through the vessel of the Sun in Sagittarius, what kind of imagination does he possess? If he came to consult you and asked you what kind of creativity he possessed, what would you tell him?

Audience: I would tell him not to be afraid of being different.

Liz: Fair enough. But in terms of what would help him make a connection to the solar world of joy, what would you suggest?

Audience: Belief in his own originality.

Liz: Every planet can be original – not only Uranus. What is special about Uranus?

Audience: Experimentation.

Audience: Progress.

Liz: What do you mean by progress?

Audience: It is the world of ideal thoughts.

Liz: Keep going.

Audience: A science fiction writer.

Liz: Yes, that might be one possibility.

Audience: A scientist who is involved in research.

Audience: I don't think that's very creative.

Liz: Try not to make the mistake of thinking that science is mutually exclusive of creativity. The greatest scientific discoveries have come through inspiration, not through the hard slog of Saturn – although Saturn is necessary to give form and viability to the inspiration. Science in the ancient sense depended as much on inspiration as it did on the accumulation of facts. Now we define science as the testing of facts, but the inspirational element is Uranian. Political creativity is also Uranian. We might not think of politics as a particularly creative sphere, but good politicians must, of course, be able to make things up as they go along. Inspiration is vitally necessary. Any vision of a potentially perfect world, an ideal future world – whether it is artistic, technological, social, psychological or spiritual – is linked with Uranus.

Freud had the Sun conjunct Uranus in Taurus in the 7th house. That suggests a creative vision of the world which impelled him to perceive the human being within a certain ideal framework, a perfectly functioning psychological system. However dated we may think Freud's work is now, we should remember how utterly innovative, inspired, and shocking it was in his lifetime. Freud was a tremendous idealist. He believed it was possible to create a world where the *id* was not supressed, and where ego and *id* cooperated and interacted so that illnesses such as hysteria, the product of repression, would cease. Freud was a reformer at heart, driven by a vision of a potentially better, more honest, and healthier society. The creativity of Uranus looks into the future and sees what could be. How many of you have Sun-Uranus aspects? Can you see how this might apply to where you could be most creative? Virtually all of you have put your hands up. Is astrology something you would call creative?

Audience: Yes, definitely.

Liz: Astrology even has its own Muse, called Urania. It is a peculiarly Uranian study. You probably all want to know who this person is. It's Steven Spielberg. He has certainly been able to enter the transitional world of play and produce wonderful things out of it. He has also made a great deal of money, but money doesn't appear to be his chief motivation. What is motivating him?

Audience: All those Scorpio planets make me think there is some terrific struggle going on inside him.

Audience: And Moon and Chiron together seem to say something about a lot of emotional pain.

Liz: I am sure you both have a valid point. But focus on the Sun, because the 5th house planets must work through the Sun. Everything in a chart must work through the Sun. Every planet has its own kind of creativity. There is no sign or planet that lacks its own particular joyful expression. But in the end, if we are going to translate these things from the inner world to a creative product in the outer world, they must be expressed through the Sun. Here is the Sun in a fire sign in an earthy house. It is in the 6th, which is Virgo's house, but it is in Sagittarius and it is opposite Uranus. And it makes an out-of-sign conjunction with Mars, which is in an earth sign. The earth-fire tension is enormous in this chart. Let's go back to what we looked at last week. What does the Sun in Sagittarius in the 6th house need?

The Sun in the 6th: inspiration from everyday life

Audience: To create useful objects.

Liz: Yes, you could put it that way. It needs to create things from the fire world that are in some way part of ordinary life. With a 6th house Sun, he could not become an artist who lived in a garret and painted paintings which got hung in an obscure gallery where only other artists went to look at them. He would shrivel up and die. Whatever he creates, he must feel that your average Joe Bloggs enjoys and benefits from it. His creative work must be embedded in everyday life.

Audience: It has to serve the public. When *Jurassic Park* came out, a lot of my friends were really sniffy about it and said they didn't want to see it because it was too mass-market. I said, "Well, he is trying to explore and communicate a variety of ideas to a big cross-section of people." There's something in it for everyone.

Liz: Yes, Spielberg has a remarkable capacity to appeal to many different kinds of audience. His family sequences are particularly interesting because they're multi-leveled. I am not sure whether he calculates this or whether it is purely intuitive, but he never chooses actors who are extravagantly beautiful. His leading ladies are always attractive but never overwhelmingly glamorous, so any woman in the audience can relate to the actress. His leading men are always pleasing to look at but never knock-them-dead handsome or over-the-top virile, so any man in the audience can identify with the actor. If we see an exquisitely beautiful leading lady or a gorgeously hunky leading man, many people might feel, "Good God, no one I know looks like that," and there isn't any real feeling for the character. We might admire, if we aren't eaten up by envy, but we can't empathise.

Spielberg's characters are always very "ordinary". He is a master of creating dinner table squabbles that are so incredibly realistic that we forget we're in the cinema. His themes are vast, yet he is Norman Rockwell behind a camera. Every detail rings true. This 6th house placement gives the Sun a wonderful anchor in everyday life.

He has, of course, done more elevated things. After *Jurassic Park*, when everyone had pigeon-holed him, he suddenly produced *Schindler's List* and leaped out of the pigeon-hole in typically Uranian fashion. This film was heavily influenced by his background. Many of his family did not survive the Holocaust, and his Jewish roots have made him acutely aware of the suffering of the scapegoat. This may be connected with the post-war Saturn-Pluto conjunction under which he was born, with its painful consciousness of just how brutish human beings can be to each other. This generation group came into the world knowing what the Holocaust was about without ever having had to experience it directly – you don't have to be Jewish to have a Saturn-Pluto conjunction – because they were conceived in the aftermath of World War II when the real horror began to dawn. Spielberg is one of a generation group that carry a dreadful awareness of how dark it can get. This conjunction squares the 5th house planets. The darkness and terror which are present not only in *Schindler's List* but also in *Jaws* and *Jurassic Park* are rooted not only in his personal background but also in the collective psyche.

Audience: I felt *Schlindler's List* touched a very traumatic place in his family and racial memory.

Liz: Yes. But the theme is timeless and archetypal, and could apply to any epoch of history where a group is scapegoated and a solitary courageous individual on the persecutors' "side" takes a stand and tries to help. This raises the perennial question: how much is a person invested in what they create?

Audience: In his case, the answer must be: a lot, but not entirely. The Sun is personal, but Uranus is universal.

Liz: I agree. These films carry Spielberg's story, but they are also everyone's story. Spielberg has given us some wonderful transitional images. Think of *ET*. It is a truly magical film. He worked that 6th house Sun in Sagittarius sextile Neptune and offered a kind of healing for both children and adults, through an imaginary character who is himself a healer.

Audience: Is it a grown-up fairy story?

Liz: How would you define a fairy story?

Audience: What you said before. A way of portraying unthinkable experiences in a form which can be coped with.

Liz: Yes. Fairy tales are imaginative portrayals of the stark reality of human life in an "as if" form. Moral, emotional, and psychological lessons which might be unbearable to look at in real life become tolerable to a child because they are in the form of images. They have been "made up". When we read about Hansel and Gretel destroying the wicked witch, the rage, destructiveness, and fear that every child experiences toward mother as witch and devourer are presented in images which are not threatening. Hansel and Gretel somehow find the resources to destroy the witch before she destroys them. A child needs to believe in the power to avert evil and destruction, especially in a destructive family environment. How many of us, as children, could actually face such emotions? But in the fairy tale it all happens in the "as if" place, and it is bearable.

Spielberg captures the essence of fairy tales in his films, particularly *ET*. Elliot, the boy who befriends ET, is the only human with the innocence and openness necessary for a relationship with this creature. Of course, the real gift of Spielberg's extra-terrestrial is that he can heal. He is wise but uncorrupted, a kind of divine child himself. In a fairy tale form, Spielberg presents a brutal fact of life. We will lose everything which is precious, innocent, and in harmony with nature because of our greed and callous exploitation of everything we encounter in the world. We do not respect the natural order of things, and so we destroy them.

This is a Virgoan, 6th house theme. Only Elliot respects ET's reality enough to keep him from the clutches of those who would exploit his abilities. The gift ET offers in return is only hinted at when he touches Elliot's forehead and says, "I'll be right here." The parallels to inner religious experience are obvious, but Spielberg never rams a spiritual message down anyone's throat. This is a transitional world which presents us with psychological reality in an "as if" form. That is Spielberg's genius.

Charts from the group

Now we need to look at some charts from the group – first from the perspective of what might obstruct a person's ability to work creatively with the "as if" world, and second from the perspective of how one's special solar creativity is connected with vocation. We just looked at a larger-than-life example of a highly creative individual. Now we need to focus on ordinary folk who don't create films like *ET*. Can I ask first if anyone is having any problems with the material so far?

Audience: I noticed that you avoided mentioning the Sun in Leo last week. Could you say something about it now?

Liz: I don't think I was trying to avoid it. I only talked about a few of the Sun-signs last week. This was partly because of time limits, partly because I worked with charts from the group and there wasn't a Leo in the group who offered a chart to discuss, and partly because the object of the seminar was not to present a cookbook list of the Sun in all the signs. If you understand the Sun, you should be able to work the rest out for yourself. Leo is, after all, the most transparent vehicle for the Sun's expression because the sign's nature is solar. The Sun in Leo is the easiest Sun-sign to understand because it doesn't involve a blend of planetary energies, as does the Sun in all the other signs. Hopefully there will be a Leo example here. I presume you are a Leo, and that's why you are upset at being overlooked? Would you like your chart used as an example?

Audience: I didn't bring it on a transparency.

Liz: Then I can't put it on the overhead projector, can I? I believe that is what is known as a double message. Perhaps you will be less ambivalent on another seminar. Meanwhile, here is a chart from someone else in the group. Perhaps we could focus on what helps or hinders the Sun, as well as what its sign, house, and aspects might tell us about avenues of creative expression. Here is the Sun at 15° Taurus, right at the IC, which is at 12° Taurus. The Sun squares Chiron, which is in Leo on the cusp of the 8th house with the north Node, also in Leo, at the end of the 7th. The Sun closely sextiles Mars in Pisces in the 2nd

house, and makes a sesquiquadrate to Neptune at the end of Virgo in the 8th. The Sun also makes a sextile to Jupiter in Cancer in the 7th. There are quite a few solar aspects here. Carl, do you have a particular issue you wanted us to explore?

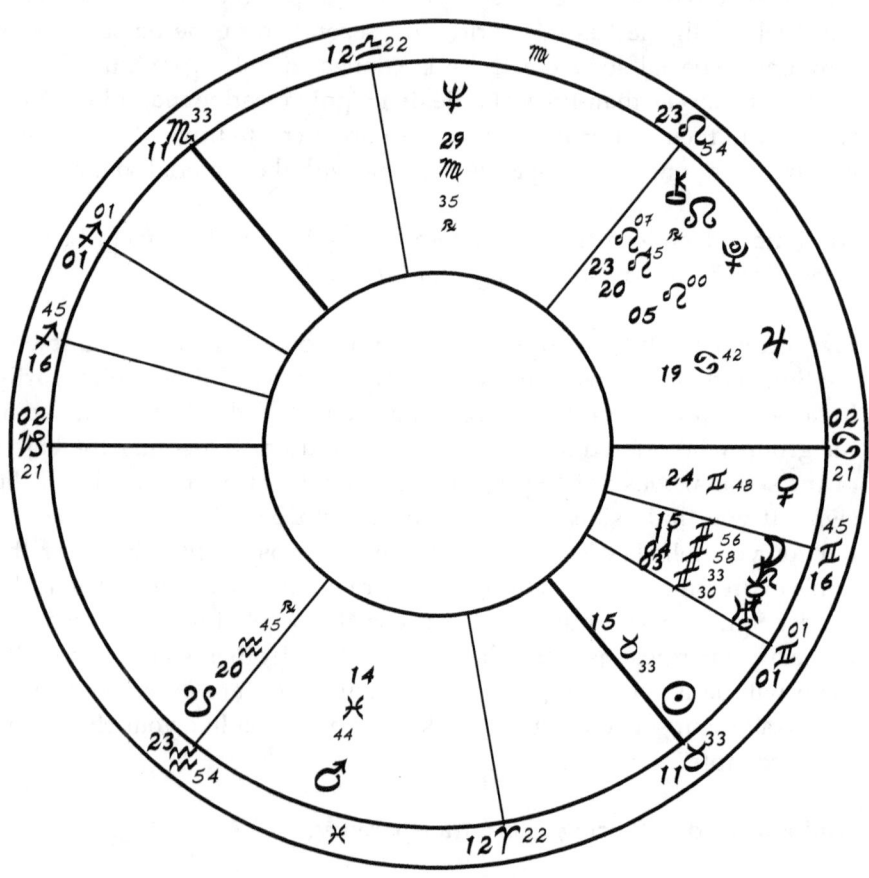

Carl
[Birth data withheld for reasons of confidentiality]

Carl: I'm not an astrologer, although I understand some of it. I'm struggling with a very damaged sense of myself. Having grown up with a lot of dysfunction in expressing myself, there is an issue around self-confidence. Over the years I have become stronger and I think also more conscious, and increasingly I am in more contact with my inner self. I want to know why I am here. There is something I have got to do, and I am not sure that I have found it through the creative work that I do.

Liz: What work do you do?

Carl: I am a documentary cameraman. I do a lot of observation work, which I find very fulfilling. At the same time, over the last few years I have wanted to put the camera down and get more involved with people.

Liz: Do you take your structure from someone else?

Carl: There is a structure from the director. I serve the production company.

Liz: So your creativity, which is essentially a way of looking at and portraying the world, has been, until now, in the service of someone else's ideas about what you should be looking at. Let's look at the Sun at the IC in Taurus. Does this speak to any of you? Does anyone have a sense of what this Sun is seeking, what it is moving toward, what its place of joy is?

The Sun in the 4th: inherited creativity

Audience: It needs to be somewhere very safe and private.

Audience: It needs to give shape to something.

Liz: Presumably the first comment relates to the Sun in the 4th house, and the second comment has to do with the Sun in Taurus. The 4th house is one of the angular houses of the chart. I think we have to look first at what this house means.

Audience: There is a deep connection with the father.

Liz: I would agree that the connection with the father is very powerful. But it may not necessarily be an obvious connection. When the Sun is in the 4th, its light is projected on the father, but this often remains quite unconscious. One isn't necessarily aware of it. Whoever father is, he will not appear as an ordinary mortal to his child. He will appear as the Sun. Then it becomes urgent to win the love of this deity who is a life-giver and a source of joy. Identification with the purpose or destiny the father wants one to have becomes an important issue at a very early age, and it is hard to break that cord and find one's own light. It sounds as though you are still tied by that cord, Carl.

Audience: Would the Sun in Taurus at the IC have something to do with a nurturing father?

Liz: I am not sure the personal father is really the issue here. My understanding of the Sun at the IC is that the father is carrying something archetypal. He appears to his child, not as a flesh-and-blood person, but as a mythic figure, a planetary god. He is Apollo. This archetypal image goes all the way back in the father's line, back into the ancestral roots. It is some kind of shining, creative spirit that, generation after generation, has wanted to be expressed. The more frustrated and unexpressed this spirit is by the personal father, the more the child with a 4th house Sun will feel driven to give expression to it. One inherits a family myth with a *daimon* which one sees first in the father. Even if this father was a very ordinary man, and even if he was absent or emotionally unavailable, there is an awareness of some solar spark which gives meaning to one's life. That is why one wants so badly to be what the father wants one to be – even if both father and child are unaware of the nature of the inheritance and the expectation.

For many people, as I said, this is unconscious. You're nodding vigorously, Carl, so it's clearly not unconscious with you. But many people don't know how important the father is when the Sun is at the IC. He assumes archetypal power because he is a stand-in for a spiritual source. This is father as giver of life – God the Father. It is the place from which the spiritual seed comes, so the personal father will carry a huge projection. The longing to be what father wants can be very great, and it can dominate later life. In order to internalise this solar joy and meaning, one has to cut the cord.

Many people with the Sun in the 4th emigrate because of the need to find an inner source. They leave their home country because they must recreate their roots. They must find a sense of origin which doesn't depend on family or the physical parameters of a particular nation. They have to get out and go somewhere else. Other people with the Sun in the 4th simply disconnect from the family. The Sun says, "I'm yours, not your father's. Introject me, own me, express me yourself instead of always projecting me on someone in authority." At the moment, Carl, it seems you are arriving at that place where you have to cut the cord. The lack of self-confidence seems to be linked with the Sun-Chiron square, and that aspect suggests that your father suffered from the same problem. Perhaps he wasn't able to express himself creatively because he felt too damaged or hopeless, so he expected too much from you or wounded you through disinterest or criticism.

Carl: That has been the basic thrust of my life over the years. I believe my father was a very creative man, but he didn't do much with that creativity. But I think it depressed him and made him very critical of me. For a long time I didn't experience any frustration working within someone else's structure. Yet now I'm feeling increasingly frustrated with the subject matter, or rather, the way the subject matter is handled in the programmes. There always seems to be a need to trivialise the profound. I find it at odds with my own views. On the one or two occasions when I have said, "You have done the wrong thing," they have told me off. So there is no feeling that I can create what I want or believe in.

Liz: Your stellium in Gemini is speaking very eloquently at the moment. Mercury and Uranus are both in the 5th along with Saturn, which conjuncts the Moon on the cusp of the 6th. Moon-Saturn in Gemini doesn't like trivialisation and superficiality. With Saturn in Gemini in the 5th, ideas should be serious. This Saturn isn't at home with satire unless it's of the biting, ironic kind. Documentary television work is an excellent choice for that group of planets in combination with the Sun in Taurus, but your own voice is not yet speaking.

Audience: With all those planets in Gemini in the 5th, especially Mercury conjunct Uranus, I would have thought Carl could be a writer of some kind. Maybe science fiction, or something innovative and startling.

Liz: Writing may be a natural talent with so many planets in Gemini. Documentary photography is also a Geminian skill, because it involves observing, recording, translating, and communicating. But ultimately the planets in the 5th must serve the Sun in Taurus in the 4th. Natural talents are not the same as a sense of vocation, which is connected with feelings of meaning and destiny. Any communication skills Carl possesses must serve the deeper purposes of the Sun.

The 5th tells us about the divine child who lives in the "as if" place. The 5th speaks about how we play, and with what playmates. When we looked at Steven Spielberg's chart, we could see, from Moon-Chiron in Scorpio in the 5th, the dark, destructive images which fuelled films such as *Jaws, Jurassic Park,* and *Schindler's List.* You can play with the eye of the camera, Carl, and the planets in the 5th portray the things that fascinate you and make you want to photograph them and tell their story. With Mercury, Uranus, and Saturn all there, you probably love showing people their ordinary world in a new, serious and disconcerting way, so that their ideas about reality are radically changed. You want to make important statements that shake people up. But the motivating power behind this ability to play lies with the Sun. That is the god you ultimately serve.

The creativity of Sun-Chiron

At the moment your 5th house planets are currently serving someone else. For you to feel fulfilled, they must serve the 4th house Sun in Taurus, and the Sun's strongest aspect is the square to Chiron. The sextiles to Mars and Jupiter and the sesquiquadrate to Neptune are all relevant, but the square to Chiron is the most energetic solar contact. This is the engine of the chart. What kind of expression does it need?

Audience: Maybe Carl's father wanted to do something important in the world and didn't achieve it, and there is a motivation to somehow be different from that – to make up for what the father wasn't.

Liz: The image of a wounded father is clear from the Sun-Chiron square. And it is a father who also wounds his son. The wounded one who wounds is as important an image for Chiron as the wounded one who heals. In fact it is more common in terms of human behaviour and the way we deal with our hurts. It is much easier to lash out at others in our pain than to contain the pain and feel compassion for others. Chiron in Leo also suggests that there is a family history, on the father's side, of blocked Leonine play and Leonine self-expression. The wound is to self-esteem and individual self-definition.

Carl: There was a point in my childhood, probably when I was approaching my teens, when my father went to Singapore with the Navy for a couple of years. That is a very conservative culture, and it made his own conservatism more extreme. It got to a point where my father stood me in front of a mirror and basically told me I was not what he wanted in a son, and that I could improve myself by becoming this, that and the other. In his way it was meant as an effort to help me, I suppose. I don't remember being dreadfully upset at the time. It was only later that I realised how much it hurt. His life was outwardly successful , I suppose, yet in himself, I believe he was always frustrated and somehow failed to become what he should have been.

Liz: You are describing a relationship which involves a great deal of expectation and disappointment, and which has inflicted great hurt to your feeling of value as an individual. I am trying to get a sense of the archetypal patterns at work behind this outward pain, because I believe such pain is somehow teleological. It leads somewhere and could contribute to something creative. Apart from the myth of Chiron himself, I am thinking of the Greek god Hephaistos. He is the artisan-god, the divine craftsman. When he is born, his mother doesn't like the look of him. She deems him ugly and therefore unfit to be an Olympian, so he is literally thrown out of heaven. He crashes to Earth and breaks both legs, and is afterward lame. For a time he is given shelter by Thetis in the kingdom of the sea, where he learns how to make beautiful objects. Eventually he is reinstated on Olympus, still lame but honoured for his gifts. He is given Aphrodite, the goddess of beauty, as a bride. He creates all the implements by which the gods have their power.

    Hephaistos is a creator-god of a very special kind. His image is connected with the ability to create beauty because one is not identified with it. The elements of vanity and possessiveness are absent. There is nothing to be gained for oneself by creating beauty, so the creative act is free of ego claims. It is as if the mother-son bond was broken in Hephaistos at birth when he was cast out of heaven, so he does not have to spend his life winning the parent's love. He knows that he is flawed, that he will never live up to the impossible standards of perfection of the other Olympians, and that frees something in him. He is the only one of the gods who can make things. Even Zeus' thunderbolt is created by Hephaistos.

There are elements of the Hephaistos myth in the psychology of both Taurus and Virgo. Alice Bailey thought that Taurus' "esoteric ruler", as she called it, is Vulcan, the Roman form of Hephaistos. The father who wanted a perfect son no longer has the power to wound, if one accepts oneself as one is and lets go of the hope of meeting parental expectations. The lack of confidence you talked about earlier may be connected with the need to live up to a standard which has been imposed on you rather than emerging from your own heart.

Carl: I find a lot of self-confidence in expressing what my father couldn't.

Liz: That's Chiron in Leo speaking. Healing is connected with recognising not only your own wound, but also your father's. Parents don't impose impossible expectations on their children unless they themselves feel inadequate. The wounder is so often also the wounded one. Scapegoats easily become persecutors of other scapegoats. And so it goes on down the family line, until someone gets fed up and begins to reflect on what is happening. Before you can get free, you will have to let go of any hope of meeting your father's expectations. You may not be fully able to play until you can relinquish the dream that, one day, if you get it "right", he will turn around and say, "Yes, you are the son I wanted." You may not want to be that son anyway. You have begun to realise that you don't like the projects they are giving you to film because they don't reflect your own values. And your father's expectations may also not reflect your own values. They reflect his values. It is not that one set of values is "better" than another. But you cannot live your Sun through any values except your own.

If you are able to free yourself from him, what does the Sun want to create? Is there anyone else here today with the Sun in the 4th? No one? What about the Sun conjunct the IC from the 3rd? Yes? Can you relate to anything we have been talking about?

Audience: Yes, totally. My Sun is in the 3rd but conjunct the IC, and also conjunct Chiron in the 4th.

Liz: Sun-Chiron contacts tend to pop up frequently in astrological and counselling circles. How many of you have this aspect? Ah, I thought a lot would. To be able to create from a Sun-Chiron aspect, what needs to be included? What is this kind of creative process about?

Audience: There needs to be an acceptance of limits.

Liz: Yes, there is that.

Audience: Some sort of woundedness in the creativity.

Liz: Get down from the abstract. What does it look like in actual life, to have "woundedness in the creativity"?

Audience: I suppose it would have to be the opposite of the Uranian kind of creativity that aspires to perfect form. There would have to be a message about the rightness of flawed things. Creative work would have to include or portray imperfection. The thing that jumps to mind as an example is working with people who are damaged, and not expecting them to be perfect. You could expect some sort of progress to be made and find it worthwhile and rewarding without expecting perfect beings as the end result.

Liz: Yes, well put.

Audience: It would involve showing the beauty in the flaw itself.

Liz: Both of you have touched on something very important. It makes me think of a book which was published many years ago called *The Family of Man*. In those days it was still permissible to use the word "man" to connote both men and women. This book was essentially a photographic essay highlighted by short extracts from literature, portraying the archetypal stages and dimensions of human life. Most of the photographs are of flawed humanity. There are images of humans not only at their happiest but also their most tragic – aged faces, foolish faces, mad faces, suffering faces. It is an extraordinary work. I don't know if it is still in print. It epitomises what you are describing – a visual journey which is both heartbreaking and ennobles the human being. By the time one has finished the book, one has a sense of belonging to a humanity which may be a mess but is nevertheless worth bothering with. The book's creative power stems not from portraying perfection, but from portraying imperfection with love.

Audience: There is a recent book called *Photo*, published by Phaidon. It includes many of the photographs from the exhibition on which *The Family of Man* was based.

Liz: *The Family of Man* is an example of what I would understand as Sun-Chiron creativity. Usually we think of the helping professions as a field where Sun-Chiron can express itself, and there is no doubt that healing is also a creative act. *The Family of Man* is an example of healing through art. Here is Hephaistos creating out of his lameness, presenting us with the paradox of the healing of ugliness through a realisation of its own beauty. Carl, all this may be quite useless to you on a practical level. But it may give you some hints about what spheres Sun-Chiron needs to explore in order to create.

Carl: I am becoming more and more detached about my present work, as I gradually find consciousness of who I am. I can even enjoy it at times, as long as I can accept the limitations. But I do have more of a sense of which way I have to go.

Liz: Good. Thank you for giving us the chart to discuss.

The Sun in the 11th in Aries: crusading for others

Now let's try something fiery as a contrast. Here is another chart from the group. Rose, what is the issue you wanted us to explore?

Rose: I am at a point in my life where I see creativity in a very different way. I am a performing artist, a singer, and I have had a fair amount of public recognition. But something is changing inside. Now I am so nervous every time I have to perform that I feel I can't do it any more. Something in me wants to find other ways of expressing myself. I feel that I am holding on to something I need to let go of. I feel very possessive of my talent, and maybe that's not a good idea. So I am trying to find a way through.

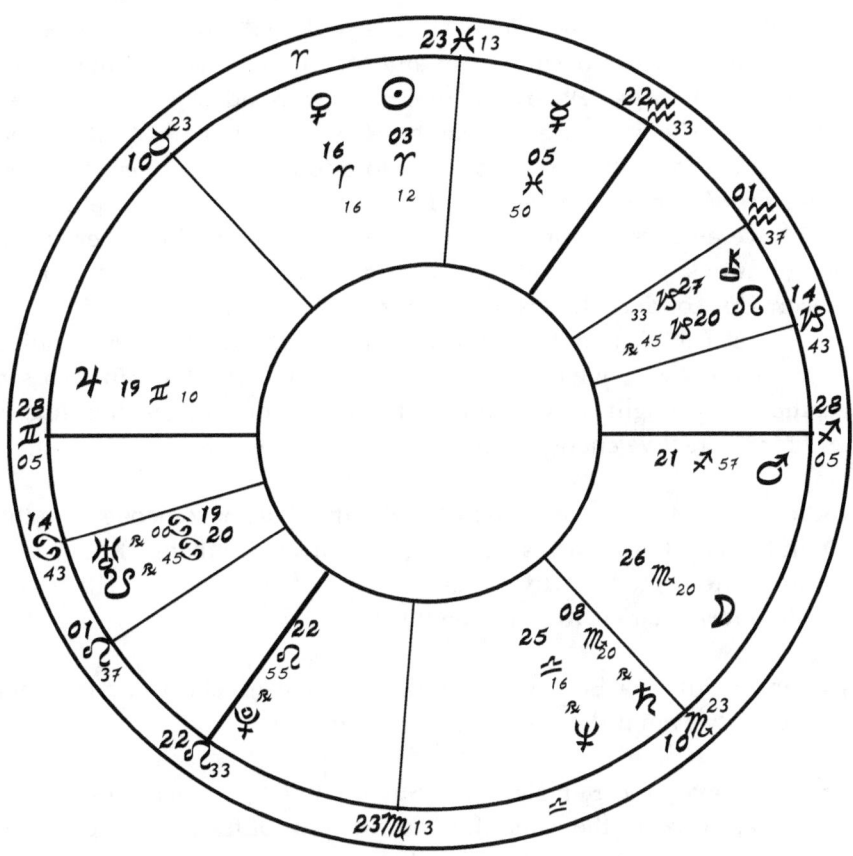

Rose
[Birth data withheld for reasons of confidentiality]

Liz: Are you concerned about what you could do if you actually left the public arena?

Rose: Yes, I suppose so. I think I do have something to say which is different and original, and I need to find a new way to say it, but I am not sure how to do it.

Liz: All right. Here is the Sun in 3° Aries in the 11th house. The Moon is in the 6th in 26° Scorpio, so the Sun and Moon are in trine, although it's an out-of-sign trine. Otherwise the Sun forms no aspects, not even minor ones. The 5th house has Neptune in it, at the end of Libra, and Saturn in Scorpio, although Saturn is close to the 6th house cusp. Given Rose's profession as a singer, I think we were expecting something in the 5th, weren't we? Neptune is in one of those powerful generational configurations, in square to both Chiron in Capricorn and Uranus in Cancer. This configuration went on for a long time during the 1950s.

Let's think about what this Sun wants, what kind of creative power it possesses, what it needs in order to shine. We can also see whether there might be something blocking it, or whether the time is right for its creative energy to find a different outlet.

Audience: Last week we were looking at the chart of someone with the Sun in the 11th in Sagittarius. There must be a similar theme. Rose needs to contribute something to the evolution of the collective. There is a wish to reform people, to enlighten them.

Audience: But this Sun is in Aries. That means she can't lose her individuality even if she is serving the group.

Liz: Whatever the Sun-sign, the Sun in the 11th must preserve its individual vision at the same time that it contributes to the welfare or education of the larger human family. That is the paradox of the Sun placed in a house opposite to its own natural house.

Rose: I've mostly worked with other musicians. Although I love doing it, it has also been very difficult for me. I always want to do things my own way and write my own lyrics. I know I need to express my own message. I can't give someone else's message. But you can't do that when you work with a group. Everyone wants to have their say, and you have to compromise. I often feel I am being domineering and autocratic when I insist on singing my own songs.

Audience: My daughter has this same placement of Sun in Aries in the 11th. She has the same problem, although she is not a musician. She works in public relations. You have to believe that you have the right to express your own message. Then you can do it. But if you don't believe you have the right, then it all goes wrong and you wind up bickering with other people all the time. My daughter has had a terrible time with the people she works with, and eventually she had to set up on her own.

Liz: Rose's Sun is in a cardinal sign. All four cardinal signs must develop their own ideas. Libra may prefer to have support and cooperation from colleagues, and Cancer may prefer to preserve a feeling of emotional intimacy and harmony, but in the end these signs too are cardinal and must pursue their own vision. Aries is the most overtly cardinal of the four. It is a crusader. It wants to change the world. A political, social, or philosophical message is often necessary for Aries, although this message may be conveyed through artistic expression rather than didactically. Ultimately the 11th house is not about art. It is about evolution and doing something to facilitate the improvement of society. It isn't surprising that a cardinal Sun would get fed up singing other people's lyrics.

Rose: Actually, not only do I write my own lyrics, but the lyrics that I sing myself, without backup, give me immense satisfaction. I suspect the satisfaction comes from giving the message. It doesn't always have to be done through singing, does it? The important thing is the message, not the vehicle.

Liz: The vehicle is less important than the message and the freedom to express the message in an individual way. Whatever is creative in you doesn't depend on one particular form of art to achieve its goals. You are trying to serve an 11th house vision. As I said, this Sun is a crusader. The real creativity is not the singing. It is the vision, and communicating the vision in a way that gets people to change something in their lives. There are Ariens who paint and Ariens who sing, and there are Ariens who don't do anything recognisably artistic at all. What, then, is their special creativity? It has to do with changing the world, making something happen, making an impact and transforming outer reality so that it is more concurrent with the inner vision, even if it's on a very small scale.

How is a crusader creative? Let's think about this figure for a moment – not the brutish fanatic of the actual Crusades, but the archetypal vision behind the historical reality. Armed only with his sword and his convictions, he charges heroically into a world which is not yet enlightened – the definition of "enlightened" naturally reflecting that particular crusader's ideology. This world is covered in darkness, held in the grip of the heretic or the heathen. The crusader brings the light. With enormous courage, with or without followers, he battles the forces of darkness to allow change, growth, freedom, enlightenment.

That is the creative energy of Aries. It doesn't matter whether Rose does this on a stage before an audience or whether she does it through running a women's group. Other placements in the chart might indicate what she would find rewarding in terms of specific vehicles. Your creativity, Rose, is not really based on whether or not you sing. And equally, there are some very talented singers about who are not really creative in the solar sense. Your chart is a good example of a very important distinction between talent and solar creativity.

Solar light on Pluto's inheritance

The Sun-Moon trine may describe another quality that needs to be brought into Rose's creative work so that the Sun can express the whole of itself. The lunar component is necessary in your working life, so you must also nourish, nurture, touch people's feelings and move them on the heart level. The lunar side of you wants to be of service in a practical way because it is a 6th house Moon. And it's in Scorpio, so it probably needs more direct, personal emotional involvement than being on the stage can give you.

Audience: I can't get my eye off Pluto in Leo at the IC. There are survival issues here. Doing some kind of creative work is really crucial for her sense of survival. It has to be done. It is not something Rose can be lukewarm about. It is absolutely compulsive.

Audience: It raises issues from the past. There is something very dark in the family background. It may not be obvious, but the compulsion comes from somewhere, and it can be traced back.

Part Two: The Sun, Creativity and Vocation

Liz: Yes, I agree. Although the Sun and Pluto are not in direct aspect, the Moon and Pluto are, and the Moon is the chart ruler. The Sun, in turn, rules the sign in which Pluto is placed. And everything in the chart must find its conscious expression through the Sun. There is a strong Plutonian theme running through this chart, and it will fuel the crusading spirit of the Aries Sun from deep within. This theme is concerned with the family history, and with the need to transform conflicts from the family past. We should remember that Apollo the Sun-god is the breaker of family curses, and Pluto at the IC, square the Moon in Pluto's sign, does suggest that there is a kind of family curse here. There is certainly a feeling of something dark and unhappy in the early family life, perhaps involving both parents, and already bubbling away before Rose's birth.

Pluto involved with the family background usually hints at difficulties which have been in the family psyche for a long time. Often there is a family member who is deeply depressed. When Pluto is involved with the Moon, that person is usually the mother. But the roots of the depression are much older than the personal mother. Because of this family darkness, the Sun's need to bring light becomes urgent. It is the only way to break free of the feeling of fatality and compulsiveness that is part of the family inheritance. Can you tell us anything about this, Rose?

Rose: My mother had very bad depressions. She also couldn't sleep well. I often felt she was haunted by something. She was an artist, a painter. My father is a very talented singer. It was assumed that I would be an artist of some kind. There are many artists and singers in my family.

Liz: So becoming a singer was "already written" for you from the beginning. That's what the word "fate" means in Latin – that which has already been written.

Audience: Yes. I was encouraged from a very early age. At the same time this was going on, my mother made several suicide attempts. Her depressions were very severe. I had a sense from her that the world was a very dangerous place. Eventually she did kill herself, quite recently.

Liz: Perhaps her death is connected with your feeling that you need to change direction. Do you know much about her family background? Or your father's? It would be worth doing some research. The light of knowledge is essential when we are dealing with Plutonian family themes.

Rose: I have done some exploration, but obviously not enough.

Liz: I can't tell what your mother's depressions were about just by looking at your chart. I would need to see her chart, and your father's. But there may have been Plutonian issues – loss, emotional frustration, power battles, sexual betrayal – that weren't obvious to you as a child. A Plutonian father can sometimes be a deeply controlling father, a kind of psychological dictator. I keep thinking of the chart of Robert Kennedy, who had Pluto exactly at the IC. We all know what his father was like. Every member of the Kennedy family had to fulfil the destiny he laid out for them. It sounds as though you had to sing or die. You had to live out these family expectations, and with your mother's death something has suddenly come free. Now you don't know who you are any more, and you are beginning to ask questions rather than submit blindly to the family fate.

Rose: Yes. I keep telling my father that I can't imagine myself not singing. But it also feels like a kind of prison. I need to be able to imagine myself as something else.

The creativity of Sun-Moon

Liz: It seems the creative expression of your Aries Sun has been compromised or dominated by Plutonian issues from the family past. Paradoxically, the Sun-Moon trine may have made it more difficult for you to follow your individual destiny. This doesn't mean that Sun-Moon aspects are not creative. But the characters of the inner world of Sun-Moon trines always live happily ever after. This is an aspect of harmony between the great archetypal poles of life, and therefore all the stories generated by these inner characters end with a satisfactory resolution of conflict. As in many fairy tales, everyone goes home pleased, the prince and princess ride off into the sunset, and the kingdom is saved from harm. Sun-Moon trines and sextiles reflect a great capacity for contentment and hope. In one's inner world of play, the characters always seek, and usually find, workable solutions for their difficulties. So one always believes this is possible in outer life. I think you can all see how immensely creative this can be, because the voice of Sun-Moon trines speaks to that part in all of us which seeks a happy ending. There is a gift for expressing images and ideas which convey the possibility of the resolution of conflicts.

This is very different from the Sun-Chiron inner world, in which the characters know that the resolution of conflict may be impossible. Many kingdoms aren't saved, and more often that not, the prince and princess end up in the divorce courts. This can sometimes be a cynical and even bitter vision of life, if it isn't leavened with compassion and acceptance. But therein lies its strength, and therein lies the weakness of the Sun-Moon trine. Carrying a vision of "and they lived happily ever after" means that, when one is not living happily, the Sun-Moon trine says, "I don't want to know about this. I don't want to look at it. I will go on believing that everything will be all right in the end. I don't accept the idea of wounds that won't heal. It's clearly someone else's negativity or destructiveness at work."

There is a curious lack of self-reflection with Sun-Moon contacts, particularly with the conjunction. And with a Sun-Moon trine, it's often difficult to find the impetus to fight, which is quite paradoxical in Rose's case because Aries is usually a good fighter. But a Sun-Moon trine carries a deep conviction that, if only everyone could be friends and could be good to each other, the problem would be solved. In this inner landscape, the nature of play is always peaceable, friendly, and harmonious. If it gets a little rough at times, well, that may be unpleasant, but it's quickly forgotten once everyone is friends again. An aspect like Rose's Moon in Scorpio square Pluto isn't allowed into the closed world of the trine. Perhaps, Rose, you couldn't have broken the family curse until time, death, and fate brought you to the point where you were freed naturally rather than forcibly fighting to free yourself. Maybe you couldn't have done it any other way, nor should you have.

Rose: Everyone in the family always worked very hard. But yet we all had it very easy because we were talented. I suppose deep down I have always known that my talent made me special. There is a kind of assumption that I am special. It's a sort of complacency.

Liz: That complacency is characteristic of the Sun-Moon trine. You are being very honest about it, which can help enormously. Many people with Sun-Moon trines, sextiles, and conjunctions aren't willing to be that honest. They are unconscious of their assumption of special privileges. Pluto in Leo also contributes to that innate assumption of specialness, although this is not unique to you. In your chart, Pluto is one of the father-significators, which suggests that he carried, and passed on, this profound belief in individual specialness. That is not a negative thing in itself. But one must be careful not to misuse it, and if it is unconscious it can create many expectations which cause hurt to oneself and others.

The father-image in your birth chart embodies a whole generation of people for whom specialness constitutes survival. For the Pluto in Leo generation, one will not survive unless one is special, and there is no one more special than the artist. This is a message which can sometimes be as destructive as the opposite one: "You are not anyone special. Who do you think you are, imagining that you can be an artist?" Many people suffer from undermining of their solar light. But with you, the suffering comes from the dictum, "You must be special twenty-four hours a day, every day of the week, every week of the year, every year of your life. If you fail, you will be a disappointment to the family. And you might not even survive." It seems this message comes from your father, and your mother is a sad example of what can happen if one fails. The message may have been mixed up not only with his need to express his own talent, but also with his need for power.

Rose: So the talent is the curse?

Liz: Yes, the talent is the curse, because you are expected to always live out its full potential. And you are expected to live it out in the form dictated by earlier generations, which may not reflect the form best suited to your own life. Think of some of our famous theatrical families, like the Richardsons. What chance does any individual family member have to go off and become an accountant? And if they do, what emotional price must they pay? They are not allowed to be ordinary people. This is a Leonine family curse, a curse of too much talent.

Rose: And there is a kind of inevitability that I would perpetuate the curse.

Liz: Yes, for a while, because there is the talent to do it, and there is a Sun-Moon trine which says, "All right, I'll become what you want me to be. Anything for a peaceful life. If I accept this fate, everyone will live happily ever after."

The challenge of Chiron in Capricorn

Rose has only one planet in the element of earth – Chiron in Capricorn. This singleton in Capricorn may say something about why it is sometimes hard to live the Sun. Last week I talked about the way the Sun in every chart has to struggle. You are not unique in that, Rose. The question is not, "Is there a struggle shown in this chart?" It is, "What is the nature of this Sun's struggle?" This singleton in earth is a deeply mistrustful planet. Chiron spent a long time in Capricorn, and this generation group have suffered greatly from seeing their hope of finding true authority, true law, damaged beyond repair. In these people there is no real belief in authority. To them, all authority figures are made of straw. There is a deep yearning for a valid set of laws by which one can live, and authority figures whose integrity and wisdom one can admire. But because the world is as it is and people are as they are, authority is recognised at best as hypocrisy and at worst as a horrific abuse of power.

For people with Chiron in Capricorn, there is a sense that the mundane world is not to be trusted because the people who run it are not trustworthy. When earth is weak in a chart, the world of fantasy, the world of art, the world of specialness, will always seem more attractive as an alternative to the actual world. This is not the result of family pressure. It is something in your own nature, Rose. All charts are lopsided in one way or another, and your lack of earth has no doubt contributed to the ease with which you access your inner vision and imaginative gifts. It is much easier for you to live in a mythic world than it is to accept real-life limitations – not only other people's, but also your own. Just as your father expected too much from you, you may expect too much from yourself. This creates enormous inner pressure.

This may have slowed down the impetus to carve out your own path in life. Where you wish to go with your future may require you to develop practical skills, to develop earth faculties, and something in you resists doing that. It is easier to rely on a talent that comes naturally and is guaranteed to receive family acceptance and support – even though you may know it isn't the right path for the future.

Family curses and family gifts

Audience: Can you say more about the family curse, and the astrological significators for it?

Liz: Any planet conjuncting the MC or IC describes some archetypal pattern, some *daimon* that comes down through the family and demands to be lived. Planets on the meridian are not the only such significators, and we also need to look at placements such as planets in the 8th and 12th houses. But any planet conjuncting the 4th house cusp, as Pluto does in Rose's chart, speaks eloquently of something that is many generations old and dominates the individual from the family past. I should stress that the word "curse", as the Greeks understood it, is nothing like the "curse" which the medieval world connected with witchcraft and evil. The origins of our English word "curse" come from an Anglo-Saxon root which signifies God's anger. We are dealing with an angry god, not with gratuitous evil spawned by the Devil and his minions. In Greek myth the family curse begins as a gift, a favour from the gods. All the figures who wind up being cursed in myth start off being given some kind of special benefit by a god, and they then abuse the benefit. They don't honour the god who is the source of their gift.

For example, the curse of the house of Atreus begins with Tantalus. Although he is mortal, the gods heap honours and riches on him. He abuses this relationship by trying to trick them in order to demonstrate his superiority. Tantalus invites the gods to dinner and serves them his own child, cut up and made into stew. Will they spot the difference in what they are eating? Instead of serving a calf or a goat as the sacrificial meal, he serves a cannabalistic feast. It is a profound sacrilege, and naturally the gods recognise it at once. And so they give Tantalus a terrible punishment in the underworld, and curse his descendants. Behind the savagery of this myth we may see a not untypical attitude of arrogance toward innate talent. Instead of honouring talent as a god-given gift, the individual claims it as his or her own creation and uses it destructively, even to the point of damaging others gratuitously.

Family curses are favours, talents, or gifts given by a god to a particular individual in the family past – in other words, gifts whose source lies in the collective or ancestral unconscious – which are then abused by that individual and by succeeding generations. Until the god is properly acknowledged and the gifts are lived rightly, they have destructive effects that pass down through the generations. A planet at the MC or IC describes something archetypal which is the gift of the family inheritance. But somehow this gift has not been lived in the right way. Something has got blocked or tainted by the personal fears, needs, and greeds of family members, or by intolerable collective pressures. The individual who is born with a planet at one of these angles needs to find a new way of expressing that planet. Family curses are not portrayed in a chart by negative aspects. They look the same as family gifts. That is because they are the same. As Cassius says to Brutus, the fault lies not in our stars, but in ourselves.

Having Pluto in Leo is not a curse. It describes enormous creative power. It carries the survival instincts of a whole generation which sustains itself through the creative expression of individuality. But the gift was not used properly in your family, Rose. Something went wrong. Something is being said in your chart about the wrong use of creative power in the family. The creative power is not the curse. You must live it in a way different from your parents, but you can't reject or ignore it. You can't throw it away and open a shoe shop, unless you are designing the shoes yourself. You need to express solar creative power, but not in the way your parents did. Their misuse of their talents cut them off from the rest of humanity and made them Olympian. With your Sun in the 11th – the house of common humanity – you cannot pursue this path.

Audience: Would Pluto on the Ascendant describe the same kind of family issue?

Liz: The Ascendant doesn't describe the family inheritance. Planets on the angles are usually experienced as highly compulsive energies to which we must give shape in our lives. An angular planet dominates the chart. But planets placed on the Ascendant-Descendant axis, unless they are in the 12th and conjuncting the Ascendant, don't seem to describe the family inheritance. They describe something which is uniquely our own. Planets on the MC-IC axis describe archetypal patterns that have been processed through many generations. We experience them first in our parents, who usually provide us with good hooks for our projections. Eventually we need to recognise these archetypal images as what they are, withdraw our projections, and find a creative way of embodying them ourselves.

The angles are the cross of incarnation. This is where we are staked to the earth. Not everyone has planets on angles, and not everyone is required to embody archetypal energies in this way. But if there is a planet within orb of conjunction of an angle, on either side of the angle, the individual must find a way to give shape to the planet. If not, the planet will embody itself, and we then we feel at the mercy of powerful forces in the outer world that we believe are shaping our destiny without our consent. When there is an angular planet in the birth chart, the Sun can show us how to anchor it. The Sun points to our sense of unique purpose, our special place in life where archetypal energies can be communicated or expressed in creative ways. Rose, your Sun is unlikely to be fulfilled unless you are singing your own songs. The songs must carry your own message. Even if you choose not to sing, you still need to use your creative power to lead and to be an example of someone who is not afraid to be an individual. You are an Aries, after all, and you have to live your Pluto in Leo somehow.

Sun-sign astrology

Audience: Why Sun-sign astrology? Of all the ways to popularise astrology, it's the least accurate. Most people aren't really like their Sun signs until they are a bit older. Perhaps we should focus on the Moon rather than the Sun. Why is Sun-sign astrology so popular now?

Liz: Sun-sign astrology began in the 20th century. It was not used in ancient times.[19] A pragmatic answer to your question might be that everyone knows their birthday, but to find out one's birth time requires some effort, and finding the Moon's exact position depends on knowing the time of birth. In the USA and many European countries, birth times

---

[19] See Nicholas Campion, *Astrology, History and Apocalypse*, CPA Press, London, 2000, Part One, p. 84ff, for a discussion of the development of Sun-sign astrology.

are recorded, but in Britain we have to ask family members, which can often prove embarrassing. The Sun-sign is the only thing we know about our charts without having to look up something or ask someone. And even if we can acquire a birth time, we then have to calculate the chart, which is a terrifying prospect for many people. It is now possible to get a chart calculated on some web sites,[20] but not everyone is on the internet, and an ephemeris can be daunting to the uninitiated.

Beyond that mundane explanation, there is something in Sun-sign descriptions that resonates. Even though the descriptions are often silly and superficial, the traditional image of each sign mirrors what, on some level, we would like to become. Sun-sign portraits ring a bell somewhere. If one is a very shy and unexpressive Leo, and one reads a typical Sun-sign description of an outgoing, shining, magnetic Leonine personality, one might well think, "How absurd. That's not me." But somewhere that bell is ringing, because the Sun is concerned with inner essence. However quiet and introverted the Leo, the shining light dwells within.

Sun-sign descriptions touch something in people which a description of the Moon-sign can't really do, because the Moon is so instinctual. If our Moon-sign is described, there is almost a sense of faint embarrassment about it. The Moon-sign symbolises the way we are when we are not conscious of being an individual. We don't secretly wish to become our Moon-signs because we have always been those qualities. But the Sun-sign presents us with an image of becoming.

Audience: I wondered if the Sun-sign, for many people, is some kind of symbol for meaning.

Liz: Since the dawn of time, the Sun has represented the face of God. That great light shining in the sky makes life possible, so it has always been worshipped. The idea that we are born when the Sun is in a certain sign unconsciously triggers a feeling of belonging to some greater unity. The characteristics portrayed in Sun-sign columns may sometimes make us cringe because of their shallowness. But something about that description allows us to connect with an archetypal image of what we want our lives to mean. The better Sun-sign column writers know this.

---

[20] The best web site for instant free chart calculation, with a wide range of house and aspect options and high-quality chart drawings, is www.astro.com.

They don't drivel on about Sagittarians being good at sport and Virgos making good secretaries. They go a little bit deeper, and people respond because these portrayals touch some essence inside. The Sun-sign is what we are meant to become. We need to embody this archetype on some level, although not necessarily on the personality level. The personality level is often the last place we see the Sun-sign, because the Sun does not describe the personality. That is more the concern of the Moon. The Sun-sign describes values we need to incorporate at the core of our lives.

I don't belong to the school of astrologers who believe that Sun-sign columnists ought to be lined up against a wall and shot. Perhaps one or two should, but that is due to the stupidity of the particular writer rather than to the invalidity of Sun-sign astrology as a whole. A lot of astrologers feel that Sun-sign astrology is silly at best and, at worst, dangerous to the work and reputation of serious practitioners. But astrology is a highly complex study, and Sun-sign astrology can provide a legitimate point of initial contact. If it is handled responsibly, it can offer a valid entry into the subject. Because something rings true or resonates, people become curious and look a little further. Perhaps we should encourage Sun-sign astrologers to do the very best they can in their particular sphere of work, rather than spending our time criticising them. Their sphere of work can be extremely important. We can become altogether too precious and inaccessible.

As psychological astrologers we can also get too sophisticated. We may stop looking at the Sun-sign, and miss something as basic as the fact that a Taurean needs beauty. Whatever a Taurean creates – even if a Sun-Chiron aspect impels the person to write about or work with the wounded and the dying – there must be beauty in it. Of course the Sun in Aries doesn't like singing other people's lyrics. When has Aries ever been a follower? We may forget to look at such basic astrological precepts. We can become too complex in our interpretations before we have grasped the fundamentals. We may forget the essential need of the Sun to feel and express joy by contacting the symbols of that joy as they are described by the sign in which it is placed at birth.

The developing Sun

Solar progressions

I would like to talk now about progressions to the natal Sun, and then about transits. Once again, we can work with an example chart from the group. It should be clear by now that the Sun reflects a process of unfoldment during the course of a lifetime. We are not born with the Sun fully radiating, shining and ready to go. The Sun is always in formation. Its development is cyclical, and it must regularly experience struggle to further that development. The struggles are not always in the same form but they always involve the same archetypal theme, depending on where the Sun is placed in the birth chart. Our particular solar story will always involve the planets aspecting the Sun, as well as the house and sign in which it is placed. A process of gradual emergence is at work throughout our lives, and progressions involving the Sun can give us a lot of insight into the timing of that process.

During the course of a lifetime, we experience aspects of progressed planets to the natal Sun as well as aspects from the progressed Sun to natal planets. And we also experience the Sun progressing to aspect itself. Sun-to-Sun progressions are infrequent because the Sun progresses roughly a degree a year, by both secondary and solar arc motion. Tracking the progressed Sun offers the only occasion when the adherents of these two different methods of progression are in agreement. In solar arc progressions, all the planets move at the rate of speed of the Sun. In secondary progressions, all the planets move according to their own rate of speed, so naturally the Sun moves at the Sun's rate of speed. Aspects from the progressed Sun to natal planets will be the same whether we use solar arc or secondary progressions.

The progressed solar cycle

The progressed Sun makes its first aspect to its natal place – a semi-sextile – at the age of thirty. It makes a semi-square to its natal place at the age of forty-five, and it makes its first major aspect – a sextile – at the age of sixty. If we manage to reach ninety, it makes a square to its own place. The progressed Sun makes very few aspects to its own place in a lifetime, but they are extremely important. They occur in everyone at the same age, and they seem to describe major watersheds in life when the sense of self is activated in its purest form.

If we consider the other planetary cycles reaching critical phases around the same time as these progressed solar aspects, we can see a picture forming. At thirty we have just finished the first Saturn return, and a bit before that, at twenty-eight, we have finished the first progressed lunar return. The progressed Sun touching its own place for the first time occurs after the cycles of two planets which both pertain to family history, the past, and embodiment. The Moon and Saturn are the natural rulers of the 4th and 10th houses. They are the two planets most concerned with our inheritance from the past and the incarnating process of taking the inner potential which belongs to the world of play and putting it into form in outer life.

At thirty we experience the first really clear expression of the essential individual we are in process of becoming. We have had one Saturn cycle and therefore, hopefully, we have found out what our limits are. Because of Saturn's crystallising process, we now know what we don't wish to be, what we aren't able to become, where we are restricted, what we must accept. We have also had a progressed lunar return, so we have a sense of our feeling nature, our instinctual needs, expressed in many different arenas as the progressed Moon moves through the houses of the chart and aspects every natal planet. We have separated from the family matrix, at least to some extent. When the Sun progresses into semi-sextile to its own place, we may be a bit like Parsifal when he first sees the Grail. He doesn't ask the right question the first time around, but at least he sees it. Then he knows what he will spend the rest of his life looking for. It is as if a sign suddenly appears that says, "You are on the M40 and you are heading for Oxford." Then the sign vanishes. There is a strong sense of going somewhere, of fulfilling an individual destiny. It is the first experience of a continuity of the essential self.

At forty-five, with the semi-square, this continuity of identity is tested. It is worth thinking about the planetary cycles that occur just before this point. Transiting Uranus opposes natal Uranus, transiting Neptune squares natal Neptune, and transiting Saturn opposes natal Saturn just before this Sun-to-Sun semisquare. Depending on the Pluto generation group in which we are born, we may also experience transiting Pluto square natal Pluto as well. All these cycles reach important turning points smack in the middle of what is euphemistically known as "mid-life". This solar progression to its own place encapsulates the deeper meaning of the transiting planets' mid-life cycles, just as the semisextile encapsulates the real meaning of the first progressed Moon cycle and the first Saturn cycle just before the age of thirty. Because the Sun symbolises the centre of the individual, all planetary movements eventually feed back to that centre and help to define its purpose and meaning. At the age of forty-five, we are fighting to define who we are. There is tremendous inner conflict during this period, described by all the transit cycles that have reached critical points.

This is a time when the essential self has a chance to make itself really clear. And naturally it is a time when people get into terrible trouble. They feel that time is running out, and if they haven't become what they are meant to become, panic begins to set in. The urgency of that juncture breaks through even the most unconscious individual. "Who am I?" we ask ourselves. "What am I here for? If I haven't worked it out by now, there might not be another chance." Naturally there will always be other chances, but the older we get, the more circumscribed are the ways in which we can utilise those chances.

At the age of sixty, we experience the progressed Sun sextile its natal place. By this time we have had a pretty good chance to make peace with ourselves, because we have had our second Saturn return a year or two before this solar progression. The first Saturn return reflects the arrival of psychological adulthood. We can no longer crawl back into the family matrix because the ego has crystallised and we have become too separate and defined. We are forced to stand in the world alone and acknowledge our limits and strengths as they really are rather than as we might like them to be. The provisional spirit of youth is replaced by a sense of living within a clearly defined personality, and we know we must make the best of what we are. The second Saturn return also reflects a separation process, but it reverses its earlier orientation and points us inward toward a recognition of the purpose of our lives rather than outward toward a recognition of what we need to do in the world. Therefore we are required to make peace with what we are and have created. Our limitations are once again revealed to us, but our attitude toward them shifts to a deeper, more philosophical level.

And we know, by the time this second Saturn cycle is complete, that the inevitability of our death is not that far away.

A sextile is an aspect of making peace with something. It is an aspect of harmony, but the harmony is between two quite dissimilar things, so it's a stimulating harmony, a creative interchange. A trine is also an aspect of harmony, but it involves signs belonging to the same element. Signs of the same element are so similar that there is a kind of unconscious identification without reflection. No energy is generated. With sextiles there is enough diversity to create movement. The Sun-to-Sun sextile at sixty reflects a lively harmonising, a creative compromise or accord, between the potential we began with, reflected by the natal Sun, and the place at which we have arrived, reflected by the progressed Sun. Sun sextile Sun reflects an acceptance of one's diversity and one's history, but it is not a passive acceptance. It is stimulating and can open up new potentials, although not in a harsh or tense way. We can look back and see the road behind us very clearly. We can recognise the path we have been following. This doesn't mean we have finished travelling, but we may travel with more serenity.

If we can manage to get to ninety we experience the progressed Sun square its own place. This is a powerful turning point, and there is conflict involved – perhaps because we get a glimpse of the road stretching into the future, and the potentials we have still not lived, yet we know we will not be able to travel for much longer. This progressed square brings home to us the painful collision between the shining light of inner divinity and the inevitable limits of a mortal life. If we survive the crisis of the progressed square, we may find that we do not begrudge the curtailment death brings to the ongoing process of the Sun's unfoldment.

I find it interesting that the retirement age is currently being pushed back to sixty. Often it seems the collective creates time frames in a very arbitrary way. Yet when we look at them symbolically, they make sense. Obviously some people would prefer to retire before sixty because they feel they have done quite enough time in an unsympathetic job, and others would prefer to go on working because they wish to be useful and active. Also, for those who are self-employed, retirement may be an irrelevant concept – no one will stand over us astrologers and tell us we cannot read any more charts once we have reached sixty. We may wish to continue teaching, writing, and researching long after we are told we are "past it". But as a symbolic turning point, a movement from expressing who we are in the outer world to who we are in the inner world, setting the retirement age at sixty reflects a profound if inadvertent wisdom.

The progressed Sun changing signs

These are the great watersheds of the progressed Sun cycle. This fundamental psychological heartbeat underpins individual solar progressions to natal planets, the timing of which varies enormously from one person to another. The progressed Sun won't ever move that far in any person's lifetime. Even if we manage to get our telegram from the Queen, the progressed Sun will still not have moved more than 100° past its birthplace. We will never experience the progressed Sun travelling all the way around the zodiac. It will never even manage a trine to its natal place unless we achieve something quite extraordinary. Many of us may be able to hope for the square, but fewer will be able to hope for the telegram. It is a profound symbolic statement that, in the progressed chart, the Sun gets only a small segment of the zodiac as its individual allotment. It is as if the development pattern of the individual permits only one small slice of the pie. But perhaps that is quite enough for one lifetime.

Audience: But for some people, it can involve four signs. If you were born at the end of a particular sign, you might just make it through three whole others.

Liz: Yes, it can involve four signs. That may give more diversity to the life of a particular individual, although four signs are still only a third of the zodiac. If a person is born at 0° of a sign, they spend their first thirty years with the Sun progressing through that sign. If they are born at 29° of a sign, they don't get much of it – the Sun is off into the next one pretty quickly. It is a big psychological event when the progressed Sun changes signs, although the importance of the change may only become apparent years later. Many of you have experienced this shift. Did you notice it?

Audience: With hindsight, yes. My progressed Sun went into Libra, and that was when I decided I needed to balance my work and play. I needed to be less neurotic and driven about work and service, and create a balance that let me have more of a life. So it was very literal. But I didn't see it clearly at the time. And it took a few years to make real changes.

Liz: It is often very literal. Now, the sign the Sun moves into after its birth sign is, by nature, out of harmony with the birth sign. This is especially the case if one is a fire sign, because the next stop for the progressed Sun will, of course, always be an earth sign, and this is not an energy that is comfortable for fiery people. But the sign after earth will always be air, and there is often a sense of relief, as though one has found oneself again or rediscovered values that one lost somewhere along the way. This is because the air signs are in natural sextile to the fire signs, and the values are in harmony.

If one is born under a water sign, the progressed Sun will always move into fire. This isn't quite as uncomfortable as a fiery Sun moving into earth, but it is still alien. Those born under air signs have to contend with the progressed Sun moving into a water sign, and those born under earth signs will always experience the progressed Sun moving into air. We spend a large chunk of life with the progressed Sun moving through an element where we do not feel at home, even if there are planets in that next sign. This applies to everyone. The Sun will change signs no later than the age of thirty, and sometimes much earlier, depending on the degree of the natal Sun. As we have seen, if one is born with the Sun in 29° of a sign, the change will take place at only one year old.

All this may sound rather simplistic. But do think about it. For the Sun to find its own light, it has to spend time somewhere where it can't fully shine. It must move through an element which is alien to its own substance. But once it has arrived in a sign which is naturally sextile to its own, there is enough affinity to feel one is back on track. This is, of course, an illusion, because we are never off track.

Audience: How deep is the change? I have often wondered about that. I've experienced the Sun changing signs, and yes, there is a difference, but it's hard to explain.

Liz: Because the Sun is connected with essential values and life purpose, the change lies in the mode of our self-expression rather than its underlying impetus. Our values emerge and consolidate through experiences which challenge them. It is often very obvious in the lives of artists, whose work may undergo major developments in new directions. Some time ago, one of the CPA diploma students wrote his thesis on the work of Picasso and tracked the different "periods" of the artist's work according to the progressed Sun and other progressed planets changing signs. The same thing can be observed in writers, who may change their ideas or style according to the sign through which the progressed Sun is passing and the aspects it makes to natal planets. Sometimes it is the form that changes, and sometimes the content. And sometimes a completely different creative medium becomes necessary.

But all this is still an overlay, because the values reflected by our birth sign are inherent and unchanging. They develop and take different forms, but the archetypal core is the same. The progressed Sun changing signs certainly reflects a deep shift, but it is a shift which incorporates and adds to, rather than replaces. We don't cease to be the sign we are born under. We become that plus something more.

Audience: That's true for me. I had to take very important new experiences on board which changed me. I remember when my Sun moved from Leo to Virgo. I had been an only child for seven and a half years, and then my sister was born. I felt a mixture of things, some good and some bad, but I had to adjust to the reality of having to share. It was also the time when I really began to get to grips with school. Study became a kind of compensation. If I couldn't be first in the family, I could be first at school. That was how I thought about it.

Liz: You too are describing a literal expression of the change of signs, with a concrete event that apparently "caused" the shift in self-expression. Yet it's also a description of a process of development – the unique, solo Leo performer having to adapt in a Virgoan way to the realities of mundane life and develop skills which compensate for the loss of being at the centre of the stage. There is often an event which heralds the new field of expression when the progressed Sun changes signs. But the event is the trigger and symbol of the theme of the next thirty years of unfoldment, not its cause. Every Leo, sooner or later, has to undergo this demand by life to adapt and adjust to mundane reality, because every Leo – except those who die very young – will have the progressed Sun moving into Virgo. We could see these inevitable shifts as an essential part of every Sun-sign's journey.

The progressed Sun aspecting natal planets

Audience: Could you talk about what happens when the progressed Sun aspects natal planets?

Liz: Yes, I was about to do that. As the progressed Sun moves along, it lights up everything it touches. It brings consciousness to any planet it aspects, and gives that planet the opportunity to become part of the Sun's world of self-awareness and self-expression rather than a loose cannon operating at an instinctual, unconscious level. Apollo's dictum – "Know thyself!" – becomes a command issued to the aspected planet, and usually we become aware of that planet in a new way. This is often triggered through initially experiencing the planet through something "outside" us. But as a solar progression takes several years to complete, we have plenty of time to internalise what has been awakened. Progressed aspects have orbs just like natal aspects do, and the gradual approach of the progressed Sun to a natal planet covers a period of up to ten years, especially if a natal configuration of several planets is triggered. It is not a sudden occurrence. As the progressed Sun moves out of exact aspect to one planet, it is usually already within orb of aspecting another. Our life journey involves a lot of overlaps and gradual transitions. The progressed Sun doesn't lurch abruptly from one aspect to another, any more than the light of dawn occurs all in one instant.

Another way of putting this is that the development of the sense of self involves a gradual inclusion of other components of the personality. The Sun is the centre of the solar system and the astrological Sun is the centre of the birth chart, but our human psyches do not carry an awareness of this at birth. We become aware only gradually that we are a whole family of planets with a Great Light at the centre. Bit by bit, the Sun sheds light on the other planets and reveals the order and harmony of the system. Given that we manage to live for thirty years, the Sun will form some aspect, major or minor, to every other planet in the birth chart. Given that we manage to live for sixty

Part Two: The Sun, Creativity and Vocation

years, it will aspect every planet again, often with a major aspect where, on the first round, it formed only a minor one.

Shedding light on dark places

This process of shedding light on each planet as the progressed Sun moves along may not always be comfortable. If light is shed on Saturn, Chiron, or Pluto, it may not initially feel very good. Although the end product may be extremely positive, the experience of recognising something that has been in the dark can be quite disturbing. Even a "benefic" planet can produce great discomfort when it is woken up from sleep. There is no progressed planet that activates a birth placement as powerfully as the Sun, because we must bring that planet into consciousness – sometimes with considerable struggle. For example, Mars may be isolated and quite unconscious in the chart. It might be a singleton by element, or unaspected. We believe ourselves to be peaceable and kind – we never get angry, we never say "No!" to anyone. Then the progressed Sun begins to approach Mars, and Mars gets woken up from sleep. Apollo's chariot passes overhead and he shouts down to Mars, "Come on, you lazy sod, wake up and get in the chariot. We have work to do." And Mars is dragged out of unconsciousness and put in the light, and we can no longer avoid this energy in ourselves.

Often the first thing that happens is that the awakened planet is projected. It starts to appear "out there". This is a natural and necessary process. It doesn't reflect any pathology or lack of maturity. The experiences we encounter under solar progressions are essential to our development, although we may do our best to avoid recognising the inner component. We encounter aggression or passion in the outer world when the Sun passes over Mars, or we fall in love when it passes over Venus, or we experience material hardship or heavy responsibilities when it passes over Saturn. The first planet that the progressed Sun hits after birth is extremely important. Can you all take a minute to think about your own chart in this context?

Audience: I would think that, for most of us, it is Mercury or Venus.

Liz: In terms of conjunctions, that would be fairly common because both planets are always quite close to the Sun. But the aspect doesn't have to be a conjunction. It can be any aspect, even a minor one. A conjunction is certainly powerful. But it's more important to look for an applying aspect which is already within orb between the natal Sun and another planet. If there are none, look for the first planet the progressed Sun aspected. How old were you when this aspect became exact, and what did you experience? When the progressed Sun encounters planets this early in life, we don't realise these planets are inside us. We think they are outside, and usually we experience them in the family environment.

Applying and separating solar progressions

Solar progressions are easy to work out because the progressed Sun moves roughly 1° a year. Before you look at other progressions and transits, focus on the progressed Sun, because the shaping of individual identity is under the Sun's governance. The progressed Moon paints a picture of our emotional experiences, but the progressed Sun, even if it makes only one aspect in childhood, is the architect of our sense of self.

Planets are like memory banks. Later transits over a natal planet build on the experiences that happened when something first transited over that same planet. This is why the transits we experience in early life have such a profound effect on us. Everything that contacts the planet later in life evokes memories of what happened earlier. The same applies to progressed aspects to a natal planet. The most important and most powerful of all progressions to natal planets are the ones which are within orb and applying at birth. When the progressed Sun completes an applying aspect to a planet in the first ten years of life, it is as if a mould is made into which all succeeding sculptures are poured.

Now we can look at another chart from the group, and see what has happened with the progressed Sun. This is Paula's chart. The natal Sun is at 8° 05' degrees Sagittarius in the 1st house, conjunct Jupiter at 11° 49' Sagittarius. That is an applying conjunction. At approximately three and a half years of age, the Sun progressed into exact conjunction with Jupiter. Then, at around ten years old, the progressed Sun reached the Moon, which is at 18° 02' Sagittarius. Remember that the progressed Sun moves roughly a degree a year. Here are two major points in childhood,

Part Two: The Sun, Creativity and Vocation   185

at three and a half years and at ten years, when the progressed Sun made an exact aspect to a natal planet.

Progressed Sun separating from natal Pluto

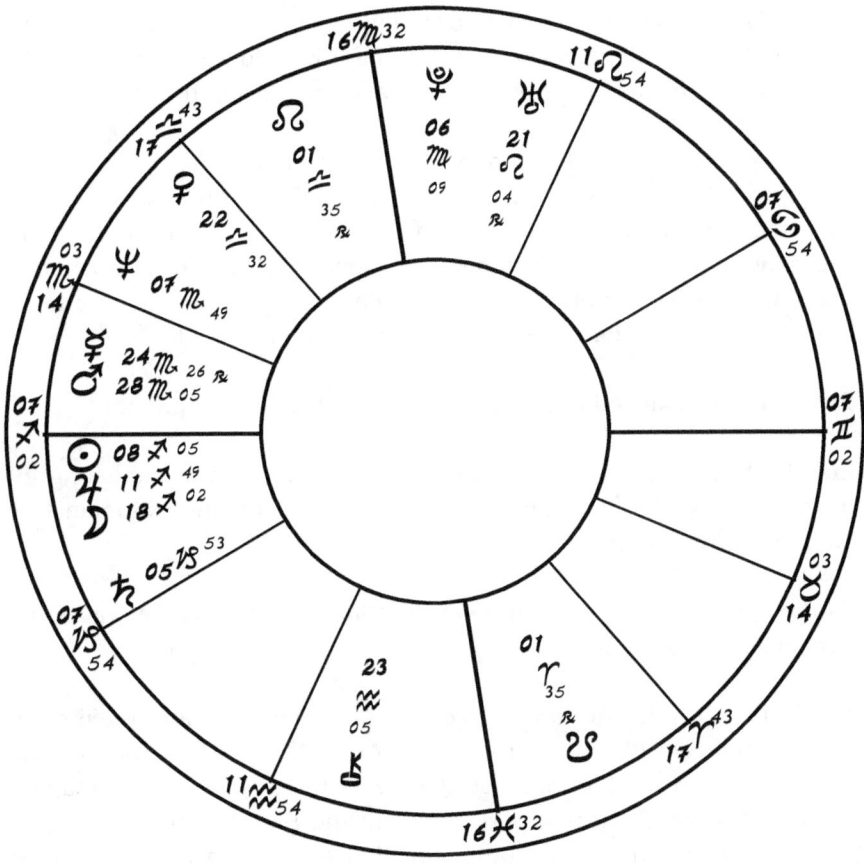

Paula
[Birth data withheld for reasons of confidentiality]

The natal Sun is also square Pluto. But it is a separating square – by converse progressed motion, it was in exact square two years *before* birth. Paula, if you want to get into really fascinating material, try to find out what happened two years before you were born, before you were a mere gleam in your father's eye. This separating solar aspect will tell you something about your father and your paternal inheritance. Do you know anything about your father's life two years before you were born?

Paula: He was around nineteen or twenty years old. He had gone off to the back of beyond to make some money. He worked very hard. The year I was born was the year he came back and started the factory.

Liz: Right. Two years before you were born he was in Pluto-land, struggling for survival. Even though you didn't meet that aspect in your childhood through an applying solar progression, it is there in the background because your father is described as a Sun-Pluto person. There may be a lot more it would be interesting to find out about – for example, what was he going through emotionally at the time?

Paula: He was kicked out of the family. I just remembered that.

Liz: So two years before you were born, in addition to vanishing into the wilderness, he had another close encounter of the Plutonian kind. He was disinherited.

Paula: That is why he went away to make his money. He was kicked out, so he left town.

Liz: All this is relevant to you, because this inheritance is in the memory of the natal Sun-Pluto square. What your father went through before you were born matters because it reflects the psychological image he presented to you, and it is part of the meaning of the Sun-Pluto square in your own nature. Your conviction that everything is a life-or-death struggle is linked with your experience of your father, who literally went through a life-or-death struggle two years before your birth.

Going back to the applying aspects, the conjunctions to natal Jupiter and Moon are the only ones the Sun made after birth. Then, as the Sun progressed further into Sagittarius, it formed other aspects. It trined natal Uranus at 21° Leo when you were around thirteen years old. Three years later, when you were sixteen, it semi-sextiled to natal Mercury. When you were twenty it semi-sextiled to Mars. Finally, when

Part Two: The Sun, Creativity and Vocation

you were twenty-two, it crawled out of Sagittarius into Capricorn. This is an example of a fiery Sun progressing into an earth sign. At that time you began to experience the hard Capricornian lessons about recognising limits, learning self-sufficiency, and surviving in the world.

Paula: It was a dreadful year.

Liz: Once the progressed Sun got into Capricorn, it began applying to natal Saturn. It reached Saturn when you were nearly twenty-eight, just before your first Saturn return. Transiting Saturn was moving along right behind the progressed Sun and reached its own place just as the progressed Sun itself reached natal Saturn. So two things happened at once – a major solar progression to Saturn and a Saturn return which also conjuncted the progressed Sun. That is a lot of Saturn.

Progressed Sun applying to natal Jupiter

Let's look at this first applying solar aspect more carefully. The progressed Sun reached Jupiter when you were around three and a half, nearly four years old. Do you remember that time at all?

Paula: It just struck me that when I was around four, or just before, I actually proposed to my father.

Liz: Did he say yes?

Paula: He said, "Wait until you are grown up!"

Liz: We will often find interesting external events synchronous with progressed solar aspects. We need to ask what the event means as a symbol of the progressed aspect. The Sun is bringing light to Jupiter in Sagittarius, so what is it stirring into awareness?

Audience: Vision. Adventure. Possibilities. Expansion.

Liz: Yes. These things would all have been projected on your father, Paula, because solar progressions tend to be experienced through the father – unless there is no father. In that case they may be projected onto the mother, or onto a brother or other figure in the immediate environment. Or the child may create a fantasy-father. Your natal Jupiter in Sagittarius describes a wonderfully adventurous spirit which works in tandem with solar creative expression and your sense of individual identity. For Sun-Jupiter in Sagittarius, the world is a great adventure playground. This youthful vision would have first appeared as an attribute of your personal father. Of course you wanted to marry him. To you he embodied Zeus, the bright and glorious king of the gods who would take you off into the ethers and show you the universe.

Paula: That's extraordinary. Yes, I suppose I was in love with him.

Liz: The way you have put that is very important. We do fall in love with things when the Sun lights them up. That's the link with the 5th house. We see something mirrored back to us of our own god, our own inner spark, and we love it. This is not Neptunian love, which seeks a state of fusion. The Sun does not seek to lose itself. It is a recognition of something shining that gives life joy and meaning. So one loves it. What you fell in love with is part of your own soul. Your early awakening to a spirit of adventure and excitement, experienced through your father, was the herald of an inner *daimon* which will lead you forward all your life. But at the age of three or four, how could you know that?

Progressed Sun applying to natal Moon

Although it was still within orb of conjunction with natal Jupiter, the progressed Sun moved on and lit up the Moon. This completed its passage over the natal conjunction of Moon and Jupiter toward which it was applying at birth. Paula was born under a new Moon which progressed to exact conjunction at ten years old. Would any of you like to try an interpretation? Any person born in the new Moon phase of the lunation cycle, with the Moon already moving away from its conjunction with the Sun, will have the progressed Sun coming up to the natal Moon very early in life.

Paula: There's something else I should have said earlier. It's taking me a while to absorb all this information and realise how it connects with my life. My father left my mother when I was four years old. I suppose that's another side of progressed Sun on Jupiter. He flew away. Then, when the progressed Sun conjuncted my natal Moon, my mother remarried.

Liz: So the *puer aeternus* side of Jupiter made itself evident *via* your father, in painful as well as positive ways. Then, when progressed Sun arrived on natal Moon, you experienced an awakening of your feeling life through your mother's second marriage. Was she happier in this second marriage?

Paula: Definitely. But I wasn't.

Liz: Of course not. You had lost your adored father. You had a Jupiterian experience of both love and loss through your father at the age of four, and a lunar experience of emotional awakening through your mother at the age of ten. Because your Moon is in Sagittarius, your emotional needs are expressed imaginatively. Both the wandering spirit and the imaginative expression of feelings are part of your own nature and need to be included in your life. But they first appeared "outside" concurrent with major solar progressions.

We won't always find events fitting quite so neatly with solar progressions as they do with Paula's. And even when they do fit, it is the inner experience that is relevant, not the external trigger. The progressed Sun lights up what it touches. In the case of the conjunction of progressed Sun to natal Moon in Paula's chart, the really important event was not Paula's mother's remarriage. It was that Paula discovered she had a Moon. She experienced feelings and needs in a new and independent way. Probably the only way to satisfy those needs was to retreat into the imaginal world. Whether or not the concrete events match, under solar progressions we always encounter something, feel something, experience something that shapes us for the rest of our lives. We learn something about the real nature of the natal planet. Whatever you felt when progressed Sun came up to natal Moon, Paula, it would have awakened your need to find security through the imagination. Maybe you began to express yourself creatively at that time.

Paula: Yes, I think I did. I made up stories.

Audience: The Moon is the ruler of the 8th. So progressed Sun on natal Moon may be more mixed, and carry something dark with it – some kind of loss or feeling of powerlessness.

Liz: Yes, well spotted. There is both a creative opening up and a confrontation with the inevitable. Also, it's important to look at the natal Moon's situation. This Moon is benignly aspected. It trines Uranus, sextiles Venus, and sextiles Chiron. Although the Moon as ruler of the 8th carries a theme of relinquishment and confrontation with fate – and aspects from the Moon to outer planets, however benign, bring their own problems – nevertheless this group of harmonious aspects to the natal Moon suggests that there is an innate capacity to accept and make the best of whatever emotional difficulties life presents. If the Moon were square Saturn or opposite Mars and the progressed Sun arrived on it, the opposition or square would be triggered, and the emotional experience would probably be harsher and leave more anger in its wake.

Audience: Could this kind of aspect indicate the psychological and physical changes of puberty?

Liz: Yes, that is a possibility if the time frame coincides, although in Paula's case, ten years old is a bit early for puberty. Sometimes progressed aspects to the natal Moon are coincident with this kind of biological change. But the progressed aspect itself isn't a literal indicator of puberty. Progressed Sun on Moon can occur at any age. If it coincides with puberty, it describes how the individual experiences the changes that occur. In that case, the awakening of instinctual feminine awareness – the realisation that one is now a woman and is able to bear a child – would be an extremely powerful psychological event. Physical experiences like the onset of menstruation or menopause, or the birth of a child, mean different things to different people depending on the planets through which the experience is perceived.

If something involving the body happens under a solar progression, then the experience becomes bound up with one's sense of identity. It contains a nugget of one's unique individual destiny, and it is a profound event on an inner as well as a physical level. For some people, in contrast, the arrival of puberty may be physically disturbing and challenging, but it is a "mere" body experience common to everyone, and does not relate to the individual's special sense of self. Paula's solar awakening to the feminine principle does not really reflect a bodily experience, especially in unmaternal Sagittarius. The inner mother, when the Moon is in Sagittarius, does not nourish with food. She nourishes with imagination and a broadening of horizons.

Audience: I was always close to my mother. She was a splendid, strong, figure. She still is.

Liz: Perhaps the deep imaginative link between the two of you was awakened when your mother remarried. The demands of a new husband meant that your relationship with her had to change, and maybe the intellectual and imaginative level became more important as the instinctual bond became compromised. Any important transit over the Moon will reawaken this important time in your childhood. When transiting Pluto reaches natal Moon, it will connect you back to the time when progressed Sun woke the Moon up at ten years old. A similar experience may occur, or the emotions you experience will be similar. Recognising this can help you respond more consciously and creatively to whatever the forthcoming Pluto transit brings.

We can only make sense of this kind of connection of past and present by looking at the movements of the progressed Sun in our own chart, and the transits that follow on its heels. After the seminar I would recommend that you all get a notebook and make some notes about the first aspect that the progressed Sun made after your birth. Most important are the aspects which are within orb and applying at birth. Try to remember what you can – inner events, outer events, people who entered your life.

Do this with all progressed solar aspects. You will find that there aren't that many of these in early life, unless the natal Sun is in a tight configuration with many planets in the birth chart. Some people have no applying solar aspects, only separating ones. The Sun may also appear to be unaspected, although usually you will find a minor aspect even if there is an absence of major ones. If the Sun makes only separating aspects, you may need to get more information on the climate in your family and the experiences of your parents in the years before your birth, coincident with when the separating aspect would have been exact by converse progression.

Once you have blocked out the time frame of the solar aspects in childhood, look at any powerful transits that occurred later, or that are occurring now, which trigger those natal planets. These transits will naturally also aspect the natal Sun, and they will connect you with the solar experience of being woken up in some way in early life. Early solar progressions mark the moment when we first understand something important about life and ourselves – something which will become part of our future destiny.

Progressed Sun trine natal Uranus

Wherever your progressed Sun is now, what is the next progressed aspect it will make? What was the last one it made? Is it moving over a configuration of planets? When the progressed Sun moves over a configuration it is within orb of all the planets in the configuration. The entire period, which may be many years, reflects a time when that natal configuration is brought to life. In Paula's chart, progressed Sun reached natal Moon at ten years old and trined natal Uranus at thirteen. Throughout this period the Moon-Uranus trine was activated.

Paula: I had a kind of nanny, a caretaker who looked after me. When I was thirteen, she left. In some ways I had more mothering from her than from my own mother. She became especially important to me when my mother remarried. I was awfully torn between the two of them. Before she left, there was a terrible dilemma of whom to support if they had a fight. When she left, it was complete misery. For a while I was very angry with my mother.

Liz: So your relationship with this nanny became particularly important when progressed Sun reached natal Moon. This seems to reflect the lunar awakening of the mother-principle. Yet it is a Sagittarian Moon. The Sagittarian expansion of horizons seems linked to this mother-experience involving someone who was not your biological mother.
Can you see how the progressed Sun activating first the Moon and then Uranus fits your experience with your nanny, focused on a time frame of three years? Uranus is in the 9th, and the Moon in Jupiter's

sign trine Uranus in Jupiter's house fits this experience of a "foreign" or non-biological mother. Although losing her was hard and painful, at the same time the archetypal pattern underpinning the experience is one of freedom from instinctual bonds. You experienced and learned about mothering from a woman who was not related to you by blood, and this set up a conflict with the woman who is biologically your mother – the woman to whom you "should" feel complete loyalty. Then the one to whom you were deeply attached, but to whom you were not related by blood, left. You had to develop special inner resources to cope with that. What were these resources? What did the progressed Sun awaken in you by activating Moon-Uranus?

Paula: Detachment.

Liz: Yes. You had to let go of the need for instinctual mothering. This process began when you received mothering from someone who was not actually your mother. It is as though something within you said, "I will cope with this by withdrawing my dependency on any flesh-and-blood person. I will become detached. If I want emotional nourishment, I will find it in my imagination. I will never again depend completely on another person." This freed something in you. It opened a route into the imagination which you have always been able to rely on. Moon trine Uranus reflects a special gift, but access to this gift requires relinquishing some part of the personal, biological level of the Moon. This is an example of how benign aspects to the Moon from outer planets can sometimes be problematic. They give us something very valuable, but they also take something away, or require us to live the Moon on a level other than the comfortable, natural, instinctual one.

Activation of natal Moon-Uranus also brought the recognition that mothering can come from someone other than one's mother. It is not just a biological process. Moon-Uranus offers a different vision of family and moves beyond the bonds of blood. It recognises the mother-principle as an archetypal principle independent of one's biological mother. One's "real" family may be one's friends or one's ideas, and often there is a separation or distancing from blood relatives to allow this recognition to take place. Paula, what you experienced under this solar progression reflects the development of a basic birth chart aspect. The outer experience activated the inner potential and brought it to life, and it thus became part of your essential character. External circumstances coincident with the solar progression required you to develop Moon-Uranus attributes because that is what you innately are and were always meant to develop. It wouldn't have mattered if the circumstances were entirely different as long as they served the same inner purpose. As Jung put it, a person's life is characteristic of the person. Events which occur under the progressed Sun have a profound teleology.

The progressed Sun brings natal configurations to life as it goes over them. It makes these configurations, both difficult and harmonious, one's own. Moon trine Uranus is a harmonious configuration, so your ability to develop the Uranian perspective seems to have come in a flowing and natural way – even though the loss of your nanny caused you a lot of emotional pain. If the Moon were opposite Uranus, detachment would have probably been far more difficult to come by, although in the end you would have had to develop it anyway. But you might have had to go through several more losses or separations until the message was clear.

As the progressed Sun moves along, it shines light on everything it touches. Something must then be integrated into our story which was always our own to begin with. Recognising this can be especially helpful when the Sun activates difficult natal configurations, because hard aspects are almost always initially dealt with by projecting one end of the aspect. The involvement of the progressed Sun gives us the opportunity to see, in a deep and complete way, what ultimately belongs to our own souls and our own life path.

Audience: What about aspects from the progressed Sun to progressed planets?

Liz: It is useful to look at the progressed Sun's aspects to other progressed planets. But these aspects don't seem to involve the same deep activation of our own destiny, our own story. It is the natal planets in their signs and houses which describe the framework of our development pattern. Progressed planets are "current" – they reflect where we are at a particular time. The birth chart reflects the underlying pattern. In thirty years the progressed Sun will make an aspect to everything in the natal chart. This may not be a major aspect – it may be a quincunx, a semisextile, or a sesquiquadrate. But the progressed Sun will touch everything before we reach the age of thirty, shedding light on the whole natal framework. Then it aspects its own place for the first time. Can you see how profound this symbolism is?

Audience: I think Paula is a person who cannot be contained within a narrow life. The experience of her nanny would have to open up her inner life. It is very much part of her destiny. It is an adventurous chart.

Liz: Yes, it is the chart of a wanderer – intellectually, spiritually, emotionally, and physically. The first time you encountered that wanderer, Paula, was when the progressed Sun moved over first Jupiter, and then the Moon-Uranus configuration. It does seem that you had to learn to let go and look to far horizons for your joy and your future. Experience forced you to develop something that was always part of your own inner shape. It invariably looks as if the outer world makes us develop character qualities. This is the cause-and-effect attitude of most people toward their lives. We believe we have formed as we have because circumstances have made us do so. But the progressed Sun reveals a great mystery here. The outer world takes the shape of something that needs to emerge into the light from inside. The circumstances, however painful, are always exactly the right ones. It is hard to articulate all of this. I hope I am getting it across to you. Solar progressions are truly awesome when we begin to explore them in depth.

Transits to the natal Sun

Here's another chart from the group. Let's look not only at solar progressions, but also at transits to the Sun. Here is the Sun in Leo conjunct Pluto in the 2nd house, although the Sun is edging towards the 3rd. Cancer is rising, and the Moon is in the 12th in Gemini. The Sun is in exact square to Mars with a 32' orb. If we think in terms of progressed motion, the Sun was not just moving towards Mars at birth, it was already hard on it, and at six months old it closed that square. Marie, you were only an infant when the progressed Sun collided with Mars in Scorpio. Could you tell us about your birth, and what was happening in your environment at the time you were born?

Apollo's Chariot

Marie: My parents lost a child eighteen months before.

Liz: When you were born, was it a difficult delivery?

Marie: I was two weeks late. I don't know if there were any complications.

Liz: Coming into life under an exact Sun-Mars square is a very powerful statement of emerging into a battleground.

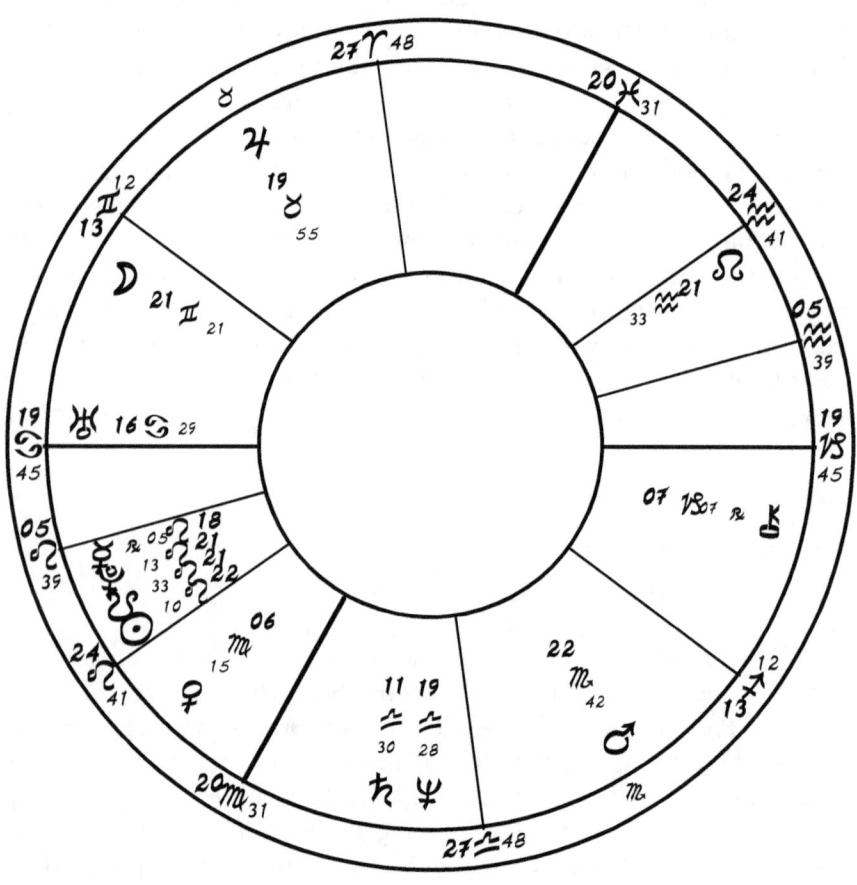

Marie
[Birth data withheld for reasons of confidentiality]

Audience: A year before birth, by converse progression, the Sun was on Pluto.

Liz: Yes, Pluto is in the past and Mars is in the immediate future. Your entry into the world is flanked on one side by Pluto and on the other by Mars.

Audience: So the Pluto converse progression could describe the loss of the child before Marie's birth?

Liz: It could describe the atmosphere in the environment concurrent with the loss of the child. It could also point to the father and what he was experiencing. Do you have brothers and sisters, Marie?

Marie: No.

Liz: So the one that was lost would have been your only sibling?

Marie: Yes. He was a boy.

Liz: From the moment of your entry into the world, it seems you had to learn how to fight, how to assert yourself in your environment. Mars is in Scorpio, so it is a life-or-death battle. I do wonder about that late birth, and whether there was physical danger involved. If the birth had not been induced, your life might have been under threat.

Audience: There must have been a lot of fear in the mother. Having lost one child, she must have been desperately worried.

The creativity of Sun-Mars and Sun-Pluto

Liz: The single theme which unites Sun-Pluto, Sun-Mars, Mars in Scorpio, and Mars square Pluto is a ferocious survival instinct. All three of these placements declare, "I'm going to live! Nothing will destroy me!" These aspects are determined to survive in the face of great danger. All the solar creative energy is wrapped up in this. It isn't playful in a frivolous sense. It is heroic. Your ability to connect with a sense of meaning requires struggle. You need a battle – otherwise you don't feel fully alive. Why did you want us to discuss your chart?

Marie: I feel I have a tremendous struggle with my creativity. I write plays. But I am always sabotaging myself.

Liz: Do you know how you sabotage yourself?

Marie: I never seem to be able to finish a play to the point where I feel I could deliver it to a director.

Liz: And what would happen if you did deliver it?

Marie: I haven't been able to see that far.

Liz: Perhaps any creative effort is attended by that sense of a life-and-death struggle. There may be great fear that your creative expression will destroy either you or someone else. If you are born, you might destroy your mother or, at the least, you might destroy your parents' dreams of the kind of child they wanted to have. What kind of plays do you write? Do they express Mars-Pluto themes?

Marie: They're certainly serious. I'm concerned with relationships, especially destructive ones.

Liz: Bearing in mind your Mercury-Pluto conjunction square both Jupiter and Mars, I think you would be very good at black comedy.

Marie: People say I am a bit Pinteresque.

Liz: Your inner landscape has a lot of darkness in it. But that darkness is actually the fuel for your best creative efforts. The fact that the Sun is so close to Mars and Pluto at birth suggests that that the life-and-death struggle was mirrored in your environment just before and immediately during and after birth. It won't help to try to remember, because one simply can't. The memory is locked in the body and might be released through certain kinds of rebirthing therapies, but it is not memory in the usual sense because there was not yet an ego to do the remembering. But whatever happened in your early environment, this heroic, battling spirit is an essential ingredient of your own soul and needs the right medium of expression. You have evidently found the medium but are experiencing a block which you call self-sabotage. Let's try to see whether this is reflected in the chart. What else does the Sun do?

Audience: It squares Jupiter. I wonder if Sun square Jupiter people sometimes play a role that they don't feel suited to. There is something in Marie's chart about the conflict between the role or expected idea of what she is supposed to create, and the sabotaging of it because it is not Plutonian, not the essence, not the truth. It is a role.

Liz: Does that make sense to you?

Marie: I'm not sure. Yes, there is some feeling that I should be living up to great expectations. I feel should be achieving a lot because I have been fortunate in some ways. I suppose that's the Sun-Jupiter.

Liz: Jupiter is in Taurus in the 11th. This Jupiter wants pleasure and good company, being liked by people, having easy and comfortable relationships with others, and enjoying being part of a congenial group. Stable friendships are important, and so are goals which achieve material security. This usually comfortable and uncomplicated Jupiter is not very comfortable co-habiting with Sun-Pluto and Mars in Scorpio, both of which want intensity, depth, and emotional truth – even at the cost of ripping the skin off everything to expose the reality beneath. Jupiter in Taurus hopes for everything to be normal, pleasant, safe, and uncomplicated. I also wonder what this says about your father, Marie, because Jupiter, Mars, and the Sun form a T-cross, with the Sun conjuncting the south Node. Can you tell us about your father?

Marie: He was a very emotional man. He was rather weak in many ways, and dependent on my mother, who was much stronger and more self-contained.

Liz: Emotional, weak, and dependent on the mother – that might fit Sun-Neptune, and there might also be elements of it described by Sun-Jupiter, but this description doesn't fit Sun-Pluto or Sun-Mars. It is always fascinating when the parental significators in a chart describe two quite different images pertaining to one parent. Parents, like everyone else, are complex beings with many different facets, and sometimes two diametrically opposite sides are described in the child's chart. "Weak" is a very interesting word because our definitions of weakness are related to our expectations of strength.

Like weakness, strength is defined in different ways by different people, and it varies according to the prevailing social norm. "Strong" in many cultures relates to traditional masculine attributes – courage in war, holding firm in the face of opposition, refusing to give way under pressure. Of course this kind of strength may not be strength at all, but mere pig-headedness. And "weak", for a child who hopes for more love from the father than she is able to get, may mean a father who takes the mother's rather than the daughter's side, and does not play the desired role in the Oedipal triangle. We feel someone is weak when they are not able to give us what we want or are not matching up to our expectations. We feel let down. Sun-Neptune's disillusionment with the father often springs from an initial idealisation and an expectation that the father will offer perfect, unconditional love. Then the parent turns out to be an ordinary flawed human who is lost, distracted, emotionally or physically absent, or a victim of external circumstances. We call him weak because he does not love us strongly enough. But Sun-Pluto and Sun-Mars are hardly weak. This suggests an entirely different dimension to the father-image. It seems that weakness sat side by side with something extremely powerful and aggressive that couldn't be expressed.

Audience: There are a lot of paradoxes in this chart. Marie describes her mother as strong and self-contained, yet the Moon is in the 12th house and trines Neptune.

Liz: It also forms a sextile to Sun-Pluto and a quincunx to Mars. Both mother and father are linked to both the Mars-Pluto square and Neptune. Both parents seem to have carried the same internal dichotomy and apportioned it between them, as couples usually do. You be the doctor, I'll be the nurse; you be the Plutonian, I'll be the Neptunian. And the same dichotomy, the same archetypal conflict between survival and dissolution, exists within you, Marie. The Sun-Neptune sextile is a separating aspect. So is the Sun-Pluto conjunction. The Sun's only applying aspect is the close square to Mars. The progressed Sun moved out of Leo and entered Virgo when you were around eight years old. This change from fire to earth suggests that you began to anchor your inner world in some external form. Once the Sun entered Virgo, it began moving toward a conjunction with natal Venus and a trine to natal Chiron.. Venus and Chiron are trine in the birth chart. This triggering of the natal trine by the progressed Sun occurred when you were between fourteen and fifteen years old. Venus is in the 3rd house and Chiron is in the 6th. What was happening to you at that age? Did you start writing at that time?

Marie: No, I started that when I was seven or eight. You are right about the change that happened when the progressed Sun entered Virgo. When I was fourteen I decided I wanted to work in the media. I knew then what I wanted to do with my life.

Liz: Progressed Sun on Venus is connected with a realisation of self-value and, often, a realisation of talents. The light of the Sun illuminates one's feelings of worth. It is traditionally an aspect of falling in love, and that happens often enough. But sometimes the love is not for another person. It may be for some artistic medium, or some innate gift which is discovered and developed. You knew you wanted to go into the media when the progressed Sun reached a 3rd house Venus. That is clear enough. The certainty you felt may also reflect your Sun-Mars-Pluto nature, which says, "I am going to do this thing, and nothing is going to stop me." Not everyone experiences such certainty, but Sun-Mars people tend to be very sure of their decisions.

Marie: I think I am afraid of being special. I am afraid I will be criticised or attacked.

Liz: That is tantamount to saying you are afraid of being a Leo – too strong, too dramatic, too defined. If this is the nature of your self-sabotage, it is connected with fearing the Sun itself and the consequences of living it. This touches on one of last week's solar themes – the fear many people have of being hurt by others' envy. But whom do you fear, Marie? Who will attack or destroy you if you are too special? You are the only child, so a lot of hopes and expectations must have been pinned on you. You were supposed to be special. What did your parents want you to become?

Marie: Yes, I was supposed to be special. But in their way, not mine.

Liz: What was "their way"?

Marie: I'm not sure. I only know that it was something other than myself. A fantasy, maybe.

Liz: Maybe it's more basic than that. Your parents lost a boy child. Perhaps, on some level, you felt you had no right to be alive because you were a girl child. You are saying that being creative implies being threatened by someone or something that will destroy you if you are special in your way, not theirs. The usual suspects are probably also involved – the envy of talented but frustrated parents, double messages given to the child ("We want you to be special, but not so special that you'll make us feel bad about our own failures!"), competitiveness and rivalry between parents and child, an Oedipal triangle gone wrong, and a child who by nature needs more emotional truth and openness than the family can possibly provide.

Audience: What do you mean by "an Oedipal triangle gone wrong"?

Liz: I mean it in a broad rather than a clinical sense. Children need to affirm their value and importance by "winning" the beloved parent and "besting" the other parent. This is natural and healthy, and not necessarily linked to the parent of the opposite sex. The beloved parent may be the parent of the same sex, or the scenario may be played out with each parent in turn. Nor do I think that sexual feelings are the core issue, as orthodox Freudians believe. A Sun-Mars or Sun in Aries child depends more than other children on this kind of "winning" to assert individual worth. That is the nature of Mars. In a relatively stable and reasonably loving family, a compromise is usually achieved and the child does indeed "win" sometimes – but not all the time, and never completely. The child's competitiveness does not unleash rage and destructiveness in the "losing" parent, and the message is clear that, however much the child is loved, the parents are a couple who cannot be pried apart.

But not all families can achieve this. Parents may have their own unconscious investment in these triangles, and the child is usually the one who suffers.[21] When family triangles go wrong, it is usually because the child either gets nothing at all from the beloved parent or gets too much because the parent, locked into an unhappy marriage, turns the child into a surrogate spouse. I suspect that, in Marie's family, the former is the case – she didn't get to win at all, and has grown up feeling that any effort to compete – in love or in creative work – will result in failure. Yet a Sun-Mars person must compete, because Martial competition and assertion of self provide the stimulus that fires the Sun to its best creative efforts. If there is no one to compete with, and no chance of winning, there is no point in trying.

Transiting Uranus opposing natal Sun

Now let's look at the approaching opposition of transiting Uranus to Marie's Sun in Leo. This transit will set off the natal T-cross as Uranus inches forward in Aquarius. It will conjunct the north Node, oppose Pluto and Mercury, square Jupiter, oppose the Sun, and square Mars, as well as forming trines to natal Moon and Neptune. And just in case any of you might think something has been left out, Uranus will also semisquare natal Chiron, which is sesquiquadrate natal Sun-Pluto and semisquare natal Mars. The configurations in Marie's chart are very tight, and transiting Uranus will set off the whole thing. Only natal Venus and Saturn remain unaffected by this transit.

Uranus opposing the Sun is a particularly important transit because it is an outer planet. Any transiting planet aspecting the Sun will kick the Sun into activity and make us conscious of ourselves in a new way, but the transiting planet will give its wakeup call in accord with its own nature. If this were a transit of Neptune, the Sun would still be awakened, but through Neptunian dreams, longings, fantasies, and disappointments. If it were a Saturn transit, the Sun would likewise be awakened, but through the experience of limits, responsibilities, failures, or separations.

Transiting Uranus will be moving through the 8th house. That will certainly wake up the survival and self-renewal instincts of Sun-Pluto. And the imaginative potential of a 12th house Gemini Moon, with

---

[21] For a further investigation of family triangles, see Liz Greene, "The Eternal Triangle", Part Two, *Relationships and How to Survive Them*, CPA Press, 1999.

its roots in the images and dreams of the collective psyche, will also be activated. The end product of this may be a powerful emergence of that tremendous drive to be something special, to create something special – not just because you wish it, but because your psychological survival depends on it. It does look as if an enormous amount of creative energy will be freed. Because Uranus is involved, there could be some sudden and unexpected loss, separation, or turbulent event in the family that mirrors the inner changes. The fact that the 8th house is involved, and also the natal Moon, suggests that the trigger may be family matters.

Audience: Natal Uranus is right on the Ascendant. That says to me that the shift may be caused by some kind of radical change in the environment.

Liz: Yes, a radical change in the immediate environment, or a radical upheaval in relationship. Uranus goes over the north Node, so there is a relationship implication. I mean "relationship" in the broadest sense, not just love relationships. Family relationships are also included under this broader umbrella. Something Uranian is likely to emerge in personal life, involving a confrontation with fate, with the inevitable. Its opposition to the Sun is like an alarm clock going off. That powerful Sun-Pluto-Mars configuration is not asleep, but it sounds a bit lethargic, as if it's been dulled by Prozac. One eye is open, but it is not really awake yet. This transit will be exact around the time of the Millennium. It is your personal Millennium, Marie – a time of new birth and new beginnings. It may involve you in loss and struggle, and the struggle may make you suddenly realise where your strengths really lie. It will be worth fighting for what you want at that time, because as a Sun-Pluto-Mars person, nothing is as creatively inspiring to you as a good struggle.

The Pluto in Leo generation group

Audience: I'm trying to work something out about the timing of these slow outer planet transits. When Pluto entered Leo, it meant that every living Leo got Pluto transiting over their Sun. And every Taurus and Scorpio got a Pluto square, and every Aquarian got a Pluto opposition. Since Uranus went into Aquarius, every Leo has had or is going to get

Uranus opposing their Sun. Is this saying something about a whole generation group? Or maybe I'm confusing this with people born with Sun conjunct Pluto in Leo. Do they all get Pluto-ed, with either the progressed Sun over natal Pluto or transiting Pluto over the natal Sun?

Liz: No to the first question – all these fixed sign people receiving aspects from transiting Pluto in Leo were born into many different generation groups. A 10° Leo born in 1910 and a 10° Leo born in 1943 would get the conjunction of transiting Pluto at the same time, but they belong to different generations, both in terms of age and in terms of their outer planet placements. Yes to the second question – all the Leos born with Pluto in Leo get Pluto-ed one way or the other.

Pluto first entered Leo in October 1937. It stationed in 0° and moved back into Cancer at the end of November. It went into Leo again in August 1938, dipped back into Cancer in February 1939, and finally moved into Leo for its long haul in June 1939. It moved into Virgo in August 1957, went back into Leo in April 1958, and returned to Virgo in June 1958. So we have a Pluto in Leo generation group – or, in simple terms, a Pluto transit – covering a time period of twenty-one years.

Not every Leo in that generation group has Sun conjunct Pluto. If Pluto is at 6° Leo and the Sun is at 23° Leo in the birth chart, the orb is too wide for a conjunction. But in that case, Pluto transited the natal Sun a few years after birth and marked an important period during childhood. If the Sun is at 6° Leo and Pluto is at 23° Leo, the progressed Sun moved over Pluto at seventeen years old. That does not have the same weight as an applying solar aspect, but it is an extremely important progressed aspect. For the Sun to make an applying or separating conjunction with Pluto, it must be less than 10° away from natal Pluto. It is true that there are a great many Leos in this generation born with a Sun-Pluto conjunction, as well as Taureans and Scorpios with the square and Aquarians with the opposition. Once Pluto moved into Virgo, many Virgos of that generation group have Sun conjunct Pluto. The same thing applies: all these Virgos, with or without natal Sun-Pluto conjunctions, have been Pluto-ed either by transiting Pluto over natal Sun or progressed Sun over natal Pluto.

At the moment many children are born each winter with Sun conjunct Pluto in Sagittarius. There are also many children born each summer with Sun in Gemini opposition Pluto. Wherever Pluto is transiting, because it moves so slowly, huge groups are born at certain seasons every year with hard natal Sun-Pluto contacts. So the Sun-Pluto component is generational in one sense. Yet it isn't generational in another sense, because the Sun's journey is always an individual journey. All individuals with the Sun contacting an outer planet seem to carry something for the collective. They need to embody and express in an individual way something of the generation group into which they have been born.

We could say this about the Sun with any outer planet. The Sun reflects a personal journey, concerned with unique destiny and individual creativity. But whatever shape our creative aspiration takes, whatever our vocation, when the Sun is linked with an outer planet it must also serve and mediate the collective psyche of the generation group to which we belong. Because Pluto is concerned with the life-and-death struggle, survival for the Pluto in Leo generation group has to do with recognition of the absolute necessity of being oneself. Without that sense of being something special, one will not survive. It is not a cerebral or spiritual thing. It is psychological death if one cannot be or express oneself. This whole generation polarises against the Aquarian ethos of the individual only being of value as a unit in a larger group.

Those with the Sun conjunct Pluto in Leo, like Marie, are particularly challenged by transiting Uranus and Neptune moving through Aquarius. It is urgent that they find the courage to be the Sun in Leo fully at this time. If the Leonine need is suppressed, it isn't only the suppression of the individual self – there is also a blocking up of the generational survival instinct. It isn't only one's own life that is not being lived. Something is pushing from behind which is collective, urgently demanding expression through the individual. There may be very strong negative repercussions, the most common of which is severe depression, if the Sun-Pluto in Leo is not expressed.

This Sun-Pluto energy can become very destructive if it is denied a positive outlet. The darkest face of the urgent need to be oneself is the outlaw, the person who destroys society in the name of individualism. It is extremely important to have a vehicle for Sun-Pluto's ferocious self-ness, because one is embodying something for a whole generation. Think of Mick Jagger, who was born under a Sun-Pluto conjunction in Leo. His music – in fact, his whole life – epitomises much of the essence of the Pluto in Leo generation. For less exhibitionist folk, the vehicle doesn't have to involve singing "Sympathy for the Devil" and rousing a crowd of twenty thousand to violence. It could be through writing. The characters in a novel, a play, or a film can easily carry Sun-Pluto.

It is salutary to remember Goethe, who had the Sun square Pluto and created Mephistopheles and Faust. The struggle between these two characters encapsulates the enactment of the square on both personal and collective levels. The creative medium needs to be able to carry the aspect. Being a bank clerk probably won't do. On the other hand, being involved with large sums of money on a global scale might suit very well. We can find Sun-Pluto in investment banking as often as at the Royal Shakespeare Company. Of course we may find it in the therapeutic world. But Pluto is not always drawn to healing or the arts. It also likes wielding power in a big way. As we saw last week, our present Prime Minister, Mr. Blair, has a Sun-Pluto square.

The Sun and vocation

Sun-Pluto in the political arena

Let's have a brief break from charts from the group. Here is another chart that I have brought. We can continue to examine the issue of the Sun and generation groups, and also begin to explore the link between the Sun and vocation. Here is a Sun-Pluto square. When Pluto was in Cancer, many people born with the Sun in a cardinal sign got a hard aspect between Sun and Pluto. What kind of vocation might be suggested by the Sun in the 11th in Libra square Pluto in Cancer?

Audience: Politics.

Audience: Espionage.

Liz: Yes, James Bond is undoubtedly a Sun-Pluto character.

Audience: Is it Mrs. Thatcher?

Liz: Of course it is. Who else?

Audience: Arthur Scargill had a Sun-Pluto opposition.

Liz: He probably still has it, unless he's discovered how to send in and get a new chart. He also has a Sun-Neptune trine. Like Marie's parents, he and Mrs. Thatcher seem to have taken opposite sides of an archetypal issue. Along with Sun-Pluto, she has a Sun-Neptune sextile and a Moon-Neptune conjunction at the MC on the 9th house side. This is the area that Gauquelin's work revealed as "hot", when planets conjunct an angle from the cadent house side. Neptune is powerful in Mrs. Thatcher's chart. Both she and Scargill had a Neptunian vision of a perfect society, and both were ruthless in implementing that vision. But their ideas about what the perfect society should look like, and the means by which it could be achieved, were diametrically opposed.

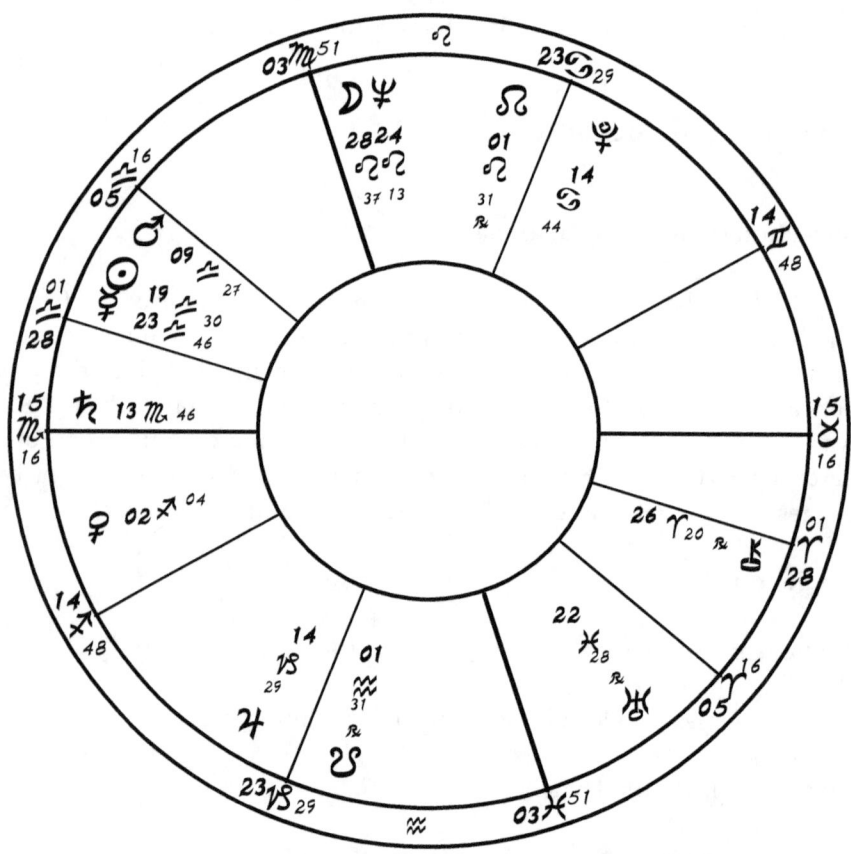

Margaret Thatcher
13 October 1925, 9.00 am GMT, Grantham, England

Mrs. Thatcher's political goals reflected her perception of a life-or-death struggle where survival depends on collective loyalty. Scargill perceived the same thing, but his loyalty was given to a different collective. "We will make our nation great again!" says Pluto in Cancer. This is not just an individual speaking. It's a whole generation born between 1912 and 1939. Some were born during World War One, others in the boom time of the 1920s, and the youngest of the group in the economic depression of the 1930s. While Pluto was in Cancer the Sun hadn't yet set on the British Empire. Pluto's generational voice says, "To survive, we must be loyal to our families, our nation" – or, in Scargill's case, "our unions, our working class". With natal Sun aspecting Pluto, this voice emerged as the basis of an individual political philosophy.

The Sun in Capricorn in the 2nd house

Perhaps we could move on to another chart from the group now. Linda, was there a particular issue you wanted us to look at?

Linda: I am definitely a late starter, with the Sun in Capricorn sextile Saturn. I think you said last week that Saturnian people often blossom late. My progressed Sun is in Aquarius now. When it progressed onto Venus recently, I began to feel I wanted more of a position of importance in the world.

Liz: The Sun is in Capricorn, an earth sign, in the 2nd house, an earthy house. In fact the whole chart is very earthy. What about that 2nd house Sun in Capricorn? What is its vocation?

Audience: Material security.

Liz: Material security isn't a vocation. Let's consider the word itself. I should remind you that "vocation" comes from the Latin verb *vocare*, meaning "to call". A vocation is a sense of special destiny, a feeling that there is something unique one is called to do in the world. Vocation is linked with purpose and meaning. The Sun's creative attributes, reflected by its sign, house, and aspects, describe the vocation as an archetypal theme. The need for material security is not a calling. It is a fundamental physical need in all of us, and for some, an important emotional need as well. But it is not linked with a sense of meaning and purpose.

The Sun in the 2nd is not really motivated by the need for material security. Vocation in the solar sense is concerned with aspirations that allow one to feel one is living a meaningful life. Certainly, when it is in the 2nd, the aspirations need to be grounded in material form. And the Moon in Taurus needs material security because material objects are symbols for emotional safety. But we are talking about the Sun, not the Moon. What would make this Sun feel fulfilled?

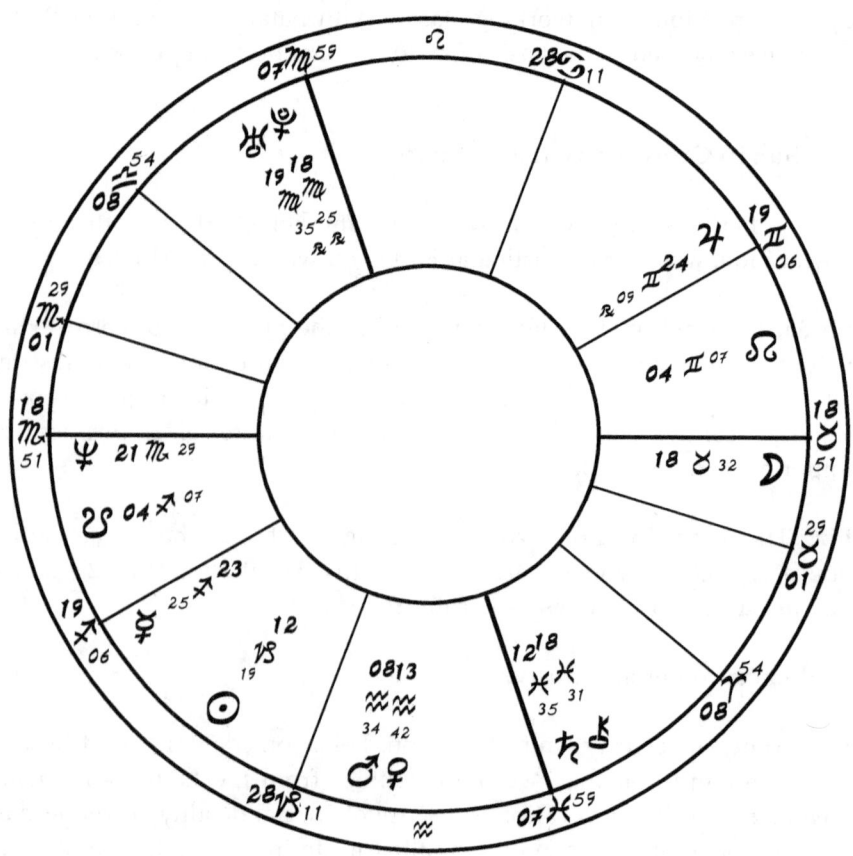

Linda
[Birth data withheld for purposes of confidentiality]

Audience: Manifest authority.

Liz: Yes, that is important for Capricorn. There is a powerful desire to build something that will last, Linda – something that will outlast your own lifetime. You need to know that you have made your mark on the world, that you have contributed something useful from a position of authority earned through expertise and responsibility. Capricorn people are not really interested in authority just for the power. They want the kind of authority which reflects the respect in which they are held by others. They need to know that they have earned their authority. You need to anchor your creative ideas in a way that affects the world around you. Your creative products must be seen, measured, and respected. This Sun wants to shine, but it wants to light up a physical landscape, not an intangible one. The aspects to the Sun will give us a clue as to what other gods wish to participate in the Sun's creative play. They will all need to be embodied as part of the Sun's story.

The creativity of Sun-Uranus-Pluto

Audience: There is a big contradiction here, because of the trine from the Sun to the Uranus-Pluto conjunction. There is an enormous drive to build. Here's somebody who could set up a traditional building, but in that building there would need to be some revolutionary, world-changing stuff going on which serves the collective in some way.

Liz: Well put. All the children of the 1960s embody, subtly or overtly, this combination of the desire to remake the world and the belief that destruction will ensue if it is not remade – violently if necessary. The bright Uranian vision of a perfect society – what is possible, what human beings could be – and the urgent Plutonian instinct for survival combine, and together they say: "We will only survive as a society if we have complete and total change. Whatever holds us back must be destroyed. If that means we have to break a lot of eggs to get the omelette, well, then, too bad for the eggs." This Uranus-Pluto conjunction can be ruthless. If we look at what happened in the world during the time this conjunction was active, we can get the flavour of it. Everywhere in the world, people rose up and fought against structures that had outlived their sell-by date.

In Linda's chart, the Sun is trine Uranus-Pluto, so it isn't as compulsive as a hard aspect. There is less inner conflict. With the trine, Linda knows that the revolutionary tendencies of Uranus-Pluto are not mutually exclusive of Capricorn's respect for structure and tradition. Change can be accomplished quietly and slowly, without breaking all the eggs. Nevertheless, it is the combination of planets rather than the aspect which matters most, and this Sun in Capricorn must participate in the changing of the world. You are nodding, Linda. When do you think you will you be able to manage this transformation of the world for us?

Linda: It might take five or ten years.

The 1960s generation

Audience: There are sextiles to the Sun from the Saturn-Chiron conjunction in Pisces. What do you think that means?

Liz: This Saturn-Chiron conjunction occurred in the mid-1960s, opposition Uranus-Pluto, and it marks a kind of sub-group within the Uranus-Pluto generation. What do *you* think it means?

Audience: I think it undermines confidence. There is a feeling of authority crumbling, and there is no structure to stand anything on. The Uranus-Pluto people want to change the world, but with Saturn and Chiron in opposition, there is a feeling of, "Why bother anyway? I'm not good enough or powerful enough to do anything about this mess. No one can do anything."

Liz: Yes, well put. Saturn represents our ego-skin, and stands as a barrier between ego-consciousness and the collective psyche. Chiron stands between Saturn and Uranus, and mediates between collective ideals of progress and individual human limits. Through Chiron we are wounded by the collective because the limits of human nature cannot accommodate the impersonal vision of Uranus without suffering. When Chiron and Saturn are in aspect, we become painfully aware of our personal failings and our lack of power to influence collective issues. This conjunction can suggest an undermining of one's strength and ability to cope, and it describes the personal and collective vulnerability of a whole generation of people. There is often a bitter awareness of how easy it is to become a victim. Saturn-Chiron in Pisces identifies readily with all living things that suffer. Paradoxically, this is its great strength. It gives the ability to empathise with the blind, suffering mass "out there". This generates deep compassion, and when this is combined with Uranus-Pluto, the revolutionary spirit is fuelled by the feeling that whole groups of people are being victimised by outworn collective structures.

Linda, your openness to collective suffering, which is described by both the Sun and Saturn aspecting this important generational configuration, must have first been triggered through what you experienced in your family. It points to your father in particular because the Saturn-Chiron conjunction is in the 4th house. Perhaps he appeared to you as one of these blind, suffering victims of collective stupidity and madness. We cannot shut out collective issues when an outer planet touches Saturn, and we need to build these issues into our vocational path when an outer planet touches the Sun. With Chiron in Pisces, the wound is portrayed as an emotional wound, a loss of trust in others, resulting in feelings of loneliness, bewilderment, emotional disillusionment, and lack of faith in the collective itself. This is a hurt which has deepened your sense of unity with other people. It can generate strong feelings of compassion that can sometimes be depressive. Saturn-Chiron often notices the misery in the world before the joy.

The involvement of Saturn-Chiron with Uranus-Pluto can increase one's determination to transform the world because one sees so much wretchedness everywhere. These aspects are linked with personal issues in Linda's chart because they are placed in the parental houses. But this configuration under which so many people were born in the mid-1960s is itself not personal. This generation group carries a finely tuned social conscience of a negatively inclined kind, which doesn't find a lot of good in life and in society. These people want revolution right now because there is such a sense of frustration. If the emotions involved are uncontained and ally themselves with destructive personal complexes, there may be a tendency toward violence, emotional or physical – especially if Mars is involved – and at the extreme end, it may contribute to the terrorist mentality. But I don't think that is the case with Linda.

Linda: Well, I'm not so sure sometimes.

Audience: Being a Capricorn, she'd have a ten-year plan for a revolution, wouldn't she?

Liz: There are checks on the anarchist tendencies in your chart, Linda. First, the Sun forms trines to Uranus-Pluto and sextiles to Saturn-Chiron. These "soft" aspects make it easier for the ego to cope with the pressure of the collective in an individually creative way. Second, the Sun is in pragmatic, cautious Capricorn – although some Capricorns, like Joseph Stalin, are not always circumscribed in their behaviour. Third, I believe other people's feelings matter a great deal to you. Neptune is rising in Scorpio, trine Saturn-Chiron in Pisces, and this reflects great sensitivity to individual suffering. Because of this, you aren't likely to subscribe to the "You have to break eggs to make an omelette!" philosophy. Fourth, your need for peace is too strong, with the Moon in Taurus trine the Sun. Earlier in the day, we explored the "happy-ever-after" dreams of Sun trine Moon. Nevertheless, despite these checks, there is a revolutionary lurking about somewhere inside.

Linda: I stopped watching the news when Pluto transited over my Neptune. I couldn't stand it. I experienced such rage and violent feelings.

Vocation and the call of the Sun

Liz: Let's look at what all this might mean for your vocation. The archetypal journey of the Sun is our vocation. As I said, vocation means a calling. The calling comes from inside, not from parental expectations or job availability or even innate talent. You have a deep and genuine calling to be involved in reshaping the world in ways where you can actually see the results. This is because you are an earth sign. "Reshaping the world", for you, doesn't mean writing a beautiful spiritual book which you hope somebody will read one day. That's not going to do a lot for you. You need to do something practical, and perhaps even something revolutionary which is disguised within a conventional profession.

Audience: I have four children, all born in the Uranus-Pluto generation. I discovered that my daughter was buying bullets for terrorist activities in Northern Ireland. That's very difficult to deal with.

Liz: I am sure it was. How did you deal with it?

Audience: I pointed out what the consequences might be, and threatened to disown her.

Liz: This group is being challenged very powerfully at the moment because Pluto is square both ends of the Uranus-Pluto-Saturn-Chiron configuration. Linda, the time is right for you to look at the inner forces that are driving you, and make something out of them. For those who don't have the self-containment, the pressure of the Pluto squares can come out in exactly what this lady has just described. A a lot of violence may emerge if the energy is frustrated, and of course it is extremely frustrated in many people of this generation.

Audience: It is easy to idealise a cause and be swept along with it.

Liz: Yes. That is what occurs when there is too little consciousness of the Sun. The individual ego must process collective issues and create an individual path. Linda, because your Sun is trine one end of the configuration and sextile the other, you have solid ego-ground to stand on. Also, because you are earthy, you are sensible. That helps you to contain the destructive potentials and work to form something useful and worthwhile out of the configuration. Do you have an idea in what direction you might want to move?

Linda: I have very strong feelings about the kind of education I received as a child. It was so irrelevant to real life and real people. I feel I learned nothing that was of any use in helping me to understand life. It was supposed to be a "good" education. But psychology in any shape or form always took a back seat. I remember so clearly what I felt when I was a child. I used to think that, if only we were taught about ourselves and each other, we could really become something grand.

Liz: So children's education is attracting your attention.

Linda: Yes. But I am also interested in the quality of education given to teachers themselves. Without well-educated teachers, we wind up with generations of badly educated children. We have to start with the teachers.

Liz: I entirely agree with you. Why are our educators not properly educated? And I don't just mean education through information. It's psychological education which is so sorely lacking, as you have pointed out. Think what a difference it would make if teachers of small children had to be in psychotherapy and study child psychology as part of their education. But the mere suggestion of such a thing would raise an outcry. Education in Britain is a political issue, not a psychological one. What will you do with your ideas? Your vocation is connected with helping to change society in practical ways. Education is an excellent vehicle in which to pursue this kind of vision. If this kind of outer planet configuration is thumping about in the chart, one does need to think big, as long as it is within realistic limits in terms of what any single individual can contribute. Your vocational path needs to be big enough to hold Uranus-Pluto, Saturn-Chiron, and Neptune. We haven't even looked at Neptune, which is also involved in the configuration.

Walking the dangerous edge

Audience: I'm sitting here thinking about my brother, who has a similar set of patterns and also has the Sun in Capricorn. He is currently engaged in supervising the building of two new ships, and is doing a lot of walking along very dangerous ledges and falling down holes. He is really trying to push the people who don't want to do the work to get everything into shape. That seems to me to be very appropriate, and he loves it. I think it is possible for that generation to get around the destructive energy. But there has to be a dangerous edge to the work.

Liz: Yes, on some level, although not necessarily physical. With Uranus-Pluto in the 10th in Linda's chart, the dangerous edge seems to be the image other people have of her, and perhaps the role she may play in future in relation to educational authorities. If she is prepared to be viewed as a complete raving looney, or a subversive who could

Part Two: The Sun, Creativity and Vocation 217

sabotage the establishment, and she is prepared to take the flak that results, then she is walking the dangerous edge.

Linda: There is a fine line between that dangerous edge and playing.

Liz: Can you say more about that?

Linda: My father played all his life, but he played in a way which seemed to me quite chaotic and mad. He hurt other people's feelings very irresponsibly.

Liz: You seem to be saying that spontaneity, which is a solar quality, is close to madness, or that it can unleash cruelty. At best, it is irresponsible.

Linda: It could be.

Liz: That sounds like something coming, in part, from your family background. If you get too wild in your play, you are crazy, irresponsible, and hurt people. It sounds like you got that message at home.

Linda: I don't know. I am talking about Neptunian play.

Liz: What is Neptunian play?

Linda: I don't know. Just pretending you're another character.

Liz: Many children do this. It is one of the most natural forms of imaginative solar play. Children invent mythic roles for themselves, which reflects an instinctive awareness of an individual destiny of some kind. They sometimes do it in an exaggerated or compulsive way to assuage personal hurts and feelings of inadequacy. But even the most emotionally secure child will do it because it is a natural creative process. For you to think there is something crazy about it suggests that you have been told it's crazy. Perhaps you should look at where this idea comes from. What you said about your father implies that your conventionality comes from the mother's side of the family, and the crazy part is coming from the father's. Yet the Uranus-Pluto conjunction is in the 10th, opposite Saturn in the 4th, which suggests that both parents carried a conflict between being "normal" and being "crazy" in their thinking. The revolutionary is always perceived as crazy by those who seek safety and social acceptance. What was it George Bernard Shaw once said? The crazy man seeks to change things, while the normal man is content with things as they are. Therefore all progress is created by crazy people.

You seem to have a deep conviction that you should be "normal". That may spring from an unease about the explosive potential of your generation group. And Capricorn carries its own in-built conventionality. It doesn't even need encouraging from the parents. Capricorn is born with an *a priori* Freudian superego. Even if the parents don't impose it, there is an inner voice that keeps saying, "What will people think?" The Sun in Capricorn is a contradiction in terms, because solar light cannot shine if one is always worrying about what others are thinking. Capricorn wants acceptance by the collective. Just having the Sun in Capricorn implies a struggle. The mythic journey of Capricorn invariably involves a battle between the self and the collective. The resolution seems to lie in being an individual who is respected for a particular creative achievement in the world. But I think there has also been a lot of pressure from your family background to be "normal".

Linda: My mother was quite unconventional when she was very young. But then she became really conventional and very frightened of other people's opinions. She talked about her youth as if she had had an illness which eventually she recovered from. Being "normal" was certainly what she taught me.

Liz: But of course she wasn't "normal" at all. No mother described by Uranus-Pluto is "normal". Perhaps your father got to act out the craziness for both of them. Mercury is the only planet in fire in your chart. It is a singleton by element. Because the Sun is by nature fiery, a chart in which there is little or no fire can give the Sun a hard time. Water and air are fairly strong, but earth dominates your chart. Earth tends to look at the fire inside – in this case, Mercury in Sagittarius – and say, "These ideas I have are quite mad. I could go right over the top, and then where would I be?" There is a fear of one's own inspirational, intuitive side. Yet this Mercury in Sagittarius is very strong, not least because it is a singleton. It is exactly opposite Jupiter and they are in

Part Two: The Sun, Creativity and Vocation

mutual reception. The Mercury-Jupiter tendency to be forcibly struck by inspirations out of the blue, to see the "big picture" and know intuitively how things are connected, is what you are calling crazy.

Audience: That is why she is interested in children and education.

Liz: Yes. It may be very important for you to pursue a vocation in education, Linda, because the need to teach is so strong in the chart. How do we communicate with children? We can't crush them with too much Saturn because they are trying to learn to be the Sun. We have to involve the two planets that are the best friends of the Sun – Mercury and Jupiter. In myth, Jupiter/Zeus is Apollo's father, while Mercury/Hermes is his brother. Hermes and Apollo have an extraordinary relationship. They are always arguing, but they love and admire each other and are always exchanging gifts. The issue of educating children, and the fine line between imagination and madness, might well provide a sphere of work in which you would feel alive and fulfilled.

Regarding future transits to the Sun, it will be a while before a really big one comes along. The one to watch is Pluto moving into Capricorn. It isn't that far away, and it would seem to be the culmination of a process which probably began in 1989, when the Uranus-Neptune conjunction in Capricorn sat on your natal Sun. What happened in 1989?

Linda: My father died.

Liz: And how did that affect you?

Linda: I formed a relationship that was a replay of my father's relationship with my mother. My father had lots of affairs. I had no idea what I was walking into. It started as a very good relationship. Then I wound up feeling like my mother must have felt. So I ended it, although it hurt a lot. That was something my mother couldn't do.

Liz: It seems you had to separate from your father and everything he represented. This came at a time when you weren't really able to understand what you were going through, and it was painful, but it cut the cord. A kind of birth began with the Uranus-Neptune conjunction moving over the natal Sun. A number of transits will trigger the Sun in the not-too-distant future – for example, Saturn will trine it from Taurus. But the time of fruition for that process which began so painfully at the time of your father's death is most likely to arrive when Pluto comes up to the Sun, trines its own place, and trines Uranus. Trines are concerned with completion and fulfillment. This is a long way ahead, but that suits Capricorn.

Audience: Could you say more about vocation?

Liz: What would you like me to say?

Audience: Anything.

Liz: Try reading Howard Sasportas' essay on vocation.[22] Many people look at the 10th house and the sign at the MC and try to define vocation on that basis. These things are certainly important and give refinement to the picture. But I believe the core of one's vocation is the Sun. Unless we can play, and feel a connection with something brighter and greater than ourselves, we are pursuing a job, not a vocation. We may also be driven into a particular sphere of work by our compulsions. Some people call their compulsions a vocation. But a vocation, by its nature, generates joy, even if it is very difficult and invokes conflict. The house, sign, and aspects of the Sun sketch the broad outline of our vocation, our "calling". Other factors in the chart provide the detail. The Sun is fundamental to vocation. We need to remember our astrological basics. If we have the Sun in the 2nd house, whatever the nature of our work, it must produce concrete results, because the 2nd house is an earthy house. And if the Sun is in an earth sign, the need to materialise one's talents is even more urgent.

If the Sun is in the 11th, we must contribute in some way – perhaps intellectually rather than tangibly – to the society in which we live and to the body of knowledge or consciousness that is compelling that society to progress. The planets aspecting the Sun must be brought along – all of them. Once we have got that spinal column, there may be many options in terms of specific work. But if the basic solar need is

---

[22] Howard Sasportas, "Vocation", Part Two of *Direction and Destiny in the Birth Chart*, CPA Press, London, 1998.

denied, there will be frustration, because there is no sense of joy and no sense that one can be creative. Vocation depends on feeling that we can make something special out of our lives. When we feel "called", we connect with the archetypal divine child. We feel we are "meant" to be doing this unique thing. It is what we are here for. Then we can play with it, even if it is something deadly serious or even dangerous.

I am afraid we have run out of time. Shall we call it a day, then? Thank you all for coming and for participating so enthusiastically.

Bibliography

Campion, Nicholas, *Astrology, History and Apocalypse*, CPA Press, London, 2000.

Greene, Liz, *Relationships and How to Survive Them*, CPA Press, 1999.

Sasportas, Howard, *Direction and Destiny in the Birth Chart*, CPA Press, London, 1998.

Winnicott, D. W., *Playing and Reality*, Routledge, 1992.

Winnicott, D. W., *Home Is Where We Start From*, W. W. Norton & Co., 1990.

Winnicott, D. W., *The Child, the Family, and the Outside World*, Perseus Press, 1992.

About the Centre for Psychological Astrology

The Centre for Psychological Astrology was founded in 1983 by Dr Liz Greene and Howard Sasportas. Since its inception, the CPA has become world renowned for its unique and inspiring application of a variety of psychological approaches to astrology.

The Centre continues to foster the cross-fertilisation of the fields of astrology and depth, humanistic and transpersonal psychology. It hosts a unique seminar and webinar programme providing an original, informal and inspiring framework for both beginners and experienced astrologers. Past seminars are available as books and e-books through the CPA Press.

For further information about the current programme of seminars and webinars, to receive mailings and browse the CPA Press astrology books, contact the Administrator, Juliet Sharman-Burke at: juliet@cpalondon.com

The **Online Introductory Certificate Course** with John Green provides a foundation in the basics of psychological astrology. Run as real time online tutorials, students can interact with the tutor and other students, ask questions and watch recorded sessions.

For further information, contact John at: webmaster@cpalondon.com

About the Mercury Internet School of Psychological Astrology

The Mercury Internet School of Psychological Astrology (MISPA) offers a Diploma Course, and students who have completed the CPA's Foundation Course are eligible to enrol.

For further information visit: www.mercuryinternetschool.com or write to info@mercuryinternetschool.com

www.ingramcontent.com/pod-product-compliance
Lightning Source LLC
Chambersburg PA
CBHW061938220426
43662CB00012B/1951